Wasp, Where Is Thy Sting?

FLORENCE KING

A SCARBOROUGH BOOK

STEIN AND DAY / *Publishers* / Scarborough House

Briarcliff Manor, N.Y. 10510

First Scarborough Books Edition Published 1980
First published in hardcover in 1977 by Stein and Day/*Publishers*
Third printing 1977
Copyright © 1977 by Florence King
All rights reserved
Designed by David Miller
Printed in the United States of America
Stein and Day/*Publishers*/Scarborough House,
Briarcliff Manor, N.Y. 10510

Excerpts from this book were originally published
in *Cosmopolitan,* May, 1975, and *Playgirl,* June, 1976.

Library of Congress Cataloging in Publication Data

King, Florence.
    Wasp, where is thy sting?

     1. United States—Social conditions—1960—
2. United States—Intellectual life.   I. Title.
HN59.K55   301.45'15'1073   76–45741
ISBN 0–8128–6025–X

942 113

Wasp, Where Is Thy Sting?

"The American WASP may have no Fifth Avenue parade, and no native dances, but now he can flaunt his foibles along with all those other lovable ethnics, thanks to this bright, very funny socio-sendup. Not that there is any such thing as a 'standard model WASP.' 'Schism is our specialty.' King then revs up a series of showcase numbers, beginning with a run-through of religions from the Episcopalians ('the Chivas Regal of Protestantism') whose clergy toss down Scotch and flirt with hostesses, through the 'Baptodistyerians,' to the Holier Than Thou Reformed Church of Wasp Crossroads, Mississippi. Then come the households of High and Low Waspdom: the High cooks dreadful messes while looped on Bloody Marys; the Low covers toilet paper with Marie Antoinette dolls and whomps up gargantuan, leaden meals (Sunday is 'plop-plop fizz fizz day'). King delves into such matters as the Wasp Prince, the Prom Queen, the Big Man on Campus, and the Great Girl, thresholds of tolerance for in-laws and embarrassing situations, distrust of sex (although the male has extraordinary staying power, sex threatens cherished self-sufficiency), etc., upon etc. A highlight is the author's hilarious reconstruction of one Sunday morning in the career of Lizzie Borden ('a case of pure Waspology'). If the Wasp once lost its sting, Ms. King has put it back."

—*The Kirkus Reviews*

FLORENCE KING is also the author of
He: An Irreverent Look at the American Male
and
Southern Ladies and Gentlemen

FOR MY AUNTS

Dicey Ruding Coyne

Ellen Beetham Sprague

CONTENTS

AUTHOR'S NOTE

I wish to thank all the people who wrote to me about my last book, *Southern Ladies and Gentlemen,* to tell me that I stereotype people and to ask them please not to write me again with the same complaint. I also do not wish to receive any more proposals, decent or indecent, from the man who addresses me as "Supergoy" and then proceeds to tell me that I stereotype people.

Stereotyping, better known as "perceptive pointing-up," is an ancient and honorable ingredient of the humorous literary genre. Betty MacDonald pointed up rural people in *The Egg and I.* Margaret Halsey pointed up the British in *With Malice Toward Some.* Cornelia Otis Skinner and Emily Kimbrough pointed up both the French and the innocent Americans abroad in *Our Hearts Were Young and Gay.* Gail Parent points up Jews in *Sheila Levine Is Dead and Living in New York.*

The wheels of American justice turn on a certain amount of stereotyping. Lawyers picking a jury are known to avoid creative people who are accustomed to dealing with subtleties of thought (i.e., writers). "The imaginative type" is the lawyer's bugbear because any lawyer wants his jury to be a human orchestra that will follow his lead. Thus, the person who would make an excellent juror is always disqualified by stereotyping. The prosecuting attorney will disqualify a journalist because he is convinced that "all those media types" are liberal; and the defense attorney's nightmare is a Presbyterian deacon named MacTavish with a Masonic emblem in his lapel.

We all stereotype to a point because we must. As my publisher

Sol Stein wrote in his novel, *The Magician:* "Thinking would be an unstructured mess if we did not poke around in this anarchy and find some guides, even if in time we adjust and change them."

So if you will read this book instead of hitting the ceiling at the mere sight of my name on it, you will discover that its purpose is to un-stereotype the Wasp and explain him with pointing-up.

The material in the Lizzie Borden chapter is the cumulative result of my eight-year study of the case and was taken from the mountain of notes I have amassed on the subject for my forthcoming book on Lizzie—a project that will undoubtedly find me accused of stereotyping Massachusetts-born ax murderesses. However, I am especially indebted in this book to Victoria Lincoln's superbly informative and entertaining work, *A Private Disgrace: Lizzie Borden by Daylight.* Because my own theories on the case come closest to those of Miss Lincoln and because she views the matter with an Anglo-Saxon woman's eye, I have limited my discussion of the Borden case to her reconstruction of it.

Naturally I have invented names for the people I describe in this book. Naturally they are mostly Wasp names, so naturally some Wasp out there is getting ready to sue me. Please don't. You'll lose. It can't be helped: authors must invent sensible-sounding names for the people in their books. Sensible-sounding ordinary names are bound to belong to a lot of people. No offense is ever meant, but a great deal of offense is always taken.

Finally I would like to thank my kinswoman, Dame Lailey King, without whose moral support this book would never have been written.

Wasp, Where Is Thy Sting?

1

INTRODUCTION

A few years ago, an editor told me, "Make your villain a Wasp so nobody will get insulted."

The once proud and powerful Wasp has lost his sting. Formerly looked up to as "the real American," he has now been shunted aside and demoted to second-class citizenship in the new dawn of ethnic awareness and anti-melting-pot trendiness.

We are the bad guys because we do not have a hyphen. There are no Anglo-Americans, just Wasps. There are English pubs and American steak houses, but no quaint Wasp restaurants. Whoever heard of Mama Nancy's or Villa Bradshaw? The three-button, three-piece conservative suit is laughingly called our uniform, but we have no native costume. The now ubiquitous blue jeans were first worn by Wasps in Wild West days, but Levi made them. We have no native instrument except perhaps the dulcimer, which no one can play except itinerant female professors with names like Ariadne Dvorak-Tzvzay; and at weddings, the only dance we do is the fox trot.

Putting down Wasps is the latest fad. Philip Roth called us "those pug-nosed little bastards from Montclair." *Cosmopolitan* writer Diane Brennan claimed that all Wasp men wear ironed boxer shorts and undershirts with sleeves. Judith Rossner's novel, *Any Minute I Can Split*, contains three digs at us:

"He had failed to see that their defenses didn't control warmth but concealed the lack of it."

". . . Wasps were born toilet-trained."

"He was just beneath the skin and to the inner core a caricature of everything the Wasp, a caricature to begin with, stood for."

It is not that Roth, Brennan, and Rossner are entirely wrong, for they all have a point; they have simply forgotten their manners. *Noblesse oblige* ordains that powerless people should not be attacked, and today's Wasp is powerless. When someone tells an ethnic or racial joke in public, watchdog societies and anti-defamation leagues spring into action with protests. When some-one tells a Wasp joke, everybody laughs. There is no Wasp-American Society, and if we formed one, everybody would laugh at *that*. Our patriotic and ancestral societies protect concepts, not people. Anyone who assumes that the DAR takes care of us is wrong; they are too busy putting brass plates on old houses and hunting for Martha Washington's thimble. We, their children, are out in the cold.

Another popular pastime in recent years is blaming Wasps for everybody's sex problems. "Our Anglo-Saxon morality" and "our heritage of Victorian repression" crop up constantly in sex manu-als, on TV roundtables, and on call-in radio shows. We are America's officially designated squares, whose idea of fun, says Diane Brennan, is *not* going to church.

We are caricatured and imitated so often that we are in the same position as John Wayne when he had to ask Rich Little to show him the John Wayne walk. People talk about us constantly, repeating one-liners they have read or heard, but no one will take the trouble to understand us. "Defining" people is a big business in the United States, provided that the subjects are ethnic, but Wasps are not considered fit subjects for ponderous foundation studies like *The Preference for Black Shirts and White Ties Among Italo-American Men Aged 15−26 in the Jersey City/Bayonne Area.* The whole point of such a tome is that Italo-American men do not wear Waspy ties, so they must be interesting. The poor Wasp must stumble unnoticed through his unhyphenated vale of tears, know-ing that his underwear will never make it to the top of the sociologist's frequency charts because he is not ethnic.

In present-day America, not being ethnic is the same as not being *there*. Matters have reached such a pass that the Wasp will soon be an endangered species unless he acquires ethnic status fast.

The best way to become an instant ethnic is to tinker with our group psyche in print. Let it be generally known that there are such things as Wasp Guilt, Wasp Conflict, Wasp Agony, and, of course, Wasp Mothers. Once cocktail-party sages start saying things like, "Well, you know, of course, she's a victim of the Wasp Daughter syndrome," our citizenship problems will be over. People will be so busy trying to understand us that we will forget we were ever misunderstood in the first place.

2

HIGH AND LOW WASPS
or
Here's the Church, Here's the Steeple

It is impossible to understand Wasps without some knowledge of our internecine warfare. There is no such thing as a standard-model Wasp. Schism is our specialty; there are Protestants and there are Protestants and the twain have yet to meet. Each Wasp's habits and personality traits down to the last little idiosyncrasy are determined by his place on that tree of many branches known as Protestantism. Our vast differences began with theological disputes, but religion has long since taken a back seat in favor of larger issues, such as social class and the psychology of mobility. Depending upon which church door you open, you will find the best people, the good people, or the ones Episcopalians call *those* people.

The Episcopal church is the Chivas Regal of Protestantism. As Vance Packard points out in *The Status Seekers*, it is the Presidents' church, the executives' church, the coupon-clippers' church, and the Ivy League church. It is the church that on Christmas, Palm Sunday, and Easter is packed with the best-dressed women ever seen outside a synagogue. Although with only three million members the Episcopal church is a Protestant minority, it continues to ooze overwhelming social mystique.

There are two kinds of Episcopalianism. The low-church version is an ordinary Protestant church with extra trimmings and a minister who is a minister. The luscious version is called high-church, or as an old beau of mine used to say, "Piscop." It is as far from shout 'n' sing Protestantism as you can get without going to Rome; and well it should be, for the point of it all is to become as Catholic as possible without becoming Catholic.

My first clear memory of the Piscop church is Palm Sunday of 1942. I was just learning to read, and like most children in this stage, I insisted upon reading aloud all signs I happened to see. When we were settled in church, I looked at the elaborately carved booth in the back and read aloud the sign, *Confession by Appointment*.

"Granny, what's confession?" I asked.

"Well, you can go if you want to but you don't *have* to, and you'd better not let me catch you in there because it's Catholic! Still, it's nice to have it there because it looks so *high-church*."

As far as I was able to tell, no one ever went to confession. The booth was always empty, and everybody limited himself to a loving glance at it as we entered and left the church. The wood was said to have come from England, which made it our version of a relic, like the foreskins of saints that are kept under Catholic altars.

Ethnics and Puritan Wasps are wiped out when they hear a Piscop refer to "Father Chillingsworth," but that is the way high-churchers like to address their pastor. Seeing Father Chillingsworth all gussied up in his lacy vestments and cloth-of-gold chasuble is enough to gag a Baptist, but Catholics, when they recover from their shock, are usually wistful. The high church reminds them of what their church used to be like before Vatican II's wrecking crew went to work. They feel quite at home except that they may miss their leather-padded kneeling rails. Many Piscop churches have purple velvet cushions. Otherwise it is the same: genuflecting, making the sign of the cross, statues of saints (but you mustn't pray to them), votive lights, and that churchy smell, which comes from the candle wax and incense and which is absent in other Protestant churches. Some high-churchers even call themselves Catholic. "Anglo-Catholic" was my grandmother's favorite way of putting it (she came down much harder on the first word). Others say Anglican, and some even say Church of England, unless they are filling out a form or answering a pollster, in which case they toss off a nonchalant "C of E."

All Episcopalians use the venerable *Book of Common Prayer* (currently in danger of being de-venerated by a modern translation in the offing), but many high-churchers prefer the British edition whose title page reads, "according to the use of the Church of England," instead of the edition that some regard as *déclassé*, which reads, "according to the use of the Protestant Episcopal Church in the United States of America." Both contain references to "Romish errors" and "papistry," but the British edition verges on schizophrenia with praiseworthy mention of that crypto-Pope, the Archbishop of Canterbury, plus numerous patriotic prayers in honor of Our Sovereign Lady the Queen—Protestant Hail Marys with an imperial touch. (The one I had as a child said Our Sovereign Lord the King.) The marriage service in the British edition I bought in London only five years ago still contains *obey* in the bride's vows; and both the British and American versions contain prayers for the ancient ceremony known as the Churching of Women, in which a newly delivered mother is blessed, purified, thanked, and sent on her way to do it again.

Looking down on both Catholicism and Protestantism is a favorite activity of high-churchers, who place themselves philosophically just outside the city limits of Rome, and sneer, first in one direction and then in the other, like spectators swiveling their heads at a tennis match. In a toss-up, however, they prefer to look down on Protestantism. There are certain manifestations of Protestant behavior that Piscops like to avoid. One is the use of the word *sermon*. The proper word is *talk*, as in "Such a good *talk*, Father Chillingsworth." *Sermon* calls up images of a ranting pulpit-thumper. Whenever Father Chillingsworth feels the spirit of the Lord upon him, he must cast it off, and remain calm and muted so that he can *talk*.

Another no-no is overly vigorous hymn singing. The best way to avoid that is to avoid overly vigorous hymns, so whoop-dee-do low-Protestant selections like "Jesus Wants Me for a Sunbeam" and "Brighten the Circle Where You Are" are out. After all, someone might get carried away and fall into religious ecstasy, and you mustn't do that sort of thing in church. Piscops prefer stately hymns like "Amazing Grace," "Abide with Me," and, of course, that Anglophile's favorite, "Nearer My God to Thee." When I was a child, the organist used to interpose a few bars of "Rule, Britannia" in the finale. When we referred to the hymn as "The Titanic Song" in Sunday school, the teacher did not correct us.

The best way to prevent people from letting loose and singing is to have such excellent soloists in the choir that no one would dare join in. The ideal Piscop calmative is that apogee of sexless-ness, a boy soprano. If these measures fail, Piscops can always drag out that quintessential anti-Protestant weapon, Anglican chanting. In the back of the hymnal you will find the Canticles, complete with delicious titles like *Te Deum Laudamus* and *Benedictus es, Domine*. There are even crowd-control instructions on how to chant, my favorite being "Breathe only at the end of a line."

Religion is a minor matter for many high-churchers. I was eight years old before I discovered that Trinity did *not* mean going to church three times a year. Piscops may not be much interested in the welfare of the soul but we are devout snobs, not above using Holy Communion as a put-down. In Roman Catholic Commun-ion, worshipers receive only the bread, which they believe is the actual body of Christ. Episcopalians, who want nothing to do with the doctrine of transubstantiation, nevertheless take both the bread and the wine, known in the prayer book as "the doctrine of both Kinds." Thanks to this arrangement, the high-churcher who really wants to show off can do a marvelous status number at Communion: take only the bread and refuse the wine. It is the absolute last word in high-churchiness. Do anything more Catholic than that and you will tumble from your high-church pedestal into an Italian abyss.

At Episcopal Communion everybody drinks out of the same chalice. The priest—that's Father Chillingsworth—merely wipes the rim with a linen cloth and passes the cup to the next soul. Nothing shocks the whistle-clean Puritan Wasp or the hypochon-driacal Jew more than this carefree Episcopalian practice. It is one small manifestation of an essentially aristocratic attitude: We happy few could not possible be dirty.

This *l'église c'est moi* attitude on the part of Episcopalians permits us to indulge in the sort of freewheeling conduct that shocks the Puritan Wasp: drinking, fornicating, and mule-skinner cussing, for example. We are perfectly capable of going from Anglo to Saxon in a trice, excusing ourselves with Tallulah Bankhead's observation, "Dahling, I can say shit because I'm a lady." A Piscop friend of mine refers to anyone who annoys her as "that piss-ass sonofabitch." I was raised by a terrifyingly elegant grandmother who nonetheless never missed a chance to call Eleanor Roosevelt "a Friday turd at a Saturday market." High-church ribaldry knows no bounds, particularly in anal matters. We take the same hearty delight in jokes about fartyng and shit-tyng that runs through Chaucer and the Elizabethans.

Our bawdy streak causes countless misunderstandings with people who do not understand it. The high-church Wasp woman must be extremely careful around a Roman Catholic ethnic man, for instance. Accustomed to the virgin-whore polarization of females, the moment he hears one of our Falstaffian observations he assumes we belong to the latter category. The Piscop man would roar with mirth and then go us one better, but the Catholic ethnic pales, then leers, then assumes he can dirty-talk us into bed. He does not grasp the difference between ordinary dirty talk, which is marked by the kind of self-conscious sniggering that can make even *damn* sound offensive to the female ear, and Piscop dirty talk, which is marked by hearty purity and an innocence born of naturalness. Jewish men are just as shocked at first, but having no madonnas to haunt them and being blessedly free of machismo, they quickly adjust. Soon they are taking it in with boyish glee and a facial expression that shows what I can only call sheer happiness.

High-church drinking is another habit that shocks the Puritan Wasp. Nothing is quite so disconcerting to him as the sight of Father Chillingsworth in a gray Brooks Brothers suit with a re-versed collar, a cocktail in one hand and a cigar in the other, flirting with the hostess. Glance over at the bar and you will see Father Chillingsworth's curates mixing martinis and flirting with the hostess's daughter. Mrs. Chillingsworth, a stunner at fifty-three, is alone with the host in his den, admiring his hunting prints as she sips a double Scotch on the rocks.

But the most horrifying thing of all to the Puritan Wasp is the Episcopal drinking that extends to the church itself. Members of a wedding party nip beforehand. Even the bride may take a snort. One of my most cherished memories is that of seeing six brides-maids holding up a Piscop bride's six-foot cathedral train so that she could get the silver flask to her lips.

The Irish have a possibly undeserved reputation as the world's greatest drinkers. Until the Puritan influence made inroads in England, Wasps may well have outdistanced their Hibernian neighbors. A seventeenth-century preacher, Thomas Reeve, called England "the dizzy iland, whose inhabitants drink as if . . .

we were nothing but spunges to draw up moisture, or we had tunnels in our mouthes."[1]

More recent commentators agree with him. Robert Lewis Taylor calls England and Scotland "traditional sinkholes of drunkenness" and cites a chart for school children published in 1900 by an American temperance group called The Band of Hope Society, entitled "The History of Drinking in England."[2]

Britons & Romans—occasionally intemperate
Saxons & Danes—great drinkers
Normans—copied English intemperance
Plantagenets—lived luxuriously
Tudors—intemperance increased
Stuarts—wild excesses
Hanoverians—drunkenness became a national vice.

It would appear that our assimilation with the Germans and the French is behind our tippling, but in any case, from 1714 to 1733, English consumption of gin rose from two million to five million gallons a year. Writes historian Eugen Weber, "Five or six *bottles* of brandy or port per man were par for an evening. Dr. Johnson once drank thirty-six glasses of port without moving from his seat—a feat in more ways than one. . . . Addison and Steele, Goldsmith and Boswell, Sheridan and Fox and Pitt and Walpole were bottomless wells of liquor, frequently drunk, often dead drunk, and little the worse for it except in health, and that only eventually. It was, evidently, an age of titans."[3]

It was also an age of English ascendancy. These men, like present-day Episcopalians, enjoyed personal status and security. Said Samuel Johnson: "All the decent people in Litchfield got drunk every night and were not the worse thought of." People who feel safe from the physical and psychological effects of prejudice tend to do as they please without giving matters a second thought. Enough centuries of feel-safe drinking might well create a biological type. Wasp tolerance for liquor could be an acquired blood chemistry like any other acquired characteristic. It is as good an explanation as any for the Piscop's notoriously hollow leg.

[1] Peter Fryer, *Mrs. Grundy: Studies in English Prudery.*
[2] Robert Lewis Taylor, *Vessel of Wrath: The Life and Times of Carry Nation.*
[3] *A Modern History of Europe.*

Episcopalians tend to be happy drunks because we feel no guilt over our drinking. Protestantism is a convenient religion because it offers denominations for drinkers and denominations for teetotalers. You pays your tithe and you takes your choice. Wets say: "Jesus drank," and drys reply: "It was really grape juice." Both groups offer the Bible in evidence of their claims, so the wets drink like Jesus, the drys abstain like Jesus, and each sees to it that they do not meet socially. Eyeing each other across the denominational chasm keeps an uneasy sort of peace marred only by mutual scorn.

One of the most intriguing aspects of high-church psychology is the Southerner's attitude toward Catholics. It has long been assumed that all Southerners hate Catholics, but that is only the gospel according to the Ku Klux Klan. The high-church Southerner is first and foremost a snob, and he may even be a bit of a Royalist in his heart. Unlike many other Protestants in other parts of the United States, he has not been raised with the admonition, "Don't play with those Catholic children." In the first place, there aren't that many Catholic children in the South to play with, but what few there are, providing they are native Southerners and not Yankee transplants, stand an excellent chance of being the *crème de la crème.*

Some of the finest and oldest families in the South are Catholic. Most are found in the Catholic "pockets"—New Orleans, Charleston, and Savannah. The latter city produced Scarlett O'Hara's mother, *née* Ellen Robillard, descendant of French aristocrats who had escaped the guillotine. (In *GWTW*, none of the neighboring families around Tara nor any of the Atlanta people minded in the least that the O'Haras were Catholic.) There are also Anglo-Saxon Catholics who are descended from Restoration cavaliers who gave their all in the service of the Catholic Stuart crown. Any connection with things Stuart is guaranteed to bring a Southerner to his knees in reverence—after all, the Stuarts had a gift for supporting star-crossed causes and aligning themselves with the losing side. In the labyrinthine recesses of the high-church Southern mind, "Catholic" triggers visions of Mary Queen of Scots sweeping into the execution hall in a red petticoat, just like Bette Davis in *Jezebel.*

My grandmother's anti-Catholicism was directed toward *foreign* Catholics who lived in that *terra incognita* that she always called North of Maryland, the border which she never crossed, physically, spiritually, or psychologically. However, she was lavish in her approval of "Maryland Catholics," as she carefully called them. These were the Calverts, the Carrolls, the Howards, descendants of Lord Baltimore himself, and all those lovely people on the Eastern Shore in places like Saint Mary's County.

Once, while attending a posh gathering as the guest of a friend from the Catholic Daughters of America, Granny saw people genuflecting to an archbishop and kissing his ring. Without hesitation, she joined the receiving line, genuflected, kissed the ring, and came home in a glow: "Oh, it was so *nice!* Why, it was just like being presented at Court!"

Some Episcopalians were born into the church, but there is a much larger group who grew into it. Becoming, rather than being, an Episcopalian is part of the American Dream. Changing one's denomination each time another rung is gained on the social ladder is standard Wasp behavior. In this way we are completely different from other socially mobile Americans. Catholics on the up and up change neighborhoods and thus parishes while still remaining Catholic. Status-seeking Jews originate in an Orthodox synagogue, move on to a Conservative one, and then when they strike gold take the final step to a Reform temple, but they do not stop being Jewish.

But the chameleon Wasp, not content to switch to a richer church of the same denomination, changes the whole church. The Jew simplifies his theology as he goes up the social scale, leaving the complex traditional version to his poorer *confrères*, but the Episcopal-bewitched Wasp goes in the opposite direction. He may have started life as a tent-dwelling hot-gospel Baptist, but when he arrives he wants velvet kneeling cushions, vestments, candles, incense, and preachers called Father.

As the provincial Illinois mother in James Jones's *Some Came Running* explained it:

It was Agnes who kept getting him to try and get her, his mother, to leave the Church of Christ, Saved, and go with them to the Methodist. Mrs. Hirsh did not have anything especially against the Methodists. It was a good enough church. At least it helped some in the fight against

Papism and the Pope. But it did not take God very seri-
ously, and was mostly a social church, where all of the
snobs who were not Episcopalian went instead. Which of
course was why Agnes wanted them to go there. Next
thing, Agnes would be wanting them all to be Episcopalians . . . Once Franklin made enough money. And
became important enough. As he was sure to do.

The Episcopal church is the inspiration for the ethnics' number
one, or Cavalier, stereotype of Wasps. According to this view, we
are all blithe, uncomplicated spirits; rich, hard drinking, wicked,
none too bright and consequently very happy. If we have any
mental problems at all, they are attributed to polo accidents.

At the same time, the ethnic harbors the number two, or
Roundhead, Wasp stereotype. That one is the Wasp in the ironed
boxer shorts whose idea of fun is not going to church. Like Oliver
Cromwell, he combines simple religion with grim businesslike
practicality: "Put your faith in God, and keep your powder dry."
He is reputed to be severe, hard working, prudish, and very
anti-sin, the personification of the pollster's catch-all category for
all unsophisticated opinions—"Middle America." Usually that's
where he lives if he is not a New Englander. That one is the Puritan
Wasp.

In its original sense, *Puritan* had nothing to do with sex; it
meant *plain*. It was spelled with an upper-case letter because it was
a proper noun—the name of a political party that wanted to tone
down the plushiness of Anglicanism, to eliminate its ritual,
hierarchy, and elegance and substitute simplicity, individualism,
grass-roots control, and God-fearing religion. Having done these
things, the Puritans became known for their strictness, which
resulted in that lower-case designation, "puritanical," an outlook
that can and usually does have something to do with sex.

Reverend Thatcher is a Baptodisterian. He likes to take his
text from things like "By the sweat of thy brow" and to wind up
with homilies along the lines of "Bread that is worked for is sweet-
er by far than the sweetmeats of sloth in the mouths of the ungod-
ly." He tries mightily to be modern and with-it, but when he reads
the church announcements from the pulpit, something comes
over him when he gets to "The sex education group will meet tonight in the basement." It sounds darkling somehow.

The old Jonathan Edwards crunch has gone out of Reverend Thatcher. He no longer rants about the fires of hell, but when he aims for the chatty, diffident style of Father Chillingsworth he falls flat on his earnestness. Father Chillingsworth quotes Kierkegaard, Gide, and Stendhal, which helps immeasurably to pass the time in an interesting fashion, but Reverend Thatcher, who means so well it hurts, quotes Phyllis McGinley and Marjorie Holmes. He is also fond of that all-purpose Indiana sermon entitled "How's Business?" which begins with a worldly anecdote. Reverend Thatcher took his car to be repaired and the mechanic, who did not know who he was, inquired, "How's business?"

"And do you know what I told him?" Reverend Thatcher asks the sea of faces before him. "Business is booming!" It goes on in this vein, with Reverend Thatcher teasing the mechanic by withholding the exact nature of his business until finally the mechanic asks him point blank what line of work he's in. Now comes the punch line, which is going to get Reverend Thatcher into trouble with some burly mechanic one of these days: "I am a fisher of men."

Reverend Thatcher is like the progressive teacher who naively believes that mathematics reduced to the mundane level of squabbles with the milkman over the monthly bill is more thrilling to the human spirit than the cold logic of pure mathematics studied for its own sake. He never stops trying to apply religion to everyday life, which is why he is so deadly dull. His flock is weary of everyday life and craves moxie, but they will never get it from Reverend Thatcher because he tries so desperately to make religion live and breathe. A variation on his favorite theme is "Jesus Was a Good Businessman," a sermon in which he tries to prove that the miracle Jesus performed at the wedding feast of Cana was (1) a good investment or (2) tax-deductible.

And it gets worse, for Reverend Thatcher is as susceptible to the spirit of the locker room as any other Wasp male in this bailiwick. When he gets in these moods he laces his sermons with reminders that "Jesus was a star quarterback . . . Jesus dropkicked sinners to salvation . . . Jesus pitched a shut-out against sin," and on and on. But he saves his best theological chalk talk for the young men's Bible group. "Jesus," says Reverend Thatcher, "was no pantywaist." To prove it, he recalls the Michelangelo paintings he saw on his trip to Europe with the National Council of Churches, a crusade that Italy has never forgotten. "Most old paintings show Jesus as a wispy, pasty, skinny, sickly fellow, but Michelangelo told it like it is. Er, was. He painted Jesus and the disciples as big muscular fellows with good builds. He knew they had to be tough to walk all those miles and rough it the way they did. And Peter and Andrew went fishing every day! You better believe they had to be in shape!"

The point of it all is that muscularity is consistent and follows through: from physical muscles spiritual muscles grow, and vice versa. Or something like that. It is hard to tell sometimes just what Reverend Thatcher is getting at because in addition to being the pride of the locker room he has an unfortunate tendency to talk like the Bible: "For if a man saith that muscles be not good, saith he not that they be not good for the soul, which is with the body yet of it not?" Reverend Thatcher's speaking style goeth far to explain the glazed eyes of his flock, and the shoulder-sagging crumple of relief when he finally stops and intones, "Let us pray."

All religions are essentially masculine, but the masculine content of Protestantism seems to increase as you go down the socio-theological scale. The Reverend Thatcher level is the median; at the bottom, where the air is laden with sulphur, Protestantism resembles a raucous, sparring-for-a-fight male club. By contrast, high-church Episcopalianism is attractively feminine. Despite Father Chillingsworth's undeniable sex appeal, he looks great in lace and swishes beautifully in the *exeunt omnes* when he keeps perfect time to "Onward Christian Soldiers."

Reverend Thatcher's flock favors labor-oriented hymns like "Bringing in the Sheaves" and tributes to heavenly parliamentary democracy like "When the Roll Is Called Up Yonder." Far from being somber, Puritan hymns are sprightly foot-tappers. Carpenters can pound nails to them, housewives can beat rugs to them, and factories can thump to them. They are music to work by.

They are also remarkably easy to sing. Nearly all of them are marked by the same simple chord structure that makes them all sound alike, so that the lyrics of one hymn are often virtually interchangeable with those of another. When Carry Nation made her first hatchet-toting foray into a Kansas saloon, she was accompanied by a lady with a hand organ. In the excitement they got their signals crossed so that Carry boomed out "Who Hath Sorrow, Who Hath Woe?" and her accompanist played "Nearer My God to Thee." Neither of them noticed the difference and both continued on with their respective numbers until the police came.[4]

Many Puritan hymns also exude an unquenchable cheerfulness that jars with the accepted somber stereotype. Smiling through salvation-induced *frissons*, bouncy references to crossing the bar, going home, gathering at the river abound. They are also notably egalitarian, like "What a Friend We Have in Jesus" and one that sets Piscop teeth on edge, "I'd Rather Have Jesus." Having a direct line to God unhampered by an intercessory hierarchy makes the Puritan Wasp feel free to approach the Deity as a lifelong buddy. Such a level of gregariousness is bound to extend beyond the church doors. It is Reverend Thatcher's Protestantism that has pinned the *Smile!* button on much of America. Wherever there is a large concentration of Puritan Wasps, there too shall ye find galloping friendliness. The hand-pumping, first-naming Kiwanian Midwest, for instance, or that land of compulsive hospitality, the South.

The Holier Than Thou Reformed Church of Wasp Crossroads, Mississippi, is led by Brother Bascom, a graduate of the Brother Bascom Do-It-Yourself Home Study Bible Institute. Brother Bascom calls himself a soldier in the army of the Lord, but his baptismal rites place him squarely in the navy. Formerly a member of the Holier Than Thou church, Brother Bascom created a schism. Convinced that every single word in the Bible is the literal truth, he objected to the way the Holier Than Thou church performed baptisms. They did it in a six-foot-square tank inside the church, and the Bible clearly stated that it was to be done in a river. That was enough for Brother Bascom; he walked out in the middle of service and started his own church, calling it the Holier Than Thou *Reformed.* (Should anyone disagree with Brother Bascom and wish to start still another church, the proper name for it would be the Holier Than Thou *Independent* Reformed.)

Brother Bascom believes in opening high. Throwing his Bible on the floor, he puts his foot on it and bawls, "I stand on the word of God!" After that he bawls, "Suddum! Suddum 'n' Gomorrah!

[4] Taylor, *op. cit.*

Jacob was a smooth man 'n' Ee-sow was a hairy man! A virtuous woman is worth her weight in rubies or she is as sounding brass!''

Then comes strong drink. "Anybody that pours Satan's own brew into the temple of the holy spirit is going to Hell in a bucket! Liquor is Hell's river! It gives you a red nose, a green liver, a black heart, and a yellow streak right up the middle of your back!''

Despite this oppressive air of certain perdition, Brother Bascom's Protestants sing the most cheerful hymns of all. No matter what gruesome Christian happening they sing about, they can punch it up. The all-purpose Brother Bascom Hymn might go something like this:

> Clap hands for spilled blood of Jesus,
> Shout it out for rapture's thorns!
> Come ye jubilant to receive Him,
> Joy beams through His empty tomb.
> Rejoice in piercèd nails defying,
> Happy hearts will quiver thus:
> Christ all gone! Cares all gone!
> Sweetly He delivered us.

The reason the Holier Than Thous are so happy is because they know they are Saved. Such knowledge accounts for the evangelistic grimace that exposes both rows of teeth that passes for a smile in these parts. It may be why they give their children names like Oral. Burt Lancaster mastered the Saved smile in *Elmer Gantry* but its undisputed mistress is that pillar of the Holier Than Thou Reformed Church, Sister Effie Lee Pringle.

Sister Effie felt sorry for folks who hadn't been Saved. Anyone who did not accept Jesus as his personal saviour was going to Hell, including all those taintless souls like the mother of the Gracchi who had the misfortune to have lived and died before Jesus was ever heard of. Bait Sister Effie on this point and she will parrot Brother Bascom back at you: "You've got to accept Jesus or you'll go to Hell." QED, not to mention PDQ.

Committed to missionary work and witnessing for the Lord, Sister Effie would hurl herself like a rocket at any unenlightened sinner she saw. Her favorite area of missionary work was "reading matter." Booklets, brochures, flyers, pamphlets, folders, anything with a soul-saving message on it. Catholics left their booklets in the rack in the church vestibule and trusted people to pay for them, but Sister Effie gave them to people free whether they wanted them or not.

Knowing that sinners liked sinful books, Sister Effie made the public library her own personal mission. Once a week she took a stack of church pamphlets to the library and spent the afternoon stuffing. By the time she got through, all sorts of inspirational messages were falling out of library books the moment anyone opened them, the way subscription cards fall out of *Time* and *Newsweek.* Sister Effie liked to watch while a sinner opened a copy of *Fear of Flying* and her pamphlet, "Are You Ready for the Second Coming?" fluttered to the floor.

Finding out what sinners liked to read was Sister Effie's only literary pursuit, for she herself did not read books. She did, however, steal them. Brother Bascom said it was a sin to sell God's word, so Sister Effie stole Bibles from bookstores. Brother Bascom approved, saying that it would sure punish those sinners and put them out of business fast because Bibles were the most expensive books in the store. Served them right for making a profit off God, he said.

Sister Effie liked to prepare her soul for the Sabbath by making Saturday her hit day. Bright and early every Saturday morning, she got her shopping satchel, took the bus to Jackson or Memphis or some other big city, and cleaned out every bookstore in town, taking special care to look for stores where an author was scheduled for an autographing party because such shenanigans distracted attention from *her* shenanigans. Sunday mornings she delivered the hot Bibles to her fence, Brother Bascom, who gave them away free to anyone who, in his opinion, needed one. In Brother Bascom's opinion, the neediest people were legislators because they passed unnecessary laws. All the laws anybody needed were right there in the Bible—the Ten Commandments.

Religious decor is a telling factor in Protestant homes. It is possible to see what level of Protestantism a family belongs to by checking out the Christian artifacts. The Episcopalian home is noted for its lack of such items. We limit ourselves to a wall cross over the bed. If it has the body of Christ on it we call it a crucifix as the Catholics do; if not we say cross. Some low Episcopalians have a crucifix, but Piscops tend to shy away from such realism, considering it too gruesome and vaguely tasteless. We prefer a Celtic cross like the ones still standing in Ireland. This is supposed to be *the* Episcopal cross, but lately it has become hard to find in denominational stores, having yielded to stark modernistic ones in blond Swedish-type wood. Recently I saw a very plain hand-carved cross made of cypress wood; when I turned it over, it was stamped *Made in Israel.*

All Episcopalians shudder at the sight of garish pictures of Jesus, but Piscops shudder harder; our reaction is more like ague or even epilepsy. To us, hanging a picture of Jesus in one's home is pure-brass effrontery because it rather implies that you are related to Him. Our walls feature daguerreotypes and chromos of antecedents; Granny in full DAR battle dress with a tricolor sash like a gun belt is all right, but not Jesus. In Southern homes you will find a cavalry saber and perhaps a bullet-torn Stars and Bars, but not Jesus. He begins to appear somewhere around the Baptodisterian level and gets Waspier looking as you go down the socio-religious ladder. The median Protestant portrait of Jesus is out of the Sears or Ward catalogue and shows a man in His late twenties or early thirties who looks very much like F. Scott Fitzgerald in a Princeton-alumnus mood. His hair is light brown, He is shown only from the waist up, and His hands are not visible. He wears a plain Roman-style toga.

Sister Effie Lee Pringle's portrait of Jesus is a sunburst of sadomasochism, a Protestant version of the Catholic Sacred Heart. Jesus wears a pink caftan and is floating upward, caught in mid-ascension. He holds His hands up, exposing reddish brown stigmata; He is long and rangy and His hair is yellow. In fact, He looks exactly like Jed Marlborough who lives up in the hills, the same Jed Marlborough whose daddy shot the Treasury man. In Sister Effie's home, Jesus is a good ole boy.

Presbyterian and Congregational homes are iffy in the religious artifacts department. Presbyterian standards are extremely complicated. Some Presbyterian churches are as rich as Croesus and have a heavy country club membership. Others, especially in the hinterland, are far more modest. A town without an Episcopal church is usually a town in which the Presbyterians are plutocrats. In that case, they do not hang pictures of Jesus. In New England, the Congregational church, a kind of Presbyterian equivalent, is often *the* church, socially speaking, and so its members do not hang pictures of Jesus, either. Generally, the people who say parlor instead of living room are the Jesus hangers of Waspdom.

At Christmastime the manger scene is acceptable to Episcopalians providing there are children in the home, but the figures must be doll-house size. The Infant Jesus must fit into the palm of the hand; anything bigger will bring forth a horrified "My God!" from Mrs. Piscop, who will hide the oversize Infant under the sink so that Father Chillingsworth will not see it when he drops by for his holiday grog. Nothing spoils a Piscop's Christmas quicker than a life-size manger scene. At the sing 'n' shout level of Protestantism the manger scene resembles that found in Detroit's Catholic ethnic areas in the front yard. St. Joseph is six feet tall, the Virgin Mary looks like a Wasp prom queen, and the Infant may be wearing a Pamper to humanize things.

The fly-specked religious calendar hanging in Sister Effie's kitchen is a fixture of Southern rural life. The illustrations underline her come-as-a-child theology. Jesus appears to be a babysitter: a child on each knee, a baby lamb under each arm, and a kindergarten of rapt listeners clustered at His feet. Jesus himself looks no more than twenty, and for once, He's clean shaven. When the calendar runs out, Sister Effie clips her favorite illustrations and sticks them in the corner of her dresser mirror, or simply tapes them on the wall.

At the other end of the scale is the Episcopal desk calendar which commemorates St. Thomas à Becket's murder with a quotation from T.S. Eliot, and records the name days for Waspy people like St. Swithin and Justin Martyr. July 12, St. Andrew's day, features the lyrics to the Orangeman's march, "Lillibulero," four bars of which guarantee the death of any whistler in Boston, and even that of the whistler's mother if she happens to be along. But the best page in the Episcopal desk calendar is March 17, which contains a quotation from the Venerable Bede pointing out that St. Patrick was actually a Briton who was kidnapped from his birthplace and taken by force to Ireland by Gaelic brigands.

3

KEEPING UP WITH MRS. JONESBOROUGH
or
The High Wasp Mother

Mrs. Jonesborough may or may not be an Episcopalian—it doesn't matter. As a member of America's upper middle class she enjoys many privileges and therefore "thinks Episcopal," even though she may belong to another church, or none at all.

Mrs. Jonesborough can be found in any part of the country. She may be an old-line Wasp whose family members have always been the pillars of the town they still dominate—the big fish in the little pond. She may be the Southern chatelaine whose picture appears constantly in the society pages, owing to her loyalty to that Victorian practice known as "giving unstintingly" to good causes in the mode of gentlewomen. Most often, however, she is the suburban Wasp whose husband is a commuting executive —the people who are universally tagged with that most Welsh of all names, Jones.

The Jonesboroughs are from everywhere and nowhere. Mr. Jonesborough was born in Iowa but works for Socony-Mobil, so he commutes to New York from Connecticut. Mrs. Jonesborough was born in Arizona for the simple reason that her mother had asthma; she met Mr. Jonesborough while they were both students at UCLA, and since then they have lived in seven states. Living the life of corporate vagabonds has robbed Mrs. Jonesborough of much of that sense of roots that all Wasps cherish; she has learned to travel light, with a minimum of those family mementos that clutter up more stationary Wasp homes, and unlike her Southern and New England counterparts, she cannot indulge in fragile antiques. However, she has something else—a college education and lots of interests, the least of which is her house. She has other things on her mind besides scrubbing floors. Those things may range from the tennis pro at the country club to the latest best-seller, but whatever it is, we may be sure it is not *Küche*, not *Kinder*, and not *Kirche*, although the latter two are often valuable for making friends in a new community.

In a sense, Mrs. Jonesborough of suburbia is the most typical Wasp mother in present-day America, for her homemaking problems, more than those of other Wasp mothers, are a direct outgrowth of Protestantism.

The concepts of individualism and equality fostered by Prostestantism took much of the sanctity out of motherhood and replaced the Perfect Drudge with another ideal. Mrs. Jonesborough is not only required to cook and clean and mother; she must also be partner, companion, accountant, consultant, hostess, geisha, and above all, mistress. The Catholic patriarch compartmentalized these various aspects of his life, thrusting different kinds of women into different niches much like the arrangement of plaster saints in his church. He did not particularly want to talk to his wife; he certainly did not want her meddling in his business affairs; and he did not even expect her to be good in bed, merely compliant and fertile. Feeling that too many interests and enthusiasms spoiled a good wife, he asked only that she mind the children, keep the house, and talk to God.

The Protestant husband, with the best of intentions, encouraged his wife to be superwoman. Knowing that she is supposed to be all things to one man keeps Mrs. Jonesborough in a perpetual state of conflict and ambivalence. Should she wash the dishes or bone up on current events so she will have something interesting to say? Should she sweep the floor or exercise her vaginal muscles? If the children are getting on her nerves, should she have another baby to prove what a good mother she really is? Whatever she decides to do, she is certain to be exhausted from decision making before she ever does it. The exhaustion tends to make her a lovable bundle of inefficiency.

The FBI compiles personality profiles by studying the contents of garbage cans. The best way to know Mrs. Jonesbororough is through her grocery list. America's most dedicated one-stop shopper, she stands revealed in the glare of her priorities:

coffee	tomato juice
Harper's	Worcestershire
Alpo	Tabasco
9-Lives	*Cosmopolitan*
cigarettes	food

Mrs. Jonesborough is the lady at the stove with a spatula in one hand and a half-finished Bloody Mary in the other. Thanks to her habit of cooking while three sheets to the wind—or even while reading a novel—her standard dessert is an upside-down cake. It didn't start out that way, but she dropped it. She picked it up because what the family doesn't know won't hurt them, and besides, the floor isn't *that* dirty. Like Mary McCarthy's famous Wasp housewife, Jane Coe, in *A Charmed Life*, she believes that germs build immunities and frequently says so. Alex Portnoy thought his mother had magical powers because she could suspend fruit in mid-Jello, but the Wasp son seldom has to wrestle with that kind of awe. Usually Mrs. Jonesborough forgets to add the fruit to the jello at all; if she remembers, the thought strikes her during happy hour. Muttering, "Oh, God," she gets to her feet, goes into the kitchen, opens a can of peaches, and throws the whole business, juice and all, into the Jello mold. The result is another standard Jonesborough dessert: *fruits gélés à la Titanic.*

Mrs. Jonesborough likes recipes that "you don't have to do anything to," meaning one-step dishes that obediently stew in their own juice in a big pot that turns itself on and off while she reads *Jaws*. The automatic crockery pot was made for the Wasp cook and could save her from herself, if only she did not have such all-American faith in gadgets. The food-conscious ethnic mother, ever solicitous of her family, does not trust the pot and keeps checking on it. Mrs. Jonesborough, feeling that the pot can do no wrong, throws in a hunk of corned beef, a head of cabbage, and six unpeeled potatoes, then disappears for ten hours. When she returns, she serves her family red rubber bands, gray leafy mush, and prolapsed potatoes.

She is the foremost exponent of the glop-it-up school, a cuisine that has been thrust upon America by that Waspy outfit, Campbell's soups. Adding a can of cream of mushroom soup to a can of tuna and calling it Tuna Surprise, which it certainly is, makes her feel like one of those women whom service magazines call "menu planners."

It doesn't take much to make Mrs. Jonesborough feel good about herself. Dumping a quivering, can-shaped blob of something into her skillet means that she is "adding" something special to what would have been an ordinary recipe were it not for her culinary talents, that is, her ability to read the helpful hints on the soup-can label. And dumping is what invariably occurs in her kitchen; when the directions say, "Add gradually and stir until dissolved," she dumps. Listen and you will hear a constant gluck-blick-gloosh-PLOP as yet another tubular mess gathers air, slides out of the can, and hits the skillet.

"Dressing up" canned foods is another specialty of hers. It involves buying a cellophane envelope of slivered almonds, which, since the envelope wouldn't "tear here," she has cussed and then ripped open with her teeth or chopped open with a gigantic butcher knife used like a meat cleaver on the poor helpless little package. She finally scatters them on top of her canned cream of shrimp soup. Sometimes she makes a *bouquet garni* with cheesecloth to boil in her canned soup. Usually it comes undone, bringing forth an exasperated cry of "God's *feet!*" If it happens to stay intact to the end, she fishes it out and swings it lariat-style in the direction of the garbage can, which accounts for the spots on her kitchen floor, and even her kitchen walls. She hits the garbage can, however, because she has an excellent aim. All that golf and tennis, and the family membership her husband took out in the Fairfield County Gun Club.

Like all Wasp women, she makes up for quality with quantity. Her motto is "If you can't cook well, cook a lot." But Mrs. Jonesborough's groaning board has only one real purpose: to camouflage her non-talents and counter any charges that she has no interest in feeding her family. Once the food is on the table, it does not matter to her what happens to it. She seldom pushes food on anyone. She could not care less if the carrot on your plate is lonesome for the carrot in your stomach; her children are lucky if she anthropomorphizes *them*, never mind the carrots. If a child whines that he isn't hungry, her standard reply is, "If you don't want it, don't eat it. Why tell me?"

Why indeed? Her children are quick to observe that food

means very little to Mother. A devotee of the theory that a woman cannot be too rich or too thin, Mrs. Jonesborough is constantly dieting. In her world, anybody over size ten is a Catholic; so her daily consumption consists of two cups of black coffee, a triscuit, three tablespoons of cottage cheese, four ounces of chopped sirloin, and a couple of daiquiris. She is not above putting a three-month-old baby on reduced rations if she thinks he is too pudgy, and her special nightmare is a fat daughter. Starting around age eleven, the Wasp daughter becomes the apple of her mother's eagle eye. At the first appreciable sign of adolescent weight gain, Mrs. Jonesborough is jerking serving dishes from her daughter's hands and declaring, "Your eyes are bigger than your stomach!"

She also warps her children's idea of good food with those ghastly concoctions that dieting women make in the blender. Something like the witch's brew that Minnie Castavet served up daily in *Rosemary's Baby*, they consist of watery skim milk, lots of nutritious herbs, and wheat germ. To convince *herself* that it's tasty, Mrs. Jonesborough downs it enthusiastically, then says, "Umm, that's delicious." Naturally the children want to taste it, too, so she gives them a sample, leading them to believe that this is what delicious is supposed to taste like.

Sniffing food to make sure it has not spoiled is a precautionary habit Wasps develop early in life, for there is no telling what might emerge from Mrs. Jonesborough's refrigerator at a full gallop. Secretly guilty over not being able to do magic things with leftovers, she saves them anyway—for weeks. Pennywise and pound foolish, she will put three string beans on a demitasse saucer and leave them in the fridge until they grow a beard. Things go from bad to worse inside the Jonesborough fridge until one day, Mother opens the door and exclaims in tones of outraged innocence, "What's that smell?" Well, there are several soggy paper bags each containing the neck, gizzard, heart, and liver of a chicken. She often forgets to remove the bags from the chicken's cavity before baking, but three months ago she turned over a new leaf and wrote herself a cautionary reminder on her kitchen blackboard: TAKE OUT GIBLETS!! She did take them out. They have been lying in the vegetable bin ever since, waiting to be transformed into giblet gravy.

A burst of housewifely energy comes over her and she does her mass-efficiency number. Throwing things out turns her on, and there is so much to throw out. Three quart cans of tomato juice, each half full of burnished brown liquid, for instance. When it's all over and some fifty dollars has been pulverized in the Disposall, she puts a fresh box of baking soda in the fridge and proudly tells her family, "I cleaned out the icebox." She fully expects them to compliment her on her precision home management.

From time to time, she really gets guilty and resolves to get with it and start cooking "from scratch." More throwing out. Out goes the Hamburger Helper, and in comes a sack of flour. Soon the family hears crashes and curses from the kitchen, view halloos that tell them Mother has gone on another cooking spree.

For breakfast there are *real* pancakes, and she just might beat the batter with the flat of her hand in good Wasp-pioneer style. She can't get the pancakes round but she feeds the oblong ones to the dog and keeps trying. As the family glues up on *real* oatmeal (she threw out the instant), she announces that there will be *real* clam chowder for dinner. Her children are so used to Campbell's soup that they will even add a can of water to their Coca-Cola; they do not care about the chowder but they insist upon staying home from school so they can watch the *real* clams spit out sand. To accompany the chowder, she decides to make *real* baked beans. It eases her guilt if she can soak something for twelve hours before she even cooks it.

Normally a salt-and-pepper woman, she now goes herb-crazy, buying the biggest bottles of chervil, tarragon, and rosemary she can find. Proudly lining them up on her spice shelf, where she also keeps her stapler and her thumb tacks, she proceeds to "dress up" her hamburgers. The first child who says, "The hamburgers taste funny," will get a tongue lashing and a royal command: "Eat! I want that plate cleaned!" Suddenly, Mother cares, but a child accustomed to gauging his own appetite is not likely to take comfort from such sudden solicitude. He is simply confused by Mother's inconsistency. Sometimes he is worse than confused, for rosemary and Swingline staples look remarkably alike after cooking.

Her housewifely enthusiasms may burn briefly, but while they burn they are incandescent. She *must* leave the house *that very minute* to go buy the 10,000 Recipes Plastic Card Filex that she saw advertised on television. The size of a small file cabinet, it contains enough menus to see her through the duration of her marriage without a single repeat. Each card has a washable finish so that it can be wiped free of what the manufacturer calls "spills" (*that's* good), and there is a beautiful full-color photo of each creation. Soon Mrs. Jonesborough is talking like the cards. Everything is now "crispy crunchy" and "zestful."

Her worst seizures involve *real* pea soup and homemade jelly. Pea soup requires a ham bone, so she buys a *real* ham and makes everybody eat it until it is coming out of their ears. If they lag behind, she prompts them: "We've got to finish that damn ham! I need the bone!"

The homemade-jelly lust comes over her so suddenly that the first time it happens she goes tearing out of the house and down to the hardware store, investing some fifty dollars or more in the necessary equipment. Naturally she expects to make her own jelly for the rest of her life, so she pooh-poohs the cost, explaining, "Homemade jelly is so much cheaper than store-bought that I'll save a fortune in the long run." Note the devotion to the concept of Wasp thrift, and that fine all-American phrase, "store-bought." Wasps never stop trying to recapture our own past, and quaint, antiquated phrases pop out of our mouths with clockwise regularity.

Soon Mrs. Jonesborough's kitchen looks like a South Seas hut, festooned with gauzy arrangements of dripping cheesecloth. This is the part that delights the children; they are little cynics on the subject of cooking, thanks to Mother's violent swings from one extreme to the other, but they love to stand directly under her "extractions" with their mouths open. It's not nourishment for the body; just a game. They know it won't last, so they like to have fun while they can.

It's as close to homemade jelly as they can expect to get, for when Mrs. Jonesborough is in these moods she wants to be one of those old-fashioned cooks who never measures anything. So she never measures anything. Something—she knows not what —goes wrong, and the jelly doesn't jell. Her raspberry soup gets shoved into the back of the refrigerator where it will sit until it ferments, which inspires her to make homemade wine. The only edible part of the entire jelly endeavor are the little round wafers of paraffin. The children acquire a taste for them and call them Mother's cookies in Show 'n' Tell.

As suddenly as her cooking spree began, it comes to a halt. The recipe Filex is stored on the topmost shelf with the six dozen Mason jars, and Mrs. Jonesborough curls up with *Ragtime*. When the children get home from school she is in no mood to stop and fix anybody a sandwich. If a child wants a glass of milk, he is welcome to help himself. Otherwise he is free to wait till happy hour and fill up on cheese ball, olives, pearl onions, maraschino cherries, lemon twists, and smoked oysters. Getting the fruit from his parents' whiskey sours and Tom Collinses makes the Wasp child feel loved, and also grown-up. However, our parents don't always realize the effect such a habit can have. My mother fed me bourbon-soaked orange slices and then asked, in honest amazement, "What's wrong with your eyes?" when they started to cross.

Manic or depressive, Mrs. Jonesborough, like all Wasp mothers, always fixes a good breakfast. As in England, so too in Waspland: Breakfast is the meal you can always trust to taste good. The incessant advice, "Eat a better breakfast, feel better all day long," to which all Americans are subjected, has its origins in this Anglo-Saxon obsession. On my first trip to London, I stayed at Mrs. 'Awkins' bed-and-breakfast. Hearing that I had just come from France, she started in on the French. "Rum lot, hain't they? A crust o' bread and a cuppa coffee. You'll get a good *English* breakfast 'ere." I did indeed. She served two eggs, two strips of bacon, two sausage links, grilled tomatoes, baked beans on toast, and *fried bread*. Eating a breakfast like this enables you to avoid an English lunch and an English dinner. Some English, like the Scotland Yard inspector in Hitchcock's movie, *Frenzy*, avoid their wives' cooking by eating breakfast three times a day.

A nightly announcement in many Wasp homes is, "We"re going to have _____ for breakfast tomorrow." We start looking forward to breakfast long before we go to bed, and conversations spring up about it, especially on Friday night when we know that two leisurely mornings lie ahead. Our feeling for breakfast is a matter of emotional security. Breakfast = a consistent mother.

The best Wasp cooks in my experience are Southerners. Southern cooking is heavy, and the Wasp cook is heavy-handed, so it works out very well. Southern women also know how to cook "by ear," as Mrs. Jonesborough of suburbia does not. Most Southern recipes were invented by black women who could not read, so the Southern white woman has had to develop a sixth sense in the kitchen. The biggest problem in Southern homes and restaurants is getting a really rare steak. Used to cooking pork, Southerners have a compulsion to cook any meat "until it's good and done." If you order a rare steak, you get medium. Tell a Southern waitress you want it blood rare and she will ask, "Are you sure?" The kitchen always wins; I have never gotten a good steak in the South unless I cooked it myself.

The Southern rural cook is both superb and terrible. Her breads and biscuits are lighter than French croissants, but the rest of the meal might well be inedible. Used to cooking for her husband's farm hands and seasonal workers (known as "the men"), she has too many different tastes to please and so gives up trying to please any of them. She will put as many as twelve vegetables on the table, all cooked without a grain of salt or anything else. Her motto is, "Do with it what ye will." Because "the men" may have spent the day slaughtering, they don't want to see any more blood, so she does her beef roast at 400° for two and a half hours. To make it juicy, she lays a strip of bacon over the top of the roast. The beef blood cooks away entirely, leaving a dry husk of gray meat that tastes like pork-flavored leather. The obligatory strip of bacon or hunk of salt pork, known as side meat or fatback, is so ubiquitous in Southern cooking that it is liable to turn up in just about any dish. Some people eat it; most of us merely fish it out and throw it away.

Cooking far too much at any one meal is a Southern tropism that has its origins in our hospitality hang-up. When my grandmother fried pork chops or baked potatoes, she would always throw on an extra for that Southern angel of death known as "our unknown guest." You never know when somebody might drop in at the last moment, so better be prepared. This way, no matter what happens, you can always say, "Sit right down, there's plenty more in the pot." *Not* saying these obligatory words is the nadir of disgrace. To this hour, despite the hermit-like writer's existence I lead, I persist in cooking for my "unknown guest." When I make cole slaw I invariably use the whole head of cabbage; I am incapable of halving anything.

In housekeeping, the Southern woman is the worst in Waspdom. Her chief problem is, of course, that she has never recovered from the Emancipation Proclamation. That one really did her in. Subconsciously she feels that she *ought* to have servants; and by servants she does not mean occasional help with the heavy cleaning—she means *servants*. Lots of them. She may or may not be a descendant of aristocrats; it does not matter because she always thinks she is. Thus she is a passionate supporter of that Southern version of *Schlamperei* which is summed up in the old saying, "Too poor to paint and too proud to whitewash." A *carte blanche* for elegant enervation, it means, "Let it rot so people will know how rich we *used* to be." Housekeepers who subscribe to this view believe that grubbiness is the patina of grandeur, and so they tend to look down on the woman whose house is excessively neat and clean. Her everlasting scrubbing and polishing are petty bourgeois habits that bar her from membership in Southern gentility. Soon all the ladies are talking about her, and before she knows it her reputation is ruined. In small towns she might even get a reputation for being insane, like Mrs. Robbins in *The View from Pompey's Head*, who "had so exaggerated an interest in housekeeping that some of the ladies in Pompey's Head called it a mania."

Far from being able to eat off the Southern woman's floors, you are lucky if you can walk barefoot across them without picking up impetigo. She takes her leaf from Christopher Fry's play, *The Lady's Not for Burning:* "What's a halo? Just something else to keep clean." The original Mrs. Nasty-Nice, as black maids have always called her behind her back, she is fussy, but about all the wrong things. The silver must be polished, but not necessarily with a clean cloth. There must be redolent fresh flowers in the house even though the dog flunked out of obedience school. If a sandwich maker drops a blob of catsup on on the kitchen floor, she wipes it up immediately—with the dish rag. Calling this item a *rag* is a disconcerting habit that jars with her elegant persona. She also uses a wash *rag* in her bath. In junior high school home ec class, we drove our Pennsylvania-born teacher wild with constant references to rags, yet in one of those typical bursts of Southern formality we called dish-wiping cloths "tea towels," which upset her even more. She never did comprehend that she had a class full of Little Misses Nasty-Nice on her hands.

Coping with the burden of history is an unavoidable frustration to Southern women who might like to be better housekeepers than they are. Every Southern home is a museum. You cannot launder a hundred-year-old flag full of bullet holes; the only thing to do is leave it on the wall with the cavalry saber. When no one is looking, dust the saber with the flag if you must; otherwise forget it. Nor is it possible to do anything about the Revolutionary War musket and powder horn on the other side of the wall. They are heavier than they look, and trying to take them down and clean them might result in a fractured skull. Besides, dust and gunpowder look somewhat alike. Ignore the dust and call it authenticity.

Besides all the junk hanging on the walls, there are cardboard boxes full of family records, deeds, land grants, quit claims in medieval Latin, genealogical charts, bloodstained uniforms, and dozens of buttons and belt buckles stamped C.S.A. They are only the beginning—the ordinary mementos that all Southern families have. Some really flaky Southerners I have known save *used* bullets, cannon balls, the rope with which an ancestor was hanged, and—so help me—a slave studbook.

At the very least, there is Grandfather's rolltop desk—it bears the scars of the shoot-out that took place in his law office—which is crammed full of old letters. Occasionally the Southern housekeeper will decide to clean it out and arrange everything neatly, but the moment she sits down and starts sifting through it all, wistful nostalgia takes over and she begins to reread her family treasures. Three hours later she is still there, having gotten no further in her task, studying the only surviving scrap of an ancestor's letter: *"Wyth a mournfull hart I take up my penn to imparte the melancholie yvents . . ."* it reads—and then stops, leaving generations of descendants in eternal suspense. What, wonders the lady of the house, were those "melancholie yvents"?

She will get so intrigued that she will spend the rest of the day on the telephone to the historical society, leaving the desk messier than it was before, the dishes in the sink, and the dirty laundry on the floor.

Old is the one small word that lies behind all the Southern woman's housekeeping problems. For one thing, she is likely to live in a very old house. Known as "big old" or "lovely old," the emphasis is always on its age. She or her husband may have inherited it, so modernistic renovations are tantamount to sacrilege. All must be left in the Southerner's favorite verb tense, the imperfect indicative: "The way it *used* to be." (My high school French class grasped the *imparfait* conjugation in a trice; even the slowest pupils took to it like ducks to water.) Thus the Southern woman's lovely old house contains rococo moldings, filigrees of every sort, a mantel that looks like an esoteric altar from some lost civilization that collapsed under the weight of its own gimcracks, and even bas relief carvings, not to mention ornate newel posts that can be dusted only with a single rabbit hair.

The lovely old apartment in which I was born and raised had seven enormous rooms complete with a Greek revival frieze, which ran around the living room ceiling. I grew up looking at cherubs with clots of dust collected in the tips of their uncircumcised penes. No one ever bothered to dust the frieze except for those times when my neat un-Southern father got fed up and swatted at the worst places with a broom. My mother and grandmother referred to the task by that dearest of all Southern phrases, "a lost cause," explaining that it would be foolish to try to dust it because, "This place will be standing long after we're all dead and buried." That is the Southern housekeeper's favorite rationale —age, death, burial, continuity, and the sacred past are all rolled up into one verbal shrug. Resignation is a Southern art form, after all: "A little dirt never hurt anybody."

Even when the Southern woman has "help," it doesn't help much. We had a black woman named Emma come in once a month for the . . . well, the heavy cleaning, but thanks to Granny nothing ever got done. After ten minutes in our apartment's darker corners, she would say, "Emma, let's sit down and have a nice glass of iced tea." Once ensconced at the kitchen table, they would put their heads together for one of their endless obstetrical seminars.

Mrs. Jonesborough's suburban house is usually modern and easily cleaned, and that helps *some*. However, despite her advantages, the best thing that can be said for Mrs. Jonesborough's housekeeping is that men are comfortable around her. She never says, "Stop! That's my good _____!"

The major problem in the Jonesborough home is Mother's favorite cottage industry: the gratis clipping bureau. No one is ever permitted to throw away a newspaper; they must be carefully saved, in the children's old baby carriage, in the cold fireplace, in the guest room bath tub, on the dining room table, until Mother gets around to cutting out the articles she has marked. After adding her usual marginal comments ("*Tant pis!*") she will read them to her club, then hand them out to her friends or send them to her expatriate son in Khartoum. Meanwhile, the newspapers sit. In the unlikely event that this devotee of current events takes a notion to dust the dining room table, she will dust *around* the newspapers, for in keeping with her ersatz definition of ship-shape, they are neatly stacked and arranged with the utmost care in order of dates. They must not be moved.

Newspapers are the only thing Mrs. Jonesborough saves. Passionately dedicated to the *theory* of Wasp puritan thrift, she has a difficult time practicing it. She never knows when her husband might be transferred to another part of the country, and so she can't amass the odds and ends, the this and the that, which her grandmother collected so lovingly. So when her race memory tells her it is time to make a patchwork quilt, she is caught without a scrap bag. (In the South it's called a rag bag.)

Undaunted, she sets about acquiring an instant scrap bag. When the patchwork quilting bee starts buzzing in her bonnet, Dad's favorite Hawaiian shirt disappears. She promises each family member a nice big handmade comforter by winter. She will see to it that her loved ones are toasty warm even if she has to strip the clothes off their backs . . . to make the quilts . . . that they wouldn't need . . . to keep them warm . . . if she hadn't stolen their clothes . . . in the first place. She means *so* well you could hug her, but after seventeen squares and numerous holes in her fingers (she can't manage a thimble), she gives up.

Next comes rug-hooking. When Mrs. Jonesborough decides to make a throw rug, female family members suddenly find that they have run out of *new* stockings. Not only that, she is not above ripping new panty hose from their packets and bisecting them at the crotch in order to plait them together. Soon the house is full of nylon pigtails; long, quivering ropes of them hang everywhere, waiting for the day when Mother acquires enough patience to sit in front of the fire for an entire winter hooking them into circular shapes. The plaiting stage of rug making is easy; she can do that while she watches "Meet the Press." But as soon as she has to look at what she is doing and read complicated directions ("My *God!*") her fervor wilts.

Now Mrs. Jonesborough decides to make her husband a belt. Lacking the attic full of usable junk that the stationary Wasp woman can turn to, she rushes out to the nearest hobby shop and buys a belt-making kit. Kits, sets, and neatly packaged do-it-yourself with reams of instructions turn Wasps on; they appeal to our self-sufficient pioneer instincts. Unfortunately, what awaits Mrs. Jonesborough is built-in frustration; whether she finishes the belt or not (she probably won't), the self-image she seeks will elude her once again. She wants to be like Jane Wyman, the wilderness wife, making do or doing without. Nobody ever told Jane Wyman to insert prong (A) into hole (B). Filmland's wilderness wife always knows how to do things already. She was taught them by her mother, who learned them from *her* mother, and on back into time. The instruction brochure issued by Fun Enterprises offers little in the way of Wasp identity.

If some enterprising businessman invented the *Waste Not, Want Not, Inc.* kit, he would make a fortune; millions of suburban Wasp homemakers would run out and buy one. Mrs. Jonesborough will indulge in Babylonian expenditures to buy back her Wasp heritage, and her internal censor will reject any suggestion that she is not the tower of thrift she believes herself to be. She is convinced that she actually uses odds and ends for her various homey projects, that she is "putting to good use" things that would otherwise go to waste. Never mind the fifty dollars' worth of quilt stuffing that never gets stuffed, or the giant crochet needle that cost ten dollars and hasn't yet touched yarn. They will be saved, at least until the Jonesboroughs move again, because "you never know when they might come in handy." Uttering these puritanical Waspisms is a great comfort to Mrs. Jonesborough. She is even capable of saying, "Wear it, wear it out" with a straight face.

However, one day throwing stuff out will become an irresistible impulse with her, because it makes her feel like a far more efficient housekeeper than she actually is. After all, throwing stuff out is the *easiest* task of all, and when it's all over, the house looks Spartan, which is almost as good as looking neat and clean. Quilt filler being a messy, bulky item to have around, it follows that *throwing out* quilt filler is going to appeal to our Mrs. J, because she is ever on the lookout for wily rationalizations. Once she throws out the quilt filler and the plaited stockings—which takes about half an hour at the most—she can bask all day in the knowledge that she got something done.

She really has raised self-deception to an art. An excellent way to get out of making the beds is to let them air. She has the airiest beds in town. If she does not feel up to washing the dishes, she lets them soak, telling herself and anyone who should happen to complain that they are really getting cleaner that way. When she finally gets around to washing them, there is nothing to wash. All she has to do is take them out of the gummy water, rinse them with boiling water, put them in the sinkside drainer— and leave them there indefinitely. Again, should anyone complain—an unlikely event *chez* Jonesborough—she simply says, "Draining is more sanitary than drying them with a towel." This is an unanswerable statement, which elevates her to the pedestal occupied by the germfree Jewish housewife.

Whether Mrs. J washes dishes by hand or in a dishwasher, her dishes seldom make it back to the cabinets. When they have finally finished soaking and draining, it's time to eat again, so she simply puts them back on the table. Her family quickly gets used to this arrangement. When the children come home from school and fix a sandwich, they bypass the cutlery drawer and head for the sinkside drainer. There, like a quiver of arrows, are all the household knives—airing. Points up, of course. Standing on tiptoe and grabbing a knife by the blade is a specialty of Wasp first-graders.

When Mrs. J uses a dishwasher, anything can happen. She frequently confuses it with the Disposall, causing floods in the kitchen and costly visits from the repairman. One of the better results of this contretemps is that item known as the funny spoon. If one of the little Jonesboroughs refuses to eat, Mother makes a crafty bargain with him which she calls "using psychology" and which psychologists call bribery. If he will eat his lunch like a good boy, she will let him use the funny spoon. It got caught in the Disposall, and the children love it. They fight over it. Should Mrs. J have three children and only one funny spoon, not to worry. Sooner or later some more will get caught in the Disposall, and she will have all the funny spoons she needs.

A special cross Mrs. J must bear are ads showing Wasp-type women standing proudly beside their long row of gleaming copper-bottom pans hung up on the wall in ascending order. Because the woman in the ad is the same physical type as Mrs. J, guilt and enthusiasm crank up simultaneously in her soul, with predictable results. "I'm going to hang up the pans!" she cries happily. She heads for the store like a woman shot out of a cannon.

Back she comes with a copper wall rack, matching copper nails, the biggest can of copper polish that Safeway carries—and three more copper-bottom pans that she happened to see in the hardware store on her way home ("I have to fill up the hooks!"). Dad puts up the rack for her—he's handy around the house—and soon she is polishing up a storm.

When all the pans are done to a mirror finish and hung up, everybody *must* admire them. Simple compliments stated once are never enough. If Dad says, "That looks pretty," she comes back, "Doesn't it? Did you ever see anything prettier?" No, he must say, he never has, never in his whole life. The next morning at breakfast, she is still fishing. Ripping open the curtains and pulling up the blinds as far as they will go, she lets the sunlight stream in upon the pans and demands, "Look! Aren't they beautiful with the sunlight on them?"

The pans gleam for a week or so, then suddenly, in the middle of scouring, Mrs. J pulls off her rubber gloves, mutters, "Oh, to hell with it," and curls up with *Poirot's Last Case.* The gleaming rack and matching copper nails are still there, but now they contain grayish-green monstrosities. Should anyone comment, Mother shrugs nonchalantly, "A pan should look like a pan."

After about a month, she stops hanging up the pans altogether. Back they go to their usual storage places—the windowsill, on top of the fridge, inside the oven—leaving a nice empty rack for Mother and the rest of the family to hang *anything* on. Some of the items you might find hanging on Wasp pan racks are transistor radios, bicycle chains, and Pan Am flight bags. Do not put it past Johnny to leave an athletic supporter there.

Mrs. Jonesborough's approach to homemaking is so bad that it's occasionally very good. Expert, in fact. Traveling the full circle of inefficiency as she does, it is quite possible for her to find herself on the side of the angels merely by default. Her standards of cleanliness are ideal for one particular kind of pan—the cast-iron skillet—for the simple reason that you aren't supposed to wash it. White-glove housekeepers always have rust problems with iron cookware because they are constantly scouring it in soap and water. The fine art of banishing rust and getting iron pots good and black comes naturally to women like Mrs. Jonesborough. Simply wipe out the grease with a paper towel and don't go near the water.

Being fond of happy hour herself, she tends to marry the kind of man who would rather drink than eat. As a result, she is an expert when it comes to "holding dinner." She knows by a kind of Wasp instinct how to keep any kind of food warm for indefinite periods of time. In fact, she can hold dinner for a couple of days if necessary—and it has been known to be necessary.

But the really superb coup of Mrs. Jonesborough's ass-backwards operation is her mastery of gourmet cooking. It boggles the mind, but it has been known to happen. Perhaps she lived for a time in Europe, or at least had Junior Year Abroad. Some memory bell goes off in her brain ten years or so later, inspiring her to enroll in a gourmet cooking class, or to buy a hundred dollars' worth of French cookbooks and teach herself. She will plug away, measuring everything meticulously and following the smallest instruction with paranoid thoroughness. This time, for reasons unknown, she sticks with it; she is so consistently inconsistent that sometimes she just might fool everybody and *stay* out of character for months. The result? The most delectable French cuisine you ever tasted—she out-Tours the Tour d'Argent. Her bouillabaisse would bring the entire city of Marseilles to its knees in reverence and win her a *cordon bleu*.

However, there's always a catch. She still can't make an ordinary American meat loaf.

4

PUTTING UP WITH MRS. BAILEY
or
The Low Wasp Mother

Like Edith Bunker, Mrs. Myrtle Bailey of Waspville, Indiana, still wears housedresses; she would not dream of owning a pair of what she calls "dungarees." Unlike Edith, she is not always lovable. Mrs. Jonesborough cannot endure five minutes of her company, and members of the Bailey family also try to avoid her. Female Baileys still have to lock themselves in the bathroom to smoke, and male Baileys have to lock themselves in the garage to drink. Someone is always saying, "Uh-oh. Here she comes!"

Mrs. Bailey is a Baptodisterian. Used to a spare, undecorated church and raised with that Puritan maxim, "Cleanliness is next to godliness, " Mrs. Bailey long ago embarked on a holy crusade against dirt. She has a disconcerting habit of picking imaginary particles of dust off her tablecloth, her furniture, and her own person. Spending most of her life in an apron (so she won't soil her housedress) has given her another even more disconcerting habit: rubbing her palms over her stomach and down her thighs after touching anything. It makes sense as long as she's wearing an apron, but when she rubs her front after shaking your hand outside the Baptodisterian church, it gives the shakee pause.

Mrs. Bailey believes that there are only two causes of divorce: (1) the man drinks, or (2) the woman doesn't keep house. She, therefore, will never be a divorced woman, or as she puts it, a grass widow. Bailey has never touched a drop. Such a good man; they broke the mold when they made him. You can set your clock by Bailey, he has such regular habits. Home every night right on the dot, except once a year when he goes to the VFW convention.

He even works hard then, attending to the concerns of the brave men who fought for their country. Poor Bailey was always exhausted when he got home from convention week; pale and trembling and too tired to eat, but bearing gifts just the same. No matter how hard Bailey worked at the convention, he always remembered to bring Myrtle a nice present.

No, never a drop passed Bailey's lips, except of course when he was taking cold, but that was different. Indiana winters were fierce, so Mrs. Bailey always kept a medicinal bottle of whiskey in the cupboard. She herself fixed him a hot toddy with her very own hands, just as her mother and grandmother, teetotalers themselves, had done for their badly chilled husbands. And children. And selves. There was nothing wrong with taking whiskey for medicine as long as you didn't take it for pleasure. And poor Bailey had so many colds; he was always saying, "Myrtle, I feel a cold coming on."

As for keeping house, Mrs. Bailey was the pride of Waspville, famed far and wide as "a real scrubber, that woman." She received the necessary inspiration for her scrubbing every Sunday thanks to Reverend Thatcher's sermons, like "Jesus Worked Overtime." The Bailey home was as neat and clean as the Bailey church. The two even smelled the same, because Mrs. Bailey, president of the Ladies Circle, bossed the gang that cleaned the church. *Chez* Bailey or *chez* God, the odor of sanctity is Lysol. All the members of the Bailey family, as well as all the members of the Baptodisterian church, had runny noses and permanently damaged nasal membranes because Mrs. Bailey had a heavy hand with the Lysol bottle.

The bane of her existence is that terrible habit some people have of putting their feet on hassocks. Bailey, of course, was an exception; he wouldn't dare put his feet on her hassocks. He did when they were first married, but he stopped. Another thing that bothered her was all the comedians on television who told jokes about Jewish mothers. As far as she could tell, they sounded like fine women, the way they kept their houses and all. Mrs. Bailey didn't have a drop of Jewish blood, but she starched her husband's pajamas, too. She didn't know any Jews, of course, but she would say one thing for them: they weren't Catholic. Catholics were the ones you had to worry about. They drank and smoked and gambled and danced and cursed and fought. The Baileys drank not, smoked not, gambled not, danced not, cursed not, and fought not. And as for the way Catholic women kept their houses—my stars! Good thing the Catholic church didn't allow divorce, or they'd all be grass widows.

Of course the Episcopalians were just as bad. Mrs. Bailey couldn't sleep nights for fear her daughter Norma Dean was getting too serious with that no-good Episcopal playboy, Keith Jonesborough, whose mother yelled, "Balls of Christ!" right in the middle of Main Street when somebody scraped her fender. You'd think a woman with all that money and all that good breeding would be more ladylike, especially seeing as how her father and father-in-law owned the whole town between them. You'd think she'd have more of a feeling of responsibility. And that time at the Inter-Faith breakfast when Mrs. Jonesborough ate her bacon with her fingers! My goodness gracious, but that shocked the Ladies Circle. You'd think any woman who went east to school at Vassar would cut her bacon in little pieces and eat it with her fork, with her little finger crooked. A terrible person, Mrs. Bailey sighed, shaking her head. No doubt about it. She *hated* people like the Jonesboroughs! Well . . . no, she didn't *hate* them because that wouldn't be Christian; she just . . . Well.

As for the Jonesborough *home*, the less said the better. All that fuss about that ugly picture Mrs. Jonesborough had had framed! Mrs. Bailey had gotten the story from Norma Dean, who had gone with Keith Jonesborough to Indianapolis to pick it up. A dirty old picture, black and white, with a big splotch on it like somebody had spilled water all over it or—knowing the Jonesboroughs— spirits. It was a picture showing a bunch of French lawyers all dressed in black. Depressing. And what they said it cost! Wasteful. You could get "Autumn Sunset" from Monky Ward's for $14.95 framed. She herself had never set foot inside the Jonesborough home, but she *heard* from Sarah Carpenter who got it from Grace Thatcher that a book called *My Secret Garden* was lying on Mrs. Jonesborough's coffee table for all the world to see. At first they had thought she was finally taking an interest in her yard, but then they found out that the book was all about s-e-x-u-a-l f-a-n-t-a-s-i-e-s. I swan! thought Mrs. Bailey.

And the worst thing of all was that Norma Dean thought Mrs. Jonesborough was "just wonderful."

Mrs. Bailey was afraid Norma Dean was having to do with

Keith Jonesborough. That very morning when Mrs. Bailey was
polishing Norma Dean's doorknob (it was doorknob day), she saw
the marked calendar on the bureau. Norma Dean hadn't fallen off
the roof yet this month.

Mrs. Bailey sighed. The only way to stop worrying was to keep
busy. There was always work to be done if you looked for it, and
she looked. The plastic runners that she kept on her carpets where
folks walked a lot needed scrubbing. Terrible how folks walked
through a house.

Nobody could say she wasn't a good wife. Never mind all that
secret garden business. The beautiful living room suit they had
bought when they were first married was still like new, she had
seen to that. In fact, it was still new. The day the store had
delivered it she had put hand-sewn slipcovers on it to keep the
upholstery nice. Then she had started worring about the slipcovers; they looked so pretty that she hated to think of anybody
sitting on them, so she had gone up to Ward's and bought clear
plastic covers to fit over the slipcovers. Now she could wash the
furniture with Lysol. Summers, when Norma Dean wore shorts,
she would get stuck to the plastic and they had to peel her off. Then
she got that rash on the backs of her legs from the disinfectant,
but—these things happened. She shouldn't wear such short
shorts anyhow.

Time to scour the bathroom. The dirt really got into those
cracks around the tiles, but Mrs. Bailey knew how to deal with it.
Pipe cleaners. She hated for anybody to see her buying them,
though, so she went all the way over to Terre Haute to get them at a
drugstore where nobody knew her. Otherwise, if she bought
them in town, people might think Bailey had taken to vice. She hid
the pipe cleaners in her sewing basket so that no one who visited
would see such things in her house. There wasn't an ashtray in the
entire Bailey home, a fact that made Mrs. Bailey very proud. No
one had ever used tobacco within these walls except that time
when they had rented the extra room to travelers, when Bailey had
the hernia and couldn't work. Then along came two Southern
hussies who smoked like a chimney. When Mrs. Bailey found
them tapping ashes into the St. Louis World's Fair saucer that had
been her mother's pride and joy, she had said, "I druther you
didn't smoke in my house," and then proceeded to give them Hail
Columbia.

Then one of the hussies went into the bathroom. There was a

lot of clattering around, then the hussy yelled to the other hussy, "Where the hell is the goddamn toilet paper?" Next to hearing someone take God's name in vain, Mrs. Bailey hated to hear anyone say toilet paper. She always called it bathroom tissue. She also hated to see it sitting right out in the open for all the world to see and *know* what it was, so she had bought a Marie Antoinette doll whose hoop skirt fit perfectly over a roll of bathroom tissue. It was just as cute as could be, and you would never know in a million years that there was bathroom tissue under it.

Mrs. Bailey loved to cover things up. She covered every bar of soap in her bathroom with plastic Easter eggs. She hated it when people put down a cake of wet soap on her clean basin. Soap dishes didn't help because they didn't have tops and you could see all that gummy mess hardening and sticking to the bottom of the dish. So she had bought the plastic Easter eggs at the dime store and trained her family to put the wet cake of soap in the bottom part, then put the top part of the egg on as a nice lid. Sometimes the wet soap and the Easter-egg halves slipped out of Bailey's hands, making him yell, "Cheese and crackers got all muddy!" When they were first married, he had had a terrible habit of yelling, "Jesus Christ God Almighty!" that he had learned during the war. Mrs. Bailey hadn't tried to *change* him, goodness no. Never let it be said that she, Myrtle Bailey, was a nag. She had just taught him to say it in a Christian way. That was kind of cute, cheese and crackers got all muddy. She didn't mind bad words as long as they were cute. She had always been broad-minded, anybody would tell you that.

My goodness, it was duck day! How could she have forgotten that? She was so proud of her six plaster ducks flying across the wall like an air force squadron. She took them down and washed them carefully in Ivory flakes. She couldn't use Lysol because it did something to the paint. Heavensakes, the arguments she had had with Norma Dean about the ducks! Every time Keith Jonesborough came to call, Norma Dean took the ducks down and Mrs. Bailey promptly put them back up again. Once they nearly broke the biggest, or leader duck, when they were yanking it out of each other's hands. Norma Dean never could tell her exactly what it was about the ducks that she resented; she just kept sobbing, "Oh, Mother, they're just so *awful!*" "They'll be yours when you marry," Mrs. Bailey had replied.

Bailey would be closing up the hardware store soon. Time to fix dinner. Let's see. . . . Pork chops, creamed corn, macaroni and cheese, baked beans from a can fancied up with molasses and brown sugar, a nice salad of canned pineapple with a cherry in the middle, lemon meringue pie, and milk.

Mrs. Bailey smiled to herself. Nobody could say she wasn't a good wife. Kissin' don't last, cookin' do.

Mrs. Bailey calls her menus "good plain food" and "something to stick to your ribs." She is right on the second count, thanks to her ironclad belief that a man should have his "supper" the moment he walks in the door. Bailey barely has time to catch his breath before she sets his piled plate in front of him. Without a pre-dinner cocktail to take the edge off his hunger and calm his workaday nerves, her leaden feast is bound to stick to his ribs, not to mention some other internal areas.

Suppertime conversation starts with grace and proceeds to snippety-snappety moral absolutes delivered by Mrs. Bailey to her spouse, who says, "Nnnnghump." Both of them pack it in since Mrs. Bailey is not given to dieting; when it's all over, Bailey rises and, still chewing, lurches in the direction of the living room sofa (davenport). As he collapses for his evening nap, Mrs. Bailey thrusts a newspaper under his feet so that he won't get the plastic slipcovers dirty. He is still there when Keith Jonesborough comes to call on Norma Dean, which explains why she is always sobbing "Oh, *Daddy!*" and can't wait to leave home.

Many heartland Wasps of the Bailey persuasion go through life thinking that all food tastes like roast beef, mashed potatoes, and peas. This is what they eat thousands of times during their youth. Then they go to a sprawling Midwestern state university whose cafeteria serves up roast beef, mashed potatoes, and peas because the head dietician is named Mrs. Elizabeth Ann York. They graduate from college, join the Junior Chamber of Commerce and the Rotary, and spend the rest of their lives attending civic luncheons that feature roast beef, mashed potatoes, and peas. If there is a salad it is usually a Waldorf, or that Wasp *pièce de résistance*, a canned pear on a lettuce leaf topped with a blob of mayonnaise.

Sundays are plop-plop, fizz-fizz day in the Bailey home. James Jones describes a typical Wasp feast and its aftereffects in *Some Came Running:*

The dinner had been heavy . . . canned shrimp in a cocktail of bitey sauce, the chopped fresh vegetable salad with a French type roquefort dressing, the thick frozen steaks and the frenchfries and stringbeans, icecream for dessert and coffee . . . the whole fare so typical they could have eaten the exact same meal . . . at the Country Club or the Elks . . . or practically any other place, road house or dinner joint . . . a Midwestern ritual of affluence; everyone . . . had eaten far too much, and Dave felt uncomfortable. He had to sit up straight to breathe easily, and the tight uniform bound him. He was damp from sweating in the heavy blouse in the warm room and the heat of the food inside him, and from time to time he wiped his palm across his forehead.

Jones's 1,266-page Wasp epic contains a number of pause-giving food scenes. The hero will not go near his mother for fear she will invite him to dinner. Her specialty is pan gravy full of grease eyes and undissolved flour and hominy drizzled with bacon grease that she keeps indefinitely in an old coffee can beside the stove. Weighing one hundred and fifty pounds at the beginning of the story (he is five-feet-six), he balloons up to over two hundred after meeting Gwen French, a typical Wasp cook who doesn't like to spend a lot of time in the kitchen. Her *tour de force* is stuffed beef heart, white potatoes, sweet potatoes, and fried apples.

The Wasp woman likes to call herself a "man's cook," a sexier way of saying that she sees nothing wrong with serving two kinds of potatoes at the same meal. To her way of thinking, anything is preferable to creative cooking, even digging your grave with your teeth. (She is now into stove-top stuffing to accompany her potaotes.)

Another habit Mrs. Bailey has is loading up the table with little dishes containing condiments: mustard pickle, watermelon pickle, chow-chow, relish, and tiny pots of marmalade with miniature spoons are faithfully brought out and just as faithfully returned to the refrigerator, where they remain until their next appearance. Nobody ever seems to eat them, which may be why they last so long.

Incredibly, Mrs. Bailey stands an excellent chance of winning first prize at the county fair cook-off, not because all the judges are Wasps, but because she knocks herself out to impress *other* people. Being known as a good cook and standing high in the opinion of strangers is more important to her than cooking well for her family every day. This streak of coldness toward those closest to us is an interesting characteristic that all Wasps seem to exhibit from time to time. In McCarthy's *The Group*, Polly Andrews was only too happy to spend time helping her ice man do his income tax, "Yet when one of her friends asked something of her, she might suddenly flush up and say, 'Libby, you can perfectly well do that yourself.' "

Mrs. Bailey's blueberry dumpling never appears on her own table, but it occupies a place of honor on the Baptodisterian table at the Inter-Faith bake sale. It's "too much trouble" to fix for the family, but that doesn't mean they can't enjoy it. As Bailey makes the rounds at the bake sale, his eyes light on the airy dumpling. Which of the ladies made that, he wonders? "Gosh, that looks good," he says—and buys it.

Building bridges of understanding between the Jonesboroughs and the Baileys is a challenge sociological engineers have yet to meet. All ethnic groups are divided into haves and have-nots to some extent, but whatever shame and resentment the subdivisions feel for each other, a bond of basic understanding exists between them.

The Jonesboroughs and the Baileys can't stand each other. Instead of looking at each other and saying, "These are my people," Mrs. Bailey looks at Mrs. Jonesborough and says, "Goodness gracious," while Mrs. Jonesborough looks at her and says, "My God!" Each resents the Wasp stereotype for which the other is responsible; the Baileys hate the Ivy League polo-playing image; and the Jonesboroughs cringe the moment anyone mentions the Silent Majority Wasp.

As if matters were not bad enough, they are hopelessly divided on the most basic issue of all: their attitudes toward the mother country. The Jonesboroughs are passionate Anglophiles while the Baileys are Anglophobes, who mutter imprecations like "pulling their chestnuts out of the fire." It is merely another aspect of their isolationist stance, but they see no difference between England and any other foreign country.

The Jonesboroughs take pride in their English ancestry, but the Baileys admit of nothing but "American" forebears. They have "always" been American, except for those few drops of Indian blood that the Baileys of Waspland like to claim. There is always a Bailey in the background who married an Indian *princess*. Needless to say, no female Bailey ever married an Indian brave.

5

MAMA WASP AND HER BABIES
or
"Johnny Who?"

The Wasp mother must be interesting; after all, Winston Churchill had one, and so did Lizzie Borden.

According to the casting office, she is a pleasant parent whose relationship with her children begins and ends with an absent-minded, "Hello, dear." This only scratches the surface but it is an excellent beginning, for she is an adult's woman — more specifically, a man's woman. Mrs. Jonesborough's attitude toward children is perfectly expressed by John O'Hara's heroine, Grace Caldwell Tate, who looked down at her pregnant belly and said, "Hurry up and get out so your daddy can get in."

Her aloofness is a fact, but not always a hard one. At best she gets along very well with her children. Everybody is on a "Hey, slugger" basis, which is relaxing, breezy, and occasionally ballsy. Conventional sentiment is rare, but she often addresses her children as "droopy drawers" or "stinkweed" in the most affectionate tones. Although she places a high value on public decorum, in the bosom of the Wasp family (32A), she can be delightfully casual and loads of fun.

Some of her worst mistakes spring from her inherent sense of fair play. As the whole world knows, "First come, first served" is an English maxim. It is said that if an Englishman sees a line, he will stand in it merely for the joy of queuing up whether he wants anything or not.

One of the Wasp mother's most cherished *idées fixes* is that the eldest child should be assistant parent. This is fair; the eldest is, after all, the eldest. He was first in line. On the face of things, that sounds like a good idea. It ought to build character—a favorite Wasp pastime—and instill in the firstborn a solid sense of responsibility.

But there's a catch. The eldest is given total responsibility for his siblings. He must watch them, feed them, protect them, and lead their games. However, he is not permitted to discipline them: it would be *unfair* to the siblings to have *another child* boss them around. Thus, in addition to the inherent contradiction, we have the makings of the most officious and dangerous sort of bureaucrat : the kind who drudges for years, seething with resentment and craving the authority that is withheld from him. At the very worst he will become a sadist; at least, a contemptible sneak, an " 'umble" Uriah Heep whose specialty, said Dickens, is "serpentining and corkscrewing people out of existence."

Whatever happens later, family unity is shot to hell. Everything deliquesces into a muddied puddle of who's-in-charge versus nobody's-in-charge, and the elder and younger children start drawing up sides and detesting each other.

Another fairness hang-up of the Wasp mother is her conviction that males *must* enjoy regular stag festivities away from women. As Ralph G. Martin points out in *Jennie,* Lady Churchill was obsessed with fears that her son did not have a man to "shape" him—so obsessed, in fact, that she whistled in several of her lovers to take Winston away from her.

The Wasp mother panics if the men in her life are not bonding enough. Somewhere, somehow, she has acquired the astounding theory that her own company is too "softening," so she encourages her son to go out with the boys. She thinks men should play together, sing together, fight together. She does not want to be a Gold Star mother as Philip Wylie implied in *Generation of Vipers,* but whenever the subject of the army comes up, her response will likely be, "It'll do him good."

Even childhood sadistic rites do not shake her up. If her son is being beaten up by a gang of schoolmates who throw his books and then him into a gravel pit, she will not interfere and go to his rescue. To her way of thinking, it would only exacerbate his peer problems to have a woman come to his rescue. It's *good* for him to be beaten to a pulp; the other boys will respect him afterward. "He's got to take his medicine," she says, and then suggests boxing lessons. She does not get upset when little girls fight and her daughter gets the worst of it, either. "You've got to learn to stand on your own two feet," she intones as she disposes of the ruined dress. However, if she sees a little boy beating up her daughter, she will send Brother to the rescue. *Any* fight turns her into the Marchioness of Queensberry. She loves rules.

Thanks to her male-bonding theories, America is overrun with teenage boys who pile into cars and spend the evening driving from one McDonald's to another "to see who's there."

That her son should be in his room doing his homework does not occur to her. After all, she's descended from the people who invented the gentleman's C. College is the place where he is supposed to learn how to hold his liquor and sing all twenty-five verses of "Tis a Pity She's a Whore." She does not want her son to be a greasy grind, and if she catches him reading too much she will insist, "Get your nose out of that book and go out and bounce a ball!" Above all, she does not want him to be a homosexual, so to ward off that fate, she encourages him to spend as much time as possible squeezed into a car with ten other horny adolescent males.

"Going out" is a Wasp male tropism. Nobody knows where "out" is, but on the other hand, nobody cares. Any McDonald's will do. A treatise on the typical Wasp evening might be called *A Natural History of Car Keys.* It is a study in adolescent wanderlust. Doorbells and telephones ring, screens slam shut, motors start, brakes squeal, as young boys roam in and out of the house asking in croaking voices:

"Is Johnny here?"

"No," says Mother. "He just went over to Bill's."

"I'm Bill. We were all supposed to go over to Bob's house, only Bob isn't home. His mother said that Ted had just left there to come over here. If you see him, would you tell him we're meeting at Jerry's instead?"

The phone rings; Mother answers it.

"Is Johnny there?" says a young male voice.

"No, everybody's over at Jerry's," she reports ecstatically.

"Well, if he checks in, would you tell him that Jerry's down at the McDonald's on Coleman Avenue? We're gonna wait there till somebody drives over to the Burger King to get Bob."

Checking in and reporting back are things Wasp children do constantly, which is why there are so many notes stuck on the icebox. As Mother hangs up the phone, a gangly boy blithely opens her kitchen door and strolls in.

"Hi, I'm Ted. I heard everybody's looking for me. I just talked to Johnny and he said that if Art comes by, would you tell him Johnny's headed for the Pizza Haven to wait for Lou?"

Of course she'll tell him; this is the sort of message that warms her heart. She knows her boy is safe. He might spoil his dinner with the six hamburgers he wolfs down, but that's all right. As she is so fond of saying, "Boys that age can digest nails." (They practiced on staples.) The important thing is, Johnny is not in the library turning queer.

She enjoys these restless evenings for another reason as well. Knowing that teenage boys think of little else besides females, she makes sure she looks her best and relishes every appreciative look she gets—and she gets a lot.

A realist about adolescent male sexuality, she is extremely tactful about inevitabilities like masturbation and nocturnal emissions. Both Mrs. Jonesborough and Mrs. Bailey change the sheets and say nothing. Mrs. Bailey deplores masturbation while Mrs. Jonesborough does not, yet both accept it. They also ignore it. To the Wasp way of thinking, the most dreadful scene in *Portnoy's Complaint* is the one in which Sophie bangs on the bathroom door, demanding, "Alex? What are you doing in there?" As my own mother put it, "What in the hell did she *think* he was doing?" When the Wasp son locks himself in the bathroom, his mother will pretend he is not really there. For that matter, she will pretend that she doesn't have a son, that he doesn't have a penis, or that masturbation hasn't been invented yet. If worse comes to worst, she will even pretend that she doesn't have a bathroom. If he stays *too* long, she will never call him herself. Instead she will send *his father* to get him and have a man-to-man talk with him. When the two of them return, she will pretend that they never left in the first place.

Even worse than Sophie's cacophony outside the bathroom door is the fact that Jake Portnoy let her embarrass Alex in such a fashion. My mother: "Why didn't he tell her to sit down and be quiet?"

The Wasp mother enjoys her children most when they turn twenty-one and take *c/o American Express* as their permanent abode. When Johnny announces his plan to hop off to Europe and find himself, she does not weep. She throws a surprise party to give Johnny the Eurailpass she has bought him. She buys the three-month one. ("You get what you pay for.")

So far, so good. It *sounds* healthy, but there's a catch. Mrs. Portnoy and Mrs. Porter both produce neurotic sons; they just have a different *modus operandi.*

Mrs. Porter's weapon is air mail.

Once Johnny is out of her hair and traversing the wilds of Khartoum, she starts paying attention to him. She becomes the most loyal and persistent correspondent any boy ever dreaded. Like Lady Randolph Churchill, she writes and writes and writes. Yet despite their length and frequency, her letters are aloof and detached. Determined not to nag ("This wanderlust has got to run its course"), she avoids writing anything that sounds too motherly. She may well be worried to death about him, but she will never say so because she is a firm believer in cutting the silver cord. ("He's got to get his sea legs.") Instead, she fills ten or fifteen pages with minute analyses of the political situation in Johnny's various host countries and a thorough run-down of her club doings. By the time she finishes, her arm is sore so she lapses into her own version of shorthand in a P.S. where, at last, she remembers to comment on Johnny's dysentery:

"Yr last ltr v. funny. Don't worry re trots. E'body has them there. Tk cr yrself & rt soon."

Translated from the Wasp, this means that she is nearly crazy from fear, she can't sleep nights, and her heart is breaking. The problem is that Johnny cannot translate Wasp because, like other Wasp children, he does not know that he has a Wasp mother. Foundations do not define us, the government does not award grants to scholars to study us, and stand-up comedians have no repertoire of Wasp mother jokes. When the Jewish mother does a number on her son he can wave a copy of *Portnoy's Complaint* in her face and say, "That's on page sixty-four!" Furthermore, the Jewish mother knows she's a Jewish mother. She may have even taken a course in herself, like the mother in Myrna Blyth's novel, *Cousin Suzanne,* who enrolled in "The Jewish Matriarch in Literature" at The New School.

Lacking a strong group identity, when our mothers hurt us with aloofness, we cannot find explanations in, or take comfort

from, a backlog of well-publicized folklore and legendary behavior. The hurt Wasp child is either puzzled and full of hate like
Lizzie Borden or puzzled and full of love like Winston Churchill.

One of the Wasp mother's favorite ways of telling her absent
child that she loves him is to send him a studio card that says,
"What I like about you is your funny-looking face."

The Wasp mama's boy? He is different, but he is just as
damned. We are short on smother mothers, but when one does
occasionally turn up, she atones for all the aloofness for which the
rest of us are famed.

Lady Porter bears a striking resemblance to Jonathan Balzer
lying in bed yelling, "Teen! I want *fresh*-squeezed!" She does not
wait on her son; he waits on her. It never occurs to her to have milk
and cookies ready when he comes home from school, and she most
certainly does not want to hear all about his day. Lady Porter
simply does not operate that way. She does everything backward,
which is why we lack a bona fide Wasp prince.

Instead we have Little Lord Alex, who spends the best years of
his life lighting cigarettes, holding chairs, opening doors, and
mixing martinis as only *he* knows how. ("Your father bruises
the gin.")

A minor scene from *My Friend Flicka* illustrates the Wasp
mother's knack for getting mileage out of her son.

> No one could do Nell's egg to suit her like Howard. She
> liked it lightly fried on one side, then lightly on the other,
> not broken. It had to be flipped. Howard poured a little of
> the hot bacon grease into a one-egg skillet and broke an egg
> in. While it crackled and spat, he salted it carefully and in a
> moment loosened the curling brown edges, then with a
> smooth motion of his wrist, gave the pan a lift and a thrust,
> and the egg rose a few inches into the air, turned a slow
> somersault, and slid back into the fat.

From little eggs, Mother hens grow. I can just see Howard count-
ing each grain of salt. It would be interesting to read more about
this family without their horses around to steal the scenes.

Like all Wasp women, Lady Porter gives men center stage.
Inflating the male ego is a kneejerk reaction with her; no matter

what dreadful deed she commits, she never openly castrates anyone. Of course, by the time she has finished, the stage is littered
with male bodies, but she will never walk *over* them; she makes
her grand exit by walking *around* them.

While Little Lord Alex is still a toddler, she starts making him
feel indispensable. "Mother can't turn unless her big boy sticks
his arm out the window. Signal a right, darling."

He is never too young to give her advice, and she goes to him
with all her problems. In *Birds of America*, honorary Wasp Mary
McCarthy paints a perfect picture of this kind of Wasp mother.
Rosamund Brown automatically turned to her son when she discovered that the local hardware store did not carry bean pots,
exclaiming, "How extraordinary, Peter! The man says they don't
make them any more. Do you think that can be true?"

Peter reflected: "She was always asking him wide-eyed, troubled questions like that one, to which he could not possibly, at his
age, know the answer; it was a kind of flattery, applied to the male
ego."

At first Lady Porter confines her pleas to male-oriented problems like driving directions. This can be good for Alex's geography grades, for he spends his formative years up to his chin in
roadmaps. But it is never long before her supplications spill over
into non-boy areas. Does he really think that Woolite does what it
claims? If he lisps out a yes, he may find himself washing out her
undies.

He must also guard her with his life. When Daddy is away on a
business trip and her ladyship hears a noise in the garage, Little
Lord Alex is torn from his trundle bed. Armed with his baseball
bat and his Cub Scout flashlight, he stalks out to the garage,
throws open the door, draws himself up to his full three-feet-
seven and shouts, "Who's there! Come out!"

It is not long before our pint-sized Cerberus views all men as
enemies out to rob him of his lady fair. The entire male sex
becomes his enemy, with Daddy leading the list. His worldview
settles into the wrong end of the telescope; his vision of delight is
to come to the rescue of Lady Porter as she frantically waves her
tattletale-gray brassiere from the castle window while Daddy-
the-Dragon breathes sulphur below.

Like all Wasp mothers she loathes sissies, so she sees to it that
Alex always behaves in a manly fashion. She buys him his first

smoking jacket when he is sixteen and teaches him how to dance. When Daddy gets home from work he is greeted with the throbbing strains of "Jalousie" and the disarming sight of Little Lord Alex lunging like a panther into her ladyship's crotch in a tango worthy of the silent screen.

By now Daddy realizes that there is something wrong with Alex, but he cannot put his finger on it. It's not that his mother has castrated him—far from it. He has an athletic letter in everything and he is a model of self-reliance. He not only shines his own shoes but all twenty-five pairs of hers.

Nor is there anything wrong with Alex's sexual adjustment. He has dated every girl in school—though never the same one twice. He definitely has high standards where girls are concerned, but then he can afford to pick and choose; all the girls are crazy about him. The phone is always ringing, and the caller is nearly always a girl asking for Alex. Otherwise, Daddy knows nothing about Alex's social life because instead of man-to-man talks in the den, Alex prefers to confide in Lady Porter. Each Sunday morning Alex tells her ladyship about the girl he took out the night before:

"She has no style."

"She doesn't know how to dress."

"Her conversation is banal."

"She can't tango."

Ever mindful of Wasp fair play and determined not to give Alex an Oedipus complex, Lady Porter remains sublimely above the battle and always takes the girl's side.

"She's young yet."

"Try to overlook her faults."

"Give her a chance."

"She's trying, Alex, she's trying."

"Naturally she doesn't have the qualities of a *mature* woman yet. Don't be unfair, dear."

By the time Alex gets out of college, he is greeting his mother with "*Ciao,* darling" and calling her by her first name. Now Daddy openly loathes his son, but they never fight. Daddy is now out of the running entirely, for the fights at Castle Porter are between Alex and Babs. Typical is the one that broke out at the country club when her ladyship got a bit tiddly. Alex had been eyeing her with tight-lipped forbearance all evening, but when she ordered her fourth martini, he spoke up.

"Do you really think you should, Babs?"

"Oh, darling, just one more? Please? Pretty please?"

"You've had enough!"

"You're mean to me!"

"Oh, come off it, Babs."

They bickered all evening, about every conceivable matter.

"You always get the fish, Babs."

"Well, I don't want it tonight."

"Everybody is looking at you."

"Let them look!"

"Will you please lower your voice, Babs!"

"Don't tell me what to do!"

"Must you always cause a scene?"

"Take me home this instant!"

When they got home, all hell broke loose. Babs stormed and wept, Alex hurled dire threats, and the two of them chased each other through the house while Daddy watched. Finally, Babs slammed into her room, and Alex pounded on the door with his fists.

"Stop being a fool, Babs, you're behaving like a child!"

"Leave me alone!"

I once witnessed an even worse Alex-and-Babs fight. The only rich boy I ever dated was a Little Lord Alex, and we became engaged. To celebrate the occasion, he, his mother, and I had dinner at the Shoreham Hotel in Washington. At some point in the Lucullan meal they started in on each other. By the time the brandy came I was definitely *de trop*, just like Daddy. She stormed out to the lobby, my fiancé stormed out behind her, and I ran after both of them. As we waited for the car to be brought around, she hauled off and slapped him. He twisted her arm; she screamed. The next day, I gave him back the ring.

What becomes of Little Lord Alex? He may turn into that brand of fuss-budget heterosexual known as an "old maid in breeches." This is the man who irons his own shirts because neither his wife nor the laundry can do them to suit him. Obviously, there is something to be said for this kind of husband if you are a Wasp woman, providing you can stand hearing, "Tsk-tsk, I'm out of Clorox," for the rest of your life.

Not surprisingly, Little Lord Alex seldom becomes gay because her ladyship, besides making him hate men, has turned him into the ultimate woman's man. He is an ideal husband for the low-sexed woman who is interested in making what is called "a brilliant marriage." He flicks the quickest cigarette lighter in the West, and is charming to his wife's woman friends. He dances with every one of them without appearing to go down a list; they absolutely *adore* him.

His biggest plus is the way he treats his mother-in-law. Provided she is chic, he absolutely *adores* her and always remembers that she likes a dash of orange bitters in her gin. Her husband never remembers, blast his hide, so Lord Alex is on the way to eroding yet another marriage while maintaining a brilliant one of his own. Soon he and *belle mère* are *ciao*-ing each other and swapping catty criticisms about the way Jackie Onassis wears her hunt derby.

Alex's eroded father-in-law may feel a bit stunned, just as his own father did, but he won't make any trouble. Who could object to such a high level of civilized behavior? After all, this is drawing-room incest. Alex never has trouble with men; they simply fade away. However, if he is a real bastard he can play Babs and *belle mère* off against each other. He has an instinct for that sort of thing and does it simply for the sheer pleasure it gives him, the way Iago stole handkerchiefs. Soon Babs and *belle mère* are doing everything simultaneously. When one pulls out a cigarette, the other follows suit. When one finishes a cocktail, the other gulps hers down so that she will be ready for a refill, too. Alex has never been happier. What of his wife? Not to worry; she can always talk to her father-in-law.

Like Sister Ingrid in *The Bells of St. Mary's*, Babe Porter gives boxing lessons. Unlike Sister Ingrid, she is good at it. A tomboy from her playpen days, the Babe is not her son's best girl, she is his best pal. They sweat together. Thanks to all the nonsense in Waspdom about masculinity, the Babe believes that *everybody* should be a real man, herself included, so she smothers her son by competing with him in the arena. She does not castrate him, she simply grows a bigger pair of her own. When she instructs, "Keep it *up*, Alex!" he knows she means his right.

The Babe's husband may be ineffectual, or simply absent. Often, he is so busy riding around the country on planes that he cannot contribute anything to his son except miniature Jack

Daniels bottles. He collects them faithfully, his own and those of other passengers, and brings them home. Alex saves them just as faithfully, lining them up on a shelf in his room, where they look strangely ladylike and tiny next to the Babe's gifts—punching bags, shoulder pads, and cleated shoes.

The Babe flays her husband to ribbons every time he exhibits anything less than troglodytic masculinity. Whenever he has the slightest difference of opinion with a gas station attendant or a waiter, she demands, "Why didn't you hit him?" Observe that this is not nagging; Wasp women do not nag, but our Babe Porters bully, and Alex follows suit. Perceiving that his mother is not happy unless men are killing each other, he moves in on his father, too: "Jeez, Dad, you didn't have to take that off of him."

Alex and the Babe now have yet another game to play. Soon Dad has no friend except Jack Daniels.

While Dad is looking at life through a veil of sour mash, the Babe spends her time peering through mesh. She wears a lot of protective shields. During sparring sessions she uses a teeth guard, which she usually remembers to spit out before she kisses anybody, but her favorite accessories are those of a baseball catcher. Alex regularly sees his mother dressed up in all the goodies associated with the receiving end of murderous balls. She takes a childlike joy in putting her cap on backward, then donning a face mask, calf protectors, and, of course, my lady's stomacher. It is during these sweatsockie moments that Alex enjoys the ultimate mother-son intimacy: there is the Babe directly in front of him; squatting, her thighs spread, wiggling her fingers in her crotch to give him the proper pitching signals.

If Dad joins the fun at all, it's from behind a stopwatch; he makes an excellent scorekeeper and serves as medic when mother and son knock each other down. Like the average female in phys ed class, he manages to find some way to get excused from the game. His standard pleas are hangovers, business worries, and jet fatigue, but as manly as these things are they cannot stand up to the Babe's image. In Alex's subconscious mind, his father is the only member of the family who has cramps.

What becomes of Alex, Son of Babe? At best he will grow up to turn his wife into a pal, a carbon copy of the Babe. He will marry one of those rough-and-ready Wasp women who enjoys going hunting and fishing with men—and who is good at it. Most women are anathema in the wilderness, but we produce a type who adores guns and baits a fishhook without batting an eye. She cheerfully takes up her camp shovel and digs her own latrine, and when the grueling day is over she turns into the best poker player since Sam McGee. As marriages go, theirs is far from the worst; they are certainly compatible, and they never stop communicating. ("Gee, that's a dandy telescopic sight.")

As long as there are Wasps there will be Babe Porters, Annie Oakleys, Calamity Janes, and Tugboat Annies. The tomboy is endemic to us. Protestantism encourages the masculine woman, or at least tolerates her, in a way that Catholicism does not. Joan of Arc's chief sin in the eyes of many of her judges was not her political and military activity but the fact that she wore men's clothes. Birthed on a wave of individualism, Protestant Christianity diluted the patriarchal content of the Roman faith and gave women some measure of equality. During the era of exploration, settlement, and colonial growth, Anglo-Saxons conceived the doctrine of *rugged* individualism. Mollie Pitchers were needed, and so Wasps produced them. Women who are told to stand shoulder to shoulder with their men and fight off Indians, put out fires, and build log cabins are bound to absorb a certain amount of masculine psychology, interests, and abilities. Some women absorb too much; the result is Babe Porter, who wants to get into the game with the fellas.

The Babe Porter syndrome exists throughout Waspdom. The ladylike Southern woman is least susceptible to the classic version, but the exotic South has a Babe Porter of its own. She is the ferocious "hunt matron" who is entirely capable of kicking the dogs out of the way and killing the fox with her bare hands.

Jocasta Porter is the ironic result of a healthy situation. Thanks to our freedom from madonnas, the Wasp mother is never viewed as a font of purity. We do not indulge in much open physical affection, but our mothers are physically available in other ways. Games, practical jokes, and teasing are Wasp ways of showing affection without risking embarrassment. A touching state of affairs as a rule, it can sometimes get out of hand and become simply a near-affair.

It starts with hair pulling. Alex tiptoes up behind Jocasta and yanks her ponytail or steals her fall. Next, he sneaks up behind her and pinions her elbows. Naturally if she has a good bosom it is very much in evidence during this hammerlock, and if Alex is strong enough to hold her fast, he is old enough to appreciate the view.

His next onslaught is something he learned from his father. The Wasp man tends to be a behind-slapper; it is his special gesture of affection. Alex sneaks up behind Jocasta and lets her have it. She retaliates with a mock scream and a giggle, and like any little boy who hears mock screams and giggles from a female, he steps up his attack. Soon they are chasing each other, until Alex corners his mother and pins her to the floor. To make her scream and giggle even more, he tickles her. The logical place to tickle anybody is in the ribs, but when the ticklee is female, you are bound to touch a couple of other bases in the process.

If Alex has a brother, one boy holds her down while the other one rips off her shoes and tickles her feet with the feather duster. That done, they decide to play sandwich and mash mother between them. At some point in all this, buttons, snaps, and hooks are certain to come loose, so Alex gets bare tit before any other guy in school.

By the time he is sixteen or so, he is strong enough to carry Jocasta piggyback, a game she initiates by leaping on him when he's not looking. (By now, she's sneaking up on him.) It's all very honest and forthright when you think about it. True-blue Jocasta Porter skips the standard smother number and goes for the jackpot. She never lays a guilt trip on Alex, she simply lays herself on him.

The Wasp daughter's independence has always fascinated observers. Over a century ago Alexis de Tocqueville wrote in *Democracy in America*, "Long before an American girl arrives at the age of marriage, her emancipation from maternal control begins."

Our mother-daughter relationship is by and large excellent. Mrs. Jonesborough's idea of a curfew is not remembering to leave the night-light burning, so it would be hard to clash with her even if you wanted to. She has mastered the art of minding her own business.

When *Marjorie Morningstar* came out in 1955, everybody in our all-Wasp sorority read it. We identified with Marjorie because she was universal; what we could not fathom was her mother. Mrs. Morgenstern read her daughter's mail. Whenever one of our Peggys or Nancys looked up from the book with a shocked "Imagine!" we knew she had come to the part about the letter.

Mrs. Jonesborough leaves her daughter's mail on the hall table. Family members' rooms are so sacrosanct in the Wasp home that Mother will leave just about anything on the hall table. If she murdered her daughter she would probably leave the corpse there. Wasp dogs and cats have the run of the house and are permitted to sleep on any bed they fancy, but Wasp mothers walk a self-imposed chalk line. She would not dream of leaving her daughter's mail on her bureau or vanity because that would be prima facie evidence that she had entered daughter's room during her absence. When daughter is old enough to have secrets, Mother often stops putting her clean laundry away in her dresser drawers; there might, after all, be something in daughter's dresser that she does not want her mother to see. Birth control pills, vibrators, dildos, lewd photographs of herself with a man in every orifice, all are easily kept from Mrs. Jonesborough. Daughter simply tosses them on top of her underwear and closes the drawer. She leaves her diary on top of her desk and even feels free to buy one with MY DIARY stamped in big gold letters. For that matter, she leaves it open at the most interesting page. She ties her love letters in a pink ribbon and puts them in a box marked LOVE LETTERS. Her secrets will go with her to the grave, for Mother's motto is "It's none of my business.

The maternal exit line is a Wasp specialty. During mother-daughter talks, whenever anything too personal arises, Mother arises and leaves, tossing back over her shoulder one of the following:

"It's your life, you have to live it."
"I refuse to interfere."
"You needn't explain, I trust you."
"I know you want to do the right thing." (Southern Wasp)
"It's your decision."
"It's not my place to sit in judgment."
"You're free to choose your own friends."
"Major in anything you like."

At first glance it might seem that her disinterest kills the mother-daughter relationship entirely, but oddly enough it has the opposite effect. A mother whom nothing fazes is a mother a girl can go to in a real emergency. Like Betty Ford, she is not disturbed at the idea of her daughter having an affair. If you get pregnant, all you have to do is say so. Mother will not cry or take to her bed of pain because keeping calm no matter what happens is vital to the Wasp's *amour propre*. She will be as unhappy as any other mother, but she will never show it. She will freeze for a moment, purse her lips, then ask, "How far gone are you?"

All mothers tell their daughters to come to them if "anything happens," but the Wasp mother means it. Nowadays legalized abortion has cut into her finest hour, but in days gone by her vast knowledge of the etiquette of illegal operations was impressive, to say the least. "Knowing somebody" is dear to the Wasp heart, and knowing where to find an abortionist was Mrs. Jonesborough's version of the male Wasp's old-boy network. Just where and how she acquired such information she never revealed, nor did the Wasp daughter ask. That, after all, was Mother's business. The wink, the curt nod, the muted, confident-sounding phone call from the den, and all was "arranged," as Mother put it. Then she gave daughter a brisk pat, "Come on, I'll take you to lunch." On the way to the club, she stopped at the travel agency for some brochures about Puerto Rico, and on the way home she bought a beach towel.

It is easy to talk about sex with a mother who looks as good if not better in a bikini than you do. Mrs. Jonesborough's sex discussions contain a minimum of stiffness. My own mother even ventured into a covert lecture on the pros and cons of oral sex. While it was more confusing than helpful, at least she tried; and for a mother and daughter to get that far is pretty good. Most Wasp mothers prefer to wait for their daughters to initiate a real nitty-gritty, but she will indicate her readiness with that marvelous Wasp invitation to the dance, "If there's something you would like to tell me I'll be glad to listen." She means just that; the nicest thing about her is her gift for hearing you out without interruption. She never clutches her heart and screams, "Oh, no, I knew it!" the moment you get the first sentence out. The best time to talk to her is when she is cooking or doing the dishes because she welcomes any opportunity to stop.

My most cherished memory of my mother is a story I have dined out on for years. When I was nine, her younger sister was expecting her first baby. Since I had never received a telegram and wanted one very badly, my uncle promised to announce the baby's birth in a telegram addressed to me. The telegram arrived on a Saturday morning about an hour after I had left for a day at my friend's home. Because it was addressed to me, my mother put it on the hall table and waited for my return, even though she was dying to find out about the baby. When I came home six hours later, there it lay, unopened. My father later told me that my grandmother had suggested steaming it open and then resealing it (she would), but that my mother had said no.

Ever since, whenever I have been tempted to pry into someone else's business, I always think of the telegram.

Mrs. Bailey is a heavier cross to bear, but even she scores higher in the mother department than Norma Dean is usually willing to admit. She snoops when she scents serious sinning, but she backs off on a number of minor matters, resulting in a considerable amount of freedom for Norma Dean. A lifelong resident of the Booster Belt, she does not care how many clubs and organizations her daughter joins. She believes that girls should "go out and do things with young people," and that is precisely what Norma Dean does. Seldom does an evening pass without a meeting of some kind, and Norma Dean goes with her mother's blessing, providing she stays with a group. Once out of the house, "staying with the group" can be interpreted elastically, which is why there are so many songs and jokes about the haystacks of Indiana.

Mrs. Bailey is surprisingly liberal about trips. In her world, girls *ought* to join Y-Teens, Girls' State, Baptodisterian Youth, and a number of other groups that hold statewide conventions. As a result, Norma Dean often spends more time making speeches of her own than she does listening to her mother's. The independence and self-confidence she gains may be parochial and useful only on a very small canvas, but independence and self-confidence they are.

It is Mrs. Bailey, rather than Mrs. Jonesborough, who is the mother of the Wasp Princess. The upper-class Wasp girl is assumed to hold this title, but she is much more likely to become a rugged individualist or even a bohemian. In Waspland, being spoiled and having lots of clothes do not a princess make. Our princessy cachets are tied up with conformity, conventionality, and healthy averageness; Homecoming Queen, Corn Harvest Queen, cheerleader, drum majorette—those are the Norma Dean Baileys. The Wasp Princess must also be sweet and good, which Mrs. Jonesborough's sui generis daughter seldom is. Mrs. Bailey supervises the sweetness and goodness department, and the result is Norma Dean: USO hostess selling kisses, 4-H Club milkmaid with a dairy queen bosom, Debbie Reynolds look-alike, rah-rah girl at the game, Pep Club president, and straight-C coed. Somewhere in all this she still finds time to render that ultimate Wasp Princess service, playing the college chimes every day at five o'clock (what Mrs. Jonesborough calls Evensong and then promptly forgets about).

Mrs. Bailey serves as lady-in-waiting to her princess daughter. Armed with her Singer, she makes the uniforms, double-stitches the webcord cross-belts, polishes the shako, and always finds the money for a new pair of white cowgirl boots. Norma Dean's alter ego, the dress form, occupies a place of honor in her mother's sewing room throughout high school and college, ready for any princessy eventuality.

Sleeping with Norma Dean is like sleeping with any other kind of American Princess. As Keith Jonesborough can testify, it shouldn't happen to an Arab, for Marjorie Morningstar and Norma Dean Bailey are sisters under the skin.

There is a minus side to every ledger. In Waspland the real mama's boys are mama's girls.

Thanks to our obsession with manliness, most Wasp mothers bend over backward to avoid emasculating their sons. They also accept the fact that their sons will eventually marry and they will lose them, so they don't even bother trying to possess what, in their minds, is a temporary child. Thus the smothering Wasp mother's motto: "A son is a son till he takes a wife, a daughter's a daughter all of her life."

In a way, the mother's attitude is admirably realistic, but there is nothing good to be said for the result. Her name is Gibraltar Porter and her calling in life falls somewhere between professional daughter and only son.

Gibraltar has a couple of brothers but they don't count; Mother decided that early in the game—as soon as Gibraltar was born, in fact. "I always wanted a little girl," she cooed sweetly from her hospital bed; translated, it means that she fully intends to hitch her wagon to the pink bundle at her breast.

She makes it clear from the start that Gibraltar is her favorite child. She might even say so in front of the boys; they react by hating Gibraltar, and she reacts by hating them. Her first lesson is learned: males hate me, females love me.

Mother constantly praises Gibraltar, her favorite compliment being "You're so dependable." The praise Mother heaps on her is never for any little-girl attributes like being pretty, sweet, or cute. Instead Gibraltar is told constantly how steady, brave, stalwart, sensible, calm, orderly, logical, and strong she is. To hear Mother tell it, her daughter is Lord Kitchener. When she doesn't cry at the dentist, Mother says, "I was so proud of you, you ought to have a medal."

By now Gibraltar's place in her mother's heart, as well as her own self-image, are dependent upon maintaining and adding to the staggering amounts of self-sufficiency and initiative for which she is famed. The ideal theater for her continuing performance is that female-dominated institution, school. Naturally Gibraltar becomes teacher's pet because teachers are bound to appreciate all the sterling qualities she possesses. Soon all her teachers are saying how steady, brave, stalwart, sensible, calm, logical, orderly, and strong she is. They write what amounts to mash notes to her mother, praising her to the skies. Gibraltar is neat, punctual, polite, truthful, clean, mature, helpful, thoughtful, and *dependable*. She always remembers to feed Miss Denham's beloved goldfish; to water Miss Harrington's creeping wisteria; to beat Miss Prentiss's blackboard erasers; to empty Miss Farrar's pencil sharpener. The hamsters in biology class would have *died* had it not been for Gibraltar, who changed their water bowls over Easter.

In her world, women praise. Since men and women are different, it follows that men do not praise. Because all the praise she gets comes from women, the entire male sex threatens her because they might withhold approval. She also senses that the qualities for which she is lauded are not likely to appeal to men. Knowing that no man is going to praise her for delivering a calm, stoic, dependable, sensible, orderly, brave hump, she refuses to have anything whatsoever to do with sex. She never dates, never learns to dance, and never takes an interest in clothes except that she's neat, clean, well-groomed, pressed, polished, tied, buttoned, manicured, combed, and well shod.

She may choose not to go to college because all the teachers there are men, and besides, she usually isn't intellectually inclined. She strove for good grades merely to please all those women teachers; her cachet was being a good *pupil* rather than a real student. When she graduates from high school, she embarks on her career as Mother's escort. Her brothers marry and leave home just as Mother predicted they would, and Father has a heart attack and leaves a tidy sum so that Gibraltar usually doesn't have to work. If she does she becomes a library assistant, a switchboard operator, or a church secretary for a minister who is the kind of passive, slightly effeminate man who doesn't threaten her. Southern Gibraltars are found in all-female file departments in state government offices, or they may work for the DAR or the historical society, or write social notes for the women's page. Any quiet place with lots of women will do, and if she can land a job as an accounting clerk with the YWCA she is ecstatic.

At least one afternoon a week Gibraltar can be found driving around and around the block, one eye on the department store where Mother has been cloistered all day. It's a shame there are no parking spaces because Gibraltar can swivel a Lincoln into a VW-size hole with one flick of her wrist. It's a sight worth seeing, for she is the world's best driver, bar nuns. Watching her shift gears brings men to their knees in reverence. She never chokes in first, and she has mastered the fine art of double-clutching on a hill. Practice makes perfect; she has been carting Mother around ever since the age of sixteen.

When Mother emerges from the store, Gibraltar, who by now is a stoic nervous wreck, growls, "Well, did you break the bank?"

"Now dear, don't be mean. We can afford it."

If this or any other hostile exchange goes on too long, Mother knows how to get the last word.

"Gibraltar, what makes you so hateful? If you ask me, I think you need a man."

What can Gibraltar say? "Mother, I *am* a man" or "Mother, I'm already married to you" are too intense to throw out in a traffic jam, which is where Gibraltar usually is when she is lured into arguments. So she subsides into her lifelong mood of silent, seething rage.

Now comes the laying-on of guilt. Mother sniffles for a while and makes cooing sounds of distress. Then, recovering from her hurt feelings, she rattles her shopping bags until she finds the package she is looking for. As Gibraltar flicks her turn signal and pulls onto the rush-hour freeway, Mother displays her peace offering: six new cardboard-stiffened, French-cuffed Ship 'n' Shore shirts. (Mother makes matters even worse by calling them blouses.)

"Do you like them, dear? I picked them out especially for you. I know you don't care for lots of ruffles and frills, or big splashy patterns. When I saw this plain checked one I said to myself, I said, my, that looks just like Gibraltar."

Go any Friday night to any Chinese restaurant near a G-rated movie, and you will find Gibraltar with a date.

"No, no, I can't eat all this," says Mother as she dumps a chunk of shrimp fried rice onto daughter's plate.

"I *said* I didn't want any!" hisses Gibraltar, who hates rice and has always hated it since the age of three. Guarding her pepper steak from Mother, who is trying to take half, she curses her parent. Mother promptly gets tears in her eyes.

"I think it's cute to trade."

During the grabby struggle, Gibraltar knocks over a glass of water, giving Mother a golden opportunity.

"My little girl is just a bull in the China shop, ha-ha."

Another hostile silence lasts until the fortune cookies come, and as luck would have it, Gibraltar's says *Romance is just around the corner*. What *is* around the corner is *The Sound of Music*. They have seen it together twelve times but Mother never tires of it.

Gibraltar is *not* the casting-office old maid, the feisty spinster who can take care of herself, thank you. Nor is she a butch. She is more likely to be soft and plump rather than lean and spindly because Mother has nothing to do except wait on her. She is the kind of woman who looks thirty between the ages of fifteen and forty and then suddenly looks sixty for the rest of her life. Her chief characteristic is an *untried* look. If she would do something, *anything* that produces growth and change it would help, but she never does. Lesbianism is beyond her despite her her need for female approval because she is beyond any form of sexual expression. Besides, being known as the best muff-diver in town is not the kind of praise she requires. It must come from older women, mother figures, and it must have a rock-of-Gibraltar ring to it.

The bona fide Wasp Gibraltar is never a protagonist of novels or movies because she is not the protagonist type. Nothing ever happens to her, so she does not lend herself to plot construction. She does appear in cameo roles to symbolize the stultifying effects of small-town life. In William Inge's *Picnic*, the next-door neighbor, Mrs. Potts, who lived with her ninety-some-year-old mother, was a kind of Gibraltar except that she had been married. Usually, however, dramatists and novelists fall into the old-maid trap when they attempt to delineate a real Gibraltar. She would even challenge the ability of Gustave Flaubert to write about utter nothingness and boredom.

Once in a great while, some Gibraltars do marry, but something weird always happens. She may leave her husband after one week and never tell anyone why. Since she is the type to have an attack of vaginismus on her wedding night, she qualifies for an annulment. If she gets a divorce, everyone knows "she tried it once and didn't like it." There was a Gibraltar in a small Mississippi town in which I once lived; her husband had died on the honeymoon. Other Gibraltar fates are husbands who commit suicide after three months of marriage, husbands with rare blood diseases, husbands who are murdered. The most normal contretemps that overtakes the Gibraltars who marry is rapid war widowhood. She marries him while he is on furlough, and he goes back to the front the next day. Two weeks later the telegram comes. It never lasts long, and Mother is always waiting in the wings.

Most Gibraltars I have known have been Southerners. The South produces a certain kind of helpless, childlike woman who needs a Gibraltar to put her together and carry her around. Mother is the eternally feminine type who subtly denigrates her daughter's femininity so as to quash the competition. When Gibraltar has no femininity left at all, Mother starts treating her exactly as she treats men, even flirting with her.

Southern mothers in general often try to outshine their daughters. Like Cousin Molly Parrington in *Old Mortality*, they secretly enjoy having an ugly daughter who never marries, permitting Mother to remain the belle of the ball. This kind of woman loves to be told that she looks more like daughter's sister than her mother, a compliment that springs so naturally to the lips of Southern men that she usually hears it once a day. Lashes aflutter behind her bifocals, the Southern mother never gives up, but sometimes her daughter does.

In the South, the Wasp Princess might just be Mother. Even when she is honestly trying to help her daughter be popular, she often outshines her by accident. One of the nicest things about the Southern mother is her eagerness to help entertain her children's friends. Like Minnie May Jekyll in Nancy Hale's novel, *The Prodigal Women*, she knocks herself out playing the piano, singing, and rolling back the rug for a jam session. The result is that every man in the house is clustered around Mother like moths at a flame while daughter runs back and forth to the kitchen with dirty glasses.

6

"JUDGE CRATER, PLEASE CALL YOUR HOME"
or
The Wasp Father

When Ma Belle says, "Someone is waiting for you to call," she means the Wasp family. Many Wasp children automatically assume it's Daddy *every* time the phone rings, which is why they say, "Hello, Daddy" when they pick it up. Daddy answers with, "Put your mother on the phone," and when Mother takes it she skips hello entirely and says, "Where are you?"

He's at some Holiday Inn. Holiday Inns are full of Wasp fathers. Mr. Jonesborough of Connecticut is in an Ohio Holiday Inn, and Mr. Jonesborough of Ohio is at a Connecticut Holiday Inn. Instead of staying in motels on business trips, they could just as well go to the nearest Wasp home and substitute for each other. The children probably wouldn't know the difference, and both Mrs. Jonesboroughs would probably enjoy a little fling.

The absent Wasp father is found on the higher rungs of the social ladder. He's the man who amuses his younger children by giving them his expired credit cards to destroy. Since the cards must be bent innumerable times before they finally break, it keeps the kids quiet for an hour or more. They also like to look on while he resets his watch. Wasp children are little experts on time zones; their favorite game is "What time is it *there*?" The gifts Daddy brings home to them always have something to do with airplanes. A miniature flight bag, a jet model, United's flight-pattern map that tells them exactly where Daddy is at any given time—over Lake Michigan, over the Rockies, over the Grand Canyon. They also have a vast collection of swizzle sticks, vomit bags, tiny paper tubes containing salt and pepper, and, of course, miniature Haig

& Haig pinch bottles to get their fingers caught in. Mother often has to get the hammer and release a child.

When Daddy is home they are likely to see even less of him, thanks to Wasp fondness for adult games. A Saturday with a father in residence means that Mr. and Mrs. Jonesborough are going to make up for lost time. One or the other is always whispering, "Where are the kids?" Getting rid of them so that Mother and Daddy can sneak upstairs to the bedroom has first priority. Daddy was too tired the night before, but now that he has recovered from his jet fatigue and knows what time it is, Mrs. J has plans for him. This is why she supports Boy Scouts, Girl Scouts, Cub Scouts, Brownies, *anything* that meets on Saturday morning. They could join the Red Guards for all she cares, as long as they met on Saturday morning. If there is no meeting, she will send them out to play and hope that they'll stay out. They don't always obey, which is why Wasp children see such interesting sights. Quite often in the middle of her fun, Mrs. J grinds to a halt and whispers, "Don't look now but I think Johnny is standing in the doorway."

Next to being on Mother, Daddy's favorite way to "unwind" (his favorite word) is shutting himself up in his workroom with his tools. Tinkering, puttering, and handymanning are the Wasp male's idiosyncratic idea of fun. Descended from people who built sod huts on the prairie "with their bare hands" and did clever things with buffalo dung, he harbors an intense conviction that he can and should repair or build anything.

He is a master fixer whose most prized possession is the great Wasp tool chest, and heaven help anybody who touches it. One of the few precision-ordered rooms in the Wasp home is the work room. There is a place for everything and everything is in its place—unlike Mother's kitchen cabinets, where the turkey platter is sitting on a teacup. Dad's number one saw is hung beside his number two saw and so on down the line. All is oiled and shining because Daddy is *fussy*. He will put up with his wife's home management, but he will not tolerate any damage to his tools. Children and work rooms do not mix very well, and anyway it's impossible to talk to Daddy in the earsplitting atmosphere. Screaming, "*What?*" over the scream of a chain saw is as far as the father-child relationship can gō.

Wasp parents don't mean to shut their children out, but that is what often happens when Mother helps Dad with home improvement. It's the Mollie Pitcher syndrome again. Side by side, they hammer, chop, slice, paint, sand, finish, and cuss.

"Damn it, hold it *up!*"

"Oh, *God!* My foot! You idiot!"

To add even more pioneer-style danger to the activity, much of the yelling is done with a mouthful of nails. It is no place for children, and neither Mother nor Daddy really wants them around at such times unless they are old enough to help, in which case the family turns into a construction gang with Daddy as foreman. He can get pretty feisty, especially with adolescent boys who are in the clumsy stage, so the result is hurt feelings as well as hurt fingers.

The same thing happens when the family goes on their boat. Daddy turns his children into a crew, with a hierarchical pattern based on their age. This is his version of Mother's eldest-child-as-assistant-parent routine. The eldest boy becomes chief bosun's mate, and the youngest is the put-upon swabby whom everyone yells at. Things get impossibly salty; the eldest son wears a yachting hat with somewhat less gold braid than his father's, while the youngest has a white gob cap pulled so far down over his ears that he presents a picture of utter pitifulness, outranked by all. Boats bring out something curt in Wasps; our seafaring heritage demands that we run a tight ship. Daddy tends to bark out orders of the "'Mr. Christian!" type, so that instead of a pleasure cruise, the family actually *is* in the navy for a few hours. Tensions mount, especially when Mother, who can't even get it together in her big beautiful home kitchen, tries to cook in a swaying six-by-six galley. It's never long before she has had it up to here with boats.

The Wasp family has its best times at backyard barbecues because *Daddy* likes to cook, and what's more he's good at it. He won't let Mother do a thing, which is fine with her; she sits peacefully on the sidelines sipping her martini in an excellent, loving mood. At these times, she adores her children.

The conflict between having money and having children has made the well-do-do father the Sophie Portnoy of Wasp literature. It's the father rather than the mother whom our writers run down. From the "stern and forbidding" type like Dombey and Sir Austin Feverel; to the peevish, asinine boobs of Jane Austen; down to the countless cigar-chewing industrialists and egomaniacal Big Daddies of American popular entertainment, the Anglo-Saxon father is the villain.

Towering above them all is George Pontifex, the insufferable professional tormentor of Samuel Butler's novel, *The Way of All Flesh*. Pontifex, well supplied with both money and children, knew precisely which he preferred, and why:

"His money was never naughty; his money never made noise or litter, and did not spill things on the table cloth at meal times, or leave the door open when it went out. His dividends did not quarrel among themselves, nor was he under any uneasiness lest his mortgages should become extravagant and run up debts which he should have to pay."

Samuel Butler suggests that the children could have responded, "He did not knock his money about. . . . He never dealt hastily or pettishly with his money, and that was perhaps why he and it got on so well together."

Pontifex's behavior, bad as it was, is understandable. He was what we call today a hard-driving executive. As a publisher of religious books, a land-office business in the pious Victorian era, his work demanded all his energies and most of his time. Add six lively little Pontifexes and the results are predictable. Today's executive-level Wasp father is in the same situation. His work not only drains him, it also accustoms him to dealing arbitrarily with people. Used to the fixed hierarchies of the corporate Wasp life, he turns his children into a boat crew instead of merely sailing for the fun of it. He likes to assign people to specific duties, thinks in terms of seniority and chains of command, and likes everything to run smoothly, just as it does in the office. He tries to be democratic about it, but he cannot hide the fact that he views his children as underlings or junior trainees—an attitude exemplified by his habit of summoning them jocularly with "team," "troops," or "gang." Teams, troops, and gangs always have leaders, and the leader is Dad.

The American Wasp has another problem that George Pontifex did not have. Victorian Englishmen took it for granted that they would have large numbers of children. Contraception was primitive, undependable, and unmanly. You were supposed to breed because God wanted you to. Children might have been necessary evils, but they were necessary; the sanctimonious, optimistic Victorian father did not question the *why* of having them.

The upper-class Wasp father sometimes does not know what children are *for*. In a country like the United States, one of the chief pleasures in having children is seeing them better themselves, so by this yardstick, the Wasp father is in trouble. He cannot bask vicariously in his children's success because he does not need to; he himself is successful. He cannot see them become the first college graduates in his family because he went to college, and so did his father. He cannot pride himself on their greater Americanization because he has generations of native-born Americans behind him. Denied these pleasures, he no longer sees the *raison d'être* of fatherhood: "What's it all about? You have children and they have children and *they* have children." The ethnic immigrant father never asked this question because he knew full well what it was all about: improvement in each generation until full-fledged American success was attained.

The children of the upper-class Wasp father often seem more like expensive pets than children, which accounts for the tipsy harangue he is wont to deliver in the commuter club car: "Why am I doing this? Who invented the rat race anyway?" *He* invented it, and what's more, he won it, so when he hears culturisms, such as "Children are the hope of the future," he is secretly puzzled. To him, the future arrived years ago.

The more involved he is in his work, the guiltier he feels, which prompts his frequent insincere complaint, "I wish I could spend more time with the kids." At the same time he is saying this, however, he is mentally planning one of those suburban escapes known as "a vacation to get away from the kids," meaning that he and Mrs. Jonesborough are going to hole up in a Bermuda hotel and screw for a week or so. Harboring such conflicts creates an exhausted, distracted, resentful, self-loathing, confused father whose chief contact with his children consists of crazy-making lectures:

"I'm sure you aren't interested in talking to me since I'm only your father, but I would appreciate a few words with you if you don't mind. After all, we *should* talk more. First of all, I don't mean to be unkind. Nothing could be further from my thoughts. It's not that I'm finding fault with you, and I don't want you to think that I don't care about you. After all, you're my son. If I didn't care about you I wouldn't take the trouble to tell you what's on my mind. That's what I'm doing now—telling you what's on my mind.

Frankly, openly, with no beating around the bush. I don't believe in beating around the bush, you know. (Pause) Well? *Don't* you know that?"

"Sure, Dad."

"Of course, you're of age now, you can do whatever you want. I can't stop you even though I'm your father. Moreover, I wouldn't want to stop you, I wouldn't dream of it. You know me. You know how lenient I've always been with you, letting you have a free rein. (Pause) Well? Haven't I?"

"Sure, Dad."

"Naturally I've guided you because that's a father's job, and I *am* your father. However, I refuse to put pressure on you. I never have, except when you needed it. But I don't believe in interfering. In fact, one of the reasons I'm sending you to college is so that you'll become independent of me. I *want* you to be independent, learn self-reliance. I also want you to know, though, that you can always depend on me no matter what happens. After all, you're my son. That reminds me: Why don't we take a vacation together, just the two of us? Go up to the lake house. There won't be anybody around at this time of year, and we could spend a whole week just talking. We need to talk more, get to know each other better. What do you say?"

"Sure, Dad."

The reason Johnny gets lured into such rambling-rose conversations in the first place is because Mrs. Jonesborough firmly believes that the father should be the head of the house. She is constantly saying, "Ask your father," even though she knows, Dad knows, and Johnny knows that she will be the final arbiter anyway. It would be better for all concerned if she would openly take command and *let* Dad be a stranger to his children, but she never will. So Johnny obediently asks his father, who goes a-rambling.

There is nothing worse than heavy-handed, forthright Wasps who think they are subtle. Mother is the worst offender. Convinced that she is a manipulator worthy of the inner sanctums of the Vatican, she works out a set of dinner-table signals, so that when the children ask permission to do something or other, Mother decides and then craftily signals Dad yes or no so that *he* can answer the petitioning child. She actually believes that the children don't catch on when she thrusts her tongue into her left cheek to signal no, and into her right cheek to signal yes. It never occurs to her that she looks as if she's having a stroke; she thinks she is a dagger flashing in a Florentine alley, the *dernier cri* of duplicity and stealth.

The father-son stag vacation is pure kneejerk Wasp. Set to the tune of "Getting to Know You," its chief characteristic is a forced heartiness that wears on the nerves of both parties. Its props are beer, vows not to bathe for a week, lots of black-and-red checked wool shirts, and enough camping equipment to start an army-surplus store. The heart-to-heart talk doesn't come off as planned. Dad may venture into the subject of condoms, and Johnny will listen respectfully even though all the girls he knows are on the pill. This realization strikes Dad in the middle of his discourse, and so he trails off, clears his throat, and says, "Well, I guess they're all on the pill now." "Yeah," says Johnny. A silence falls, then Dad takes a breath of pure country air and says, "This is the life." "Yeah," says Johnny. Most of the time they spend fishing, which means they *can't* talk for fear of disturbing the fish. They sit side by side in absolute silence, their eyes glued to their floats.

Stereotype has it that the Wasp father is *always* a workaholic executive, but such is not the case. We produce a Serenity Wasp whose motto is, "Why bother? We're all going to die someday anyhow." An old-line Wasp with too much self-esteem, his sense of identity is so strong that it has destroyed all his ambition. He feels no need to try, no need to push himself up the ladder, no need to prove himself because there is nothing to prove. He is content simply to live, and to enjoy every moment of it. He guards his regular hours zealously, declines to work overtime, refuses all promotions involving added responsibilities because he wants his time to himself—to paint watercolors, transpose *Lucia di Lammermoor* for the harmonica, or tinker around the house. Even if he is a doctor he manages to take it easy; he would rather have a general practice in a small town than be chief of staff in a big hospital. If he is a lawyer, he prefers to be a solicitor rather than a barrister, and sticks with nice old ladies' wills and the more genteel sort of boundary dispute. If he is a newspaperman he will never try to be a Johnny-on-the-spot star reporter. He would rather be a rewrite man because he doesn't have to move all day long. An indoorsman, he makes an excellent archivist because he does his best work in dim, silent marble halls. You would think he would make a great undertaker, but he doesn't; grief-sticken people are noisy and emotional, and he wants his life to be one long, even tenor.

It helps if he has an independent income, but oddly enough, many Wasps do not. It would also help if he chose his wife from his own metabolism group, but Serenity Wasps have a terrible tendency to marry women who like to dance.

Despite his faults, the Serenity Wasp makes a marvelous father. I know, because I had one.

My mother's idea of fun was fifty people all talking at once. My father's idea of fun was making boats in the bottle. Thanks to their near-total incompatibility, there were always plenty of empty bottles for his boats. He also had a thing for jigsaw puzzles and rushed home every night on the stroke of five to play with them. Ordinary dimestore puzzles were not challenging enough, so he ordered custom-made ones from a hobby shop in New York. His *pièce de résistance* was "The Battle of Trafalgar," which took up the entire dining room table and cost a hundred dollars. (Fortunately for our family finances, my grandmother had been nicely widowed three times.) We had to eat in the kitchen for two weeks until he finished Trafalgar. When he put in the last piece —Nelson's eye-patch—he looked as happy as a tycoon who has just closed a multi-million-dollar deal.

It never seemed to occur to him that he was not a "good provider." For that matter, it never seemed to occur to him that he was not a good *everything*. Born in England in 1902 at the height of Victorian-Edwardian glory, when merely *being* a British subject was *ipso facto* proof of superiority, he oozed self-contentment. He was not a good husband, but he was the perfect father for a daughter. The metabolic requirements of the Wasp father-son relationship—baseball, hunting, fishing, and other outdoor exertions—are anathema to the Serenity Wasp. Even worse is the need to set an example of the aggressive money-maker, or the aggressive anything. Consequently, when he finds that his wife is expecting, the Serenity Wasp often hopes for a girl. This rare state of affairs can do a girl more good than ten thousand women's liberation movements. There is nothing quite like knowing that you pleased your father simply by not being male.

The only real patriarch in Waspland is the Southern father. He is the strictest Wasp of all, and is often downright menacing, particularly with his sons. Famed for his soft-spoken ultimatums, he must live up to his wife's boast, "All he has to do is *look* at the children." As a result, his looks can kill. A born actor, his reprimands can get terribly dramatic. If his son is rude at dinner, Big Daddy will roar, "Sir, you are at your mother's table!" When Mother disciplines, she draws herself up in a good Southern huff and intones, "Don't you dare say such a thing in your father's house." Because he is clay in his daughter's hands, Big Daddy must salvage his pride by playing the heavy with his sons. The result is a quivering bundle of son, like Gooper in *Cat on a Hot Tin Roof*. "Big Daddy told me to get married, so I got married. Big Daddy told me to live in Memphis, so I lived in Memphis." The number of grown men who are terrified of their fathers astounds the Northern woman who goes to live in the South and starts dating, and perhaps marrying, Southern men.

Big Daddy's approach to son raising is something like that of the Emperor Franz Joseph, who ordered Crown Prince Rudolph's tutor to fire guns beside his head to steady his nerves. We all know what Rudolph's nerves were like. The gun ritual is Big Daddy's favorite number. Sometime between the ages of ten and thirteen, it is time for Sonny's first gun. It's the Southern Wasp version of the bar mitzvah, and before long Sonny has as many guns as Seymour has fountain pens.

The classic Southern family situation is like the classic Greek drama. Mother is Clytemnestra, unable to stop talking, hovering on the brink of hysteria; Sonny is a much-beset Orestes; daughter is a Daddy-struck Electra; and towering above them all is Agamemnon after Sidney Blackmer.

Generally, the Wasp shortage of patriarchs results in some very good father-daughter relationships. They can be buddies, like Moses Pray and Addie Loggins in *Paper Moon*, combining shouting matches with a silent understanding of each other's natures that is very moving.

Sometimes, the silent understanding is too silent. When Norma Dean Bailey sobs, "Oh, *Daddy*!" it is more than a cry of exasperation over his latest *faux pas*. Bailey regards his daughter with a kind of puzzled awe and a mute deference that makes her feel both loved and shut out at the same time. Unsophisticated Wasp fathers like Bailey are embarrassed around their daughters and try mightily to avoid any acknowledgment of their budding sensuality. Bailey does not know how to compliment Norma Dean, or how to tease her with the affectionate jauntiness that comes naturally to Mr. Jonesborough. The feet-off policy that Mrs. Bailey maintains over her hassocks becomes a hands-off policy in the matter of raising daugthers. Let *me* worry about Norma Dean, she tells her husband, whenever he ventures any thoughts on the matter. While she and Norma Dean argue in the sewing room about a revealing décolletage, Bailey tunes out and reads his newspaper.

Most Wasps have a difficult time showing love, but Bailey is the greatest casualty of Wasp emotional repression. In fact, he and Norma Dean often remain total strangers until her wedding day, when Bailey finally breaks down. In the vestibule of the church, just as they are due to start marching up the aisle, he turns to her, gulps, and says, "Honey, I just want you to know that . . . well, I love you." Whereupon Norma Dean bursts into tears and says, "Oh, Daddy, I love you, too!" Tears form in Bailey's eyes and spill down onto his cheeks. He tries manfully to hold them back, but he can't, so father and daughter make their sodden way to the altar. Everyone present is astonished, for they never realized that Bailey was so fond of his daughter. Bailey and Norma Dean never realized it either.

7

WE DON'T KITH OUR KIN
or
Those No-Neck Monsters

The possibilities for culture shock between Wasps and ethnics are endless, thanks to our vastly different attitudes toward family. When my agent first mentioned a Jewish family custom called the Cousins Club, I assumed it was the preamble to a joke. I waited, but no joke came. As he spoke of collecting dues and planning birthday celebrations, it gradually dawned on me that this was a real club.

"Dear God," I said, "it sounds dreadful. How can you stand it?"

"It's fun."

"It *is*?"

We ended up staring, bemused, at each other across the lunch table, two people in search of a wavelength.

Novelist Fannie Hurst recounts her first experience with Wasp kinship attitudes in her memoir, *Anatomy of Me*: "A chance acquaintance in an English railway carriage, a member of the peerage, once said to me in four unadorned words: 'I hate my mother.' It was the first time I had heard such blasphemy uttered. Surely God would strike him dead."

Miss Hurst must have received an even greater shock if she read John O'Hara's *From the Terrace*. It contains an upper-class version of the sort of Wasp estrangement that social workers encounter in our humbler ranks:

My son Jack? I haven't the faintest idea. He must be forty. No, he's thirty-nine, almost forty. I haven't heard a word from Jack since before his mother passed on. I sent him three thousand dollars in care of a bank in Hong Kong, China. He never even wrote and thanked me.

Wasp family attitudes got their start in the very bogs of time. "The English," wrote G.M. Trevelyan, "have always been singular for caring little about their cousins and ignoring their distant relatives."[1] Trevelyan carefully says English instead of British. Ancient Britain was a Celtic country and Britons, like present-day Celts in Scotland, Wales, and Ireland, were clan-oriented people. Their concept of loyalty underwent a drastic change in the fifth century with the Anglo-Saxon invasions. The Teutonic invaders stamped out Celtic tribalism and introduced the concept of loyalty to an elected warrior king. The practice of swearing allegiance to the head of a family-based clan lived on in the north and west, but in England, where the Saxons settled, it quickly died out. Britons became Englishmen, and relatives took a back seat.

Our later history made kinship even less important. We are history's lucky people: neither Cossacks, Hussars, nor secret police have ever come for us in the middle of the night. Security has been one of our blessings, and the feelings of safety and self-confidence we derived from it convinced us that we could go it alone: we do not *need* to stick together.

Finally, the Wasp in America has something to take the place of relatives: ancestors. Ancestral societies fill the same need in us that actual family gatherings do in others. We get more out of our great-great-great-granduncle than we get from "that goddamn Uncle Jim and his crazy wife." The difference between ancestors and relatives to us is what the difference between books and friends was to Lord Macaulay:

> Plato is never sullen. Cervantes is never petulant. Demosthenes never comes unseasonably, Dante never stays too long. No difference of political opinion can alienate Cicero. No heresy can excite the horror of Bossuet.

Our kinship attitudes long ago shaped the English language. Rugged individualists, we capitalize "I" but leave "you" in lower

[1]*History of England*, vol. I.

case. We have eliminated the intimate form of the second-person pronoun, refusing to address anyone familiarly, except of course God, whom we call Thee. English has no words to denote the relationship between one in-law and his or her opposite number. In Yiddish the father-in-law is the *machuten* and the mother-in-law the *machetayneste,* and any relatives by marriage are called *machetunim.* In Waspish they are called "Oh, *God,* here they come!" By forcing us into tongue-twisters like "my daughter-in-law's brother's father-in-law," English discourages us from even talking about them, much less bothering with them.

Wasps have developed certain speech habits to build barriers of respect between family members. My normally indulgent father insisted that I observe a strict British rule: I was never permitted to use a pronoun to refer to my mother. If I said "she" instead of "Mama," my father would snap, "She is for she-goats!" The English apparently feel that if a gulf of formality can be created between mother and child, the battle for general aloofness is more than half won.

In some upper-class or sophisticated Wasp homes, children first-name their parents. But instead of bringing parent and child closer, it has the opposite effect: the parent is demoted to the status of buddy, and the blood between them is cooled. (I grew up with a girl who called her mother Winnie but got yelled at if she said "she" or "her.")

First-naming of lateral relatives is another habit of some Wasp children. In college I received a great shock when I acquired my first Italian friend. Not only did she have an aunt who was a mere four years older than she—incredible enough in my experience—but she carefully called her Aunt Theresa and even referred to her as such. My aunts and uncles were all contemporaries of my parents, and I called them by their first names. My cousins addressed my parents in the same fashion.

The Anglo-Saxon's special weapon against strong feelings is nicknames. Whenever passions of any kind threaten, we bring one out. The Wasp male uses nicknames to establish a comfortable distance between himself and kinswomen; they are a safe way of showing verbal affection without saying anything mushy. Harry Truman infused a great amount of warmth and love into his favorite name for Bess, "the Boss." Many Wasp men of the rough-and-ready persuasion achieve the same effect when they nickname their wives "Dutch." It is not very flattering, but Wasp women have a third ear for this sort of thing. As Edith Bunker explained it, "Whenever he says dingbat, I know he really means sweetheart."

Royal nicknames are convenient for elevating women beyond reach. Warren Harding called his wife "the Duchess," a sobriquet that became so customary in the White House that it even slipped out during the Teapot Dome hearings. My father called my grandmother the Queen Mum and my mother Your Ladyship. When he really wanted to avoid her he used the third person and said Her Ladyship. The world's most famous Wasp Dutchman, Franklin D. Roosevelt, referred to Eleanor with a tag that gentleman farmers are accustomed to hearing from servants: the Missus.

Our nicknaming can go wild. Lady Randolph Churchill's third husband, Montague Porch, was called Porchie. Her brother-in-law Moreton Frewen was known as Mortal Ruin owing to his unwise financial investments. Oscar Wilde's lover, Lord Alfred Douglas, was called Bosie, which even Englishmen found a little hard to take under the circumstances—Wilde's writer's ear concocted it from "beautiful boy."

The most famous nickname in the Anglo-Saxon world is probably Jack the Ripper. Whether he was a lone killer or, as the most recent evidence has it, a team of three men covering up a government scandal,[2] it is doubtful if the crimes would have become so legendary without the catchy name. Whoever coined it had an English ear. Besides describing accurately the anatomical horrors involved, it is also a summing up of Cockney life, evoking the smell of fog, the feel of slimy Whitechapel cobblestones underfoot, and the noise of the raucous drunken singing from the music halls. When the French dramatized the murders they came up with *Jacques L'Eventreur*, which simply doesn't have it. It sounds very fey and very French, a murderer out of a traveling puppet show. I don't know what the Germans call him but I can imagine. Undoubtedly they have thrown together one of their famous compounds that translates Jack Who-the-Throats-of-Women Who-Their-Bodies-to-Men-Sell-Cuts. It takes a repressed Anglo-Saxon who hides his urgent feelings under a jaunty exterior to invent living, breathing nicknames for unspeakable people.

---

[2] Stephen Knight, *Jack the Ripper.*

The whole Ripper case is rife with nicknames; even his victims had them. Annie Chapman had lived with a sieve maker, so the other harlots called her Annie Sievey. The combination of Elizabeth Stride's generous height and her surname was irresistible, so she was called Long Liz. Mary Kelly was Black Mary owing to both her disposition while under the influence and her Irish coloring. Two suspects in the case, a butcher and a cobbler, both wore leather aprons in their work, so in the press both were nicknamed Leather Apron. When it was all over, the English bestowed the name Leather Apron on a rock-hard molasses toffee. It was their quaint way of putting the horrible lust of the murders into perspective.

Our literature and popular entertainment do not lack for examples of loose family ties. A throwaway paragraph in *The Way of All Flesh* illustrates our views on the relativity of relatives. Although it is a minor point, Samuel Butler obviously felt compelled to interrupt his narrative, not only to explain it, but to apologize for it:

> No very close relations had been maintained between the two sisters for some years, and I forget exactly how it came about that Mr. and Mrs. Fairlie were guests in the house of their sister and brother-in-law; but for some reason or other the visit was paid.

Our most popular fictional character is the orphan. Charles Dickens, who was out to make money, knew what would sell in England. The Wasp orphan is not just any orphan, however. He invariably exhibits a trait that we insist on in all our orphans. As Horatio Alger decreed, he must be "plucky"—that is, he must be glad he's an orphan, not sorry.

It helps if he is left on a doorstep in a basket. If that is not possible, his mother must die immediately after giving birth so that the nursemaid can say, "Oh, the poor little one, all alone in the world." The nursemaid is a very important character because it is through her that the Wasp author makes one of his main points: People who aren't related to us by blood are the ones we love best. They are *safe*.

There begins an idyllic period in which nursemaid and orphan are Alone Together, isolated from any and all kinfolk. But then something happens to separate them, and the orphan is tossed into a Wasp's nest populated by the stingiest, most hypocritical, sadistic set of relatives that ever walked across a printed page. Each aunt or uncle is worse than the one before, and only a foretaste of the one who will adopt the orphan next. Every time he goes to live in a new home, he is greeted by a grim, hateful, bad-guy relative in a black hat who skips hello and says, in the manner of Miss Murdstone, "I don't like boys. Boys are Satan's spawn. I keep a birch rod in the corner for boys. Do you understand, boy?"

All is not lost, however, for it turns out that the little Wasp has *one* relative he loves: the old-maid aunt. She is a certain kind of old maid, of course—utterly self-sufficient, and blunt to the point of insulting. These qualities serve to keep *her* relatives, and everyone else, at bay, so that she and the little orphan can be Alone Together, wrapped in unspoken, no-nonsense Wasp love.

English writers prefer the Betsey Trotwood type of spinster; American Wasps like frontier touches. Our maiden aunt is physically self-sufficient. She is always shoveling something all by herself—snow, coal, manure, *anything*, muttering all the while, "The Lord helps those who help themselves." Unlike the Wasp matron, who is excused from blue-ribbon cooking and housekeeping, the Wasp spinster aunt, who has no one to care for except herself, must excel at both, so that her relatives will understand that she doesn't need any help and will *stay away*. Our girl with the hoe puts in a garden, harvests it, and cans two thousand bushels of vegetables, all by herself. She milks her cows, churns her butter, and refuses all help during slaughtering season—she can carve up seven pigs before breakfast, and have the pork roast in the oven for dinner the same day.

Our old-maid aunt always lives alone in a fifteen-room house. If she has not gotten rid of her relatives by insulting them, she has outlived them all, or else she had a mysterious quarrel with them long ago, resulting in that well-known plot situation that warms the Wasp heart: "They haven't spoken for thirty years."

Naturally, she has a cat. Of all the animals Wasps love, the great English cat is tops. "Cats make the best companions," says our maiden aunt—by which she means that for the last seventeen years, since the day she took in the stray kitten, she has occupied one wing of the house and the cat has occupied the other. "We keep ourselves to ourselves," says she Waspily. When she finally dies at 103, she leaves half her money to her cat and the other half to the *one* nephew in her timorous clan who refused to be terrorized by her. That, too, is a Wasp definition of love.

The Wasp author who does not write about orphans and old-maid aunts can still comment on kinfolk with a story about the plucky little boy who leaves home—at twelve. The little Wasp wanderer was immortalized in Thomas Hovenden's painting, "Breaking Home Ties," and in that favorite nineteenth-century ballad, "Where Is My Wandering Boy Tonight?" This lad either went forth to seek his fortune in the West—on foot, of course—or else he "went to sea," the cabin boy being one of our all-time favorites. Considering what maritime life was in those days, he undoubtedly was sodomized repeatedly by the entire crew, but that's better than getting loose bowels from too many nerve-wracking family reunions.

The little Wasp making his way in the world never sees his own family again, but he invariably hits it off extremely well with somebody else's family—so well, in fact, that he becomes the sole heir of a rich stranger.

"I, Edward Fairfield, in view of the fact that my four sons have not communicated with me for thirty years and have been declared legally dead, do hereby bequeath my entire fortune to Thomas Trueheart, the grocer's delivery boy. So that my sisters will not be able to interfere with my wishes in this matter, I leave them each the sum of one dollar."

The Wasp is often at his best with ships that pass in the night. This kind of relationship can have all the warmth and satisfaction anyone could desire, yet it is emotionally safe; hence some minor good turn performed by a total stranger is remembered forever and regarded, as in *Great Expectations*.

This Dickens novel also contains another kind of Wasp-soothing situation: the concealed relationship. If you must be kin to someone, it's better not to discover the fact until the very end.

The Wasp-sister plot? Two sisters loathe each other. One is plain, the other is pretty; one cleans the house, the other messes it up; one is a virgin, the other is a wanton; one wears glasses, the other can see in the dark. Father loved one and hated the other. One steals the other's bridegroom just before the organ strikes up

Lohengrin. There is what Wasps call "bad blood" between them. The movie ads say, "And then something terrible happened . . ."

If the sisters are twins, Bette Davis can play both parts, otherwise there is always Miriam Hopkins. The story opens low because the sisters are practicing that Wasp version of the family knock-down-drag-out known as "not speaking."

In a cry-havoc whisper, they start doing unsisterly things to each other. Somebody is certain to drown. Drowning is terribly Wasp—the sea and all that. It's an easy death to arrange because they live on the North Shore or some other howling, blustery place that draws Wasps like moths to the flame. Not only that, they go back and forth to the lighthouse in a boat to pick up their mail, and the meaner of the two sisters always rows. The nicer one can't swim.

If drowning fails, one sister drives the other crazy. There are lots of subtle Wasp ways to do this. You can get up in the middle of the night and shove the furniture around. You can switch the pictures on the wall. You can fiddle with the grandfather clock that hasn't lost a second in fifty years. If you want to punch things up a bit you can chop at a tree until it's weakened enough to fall on the intended victim's side of the house during the next gale. This requires a lot of hard work, but after all, she's your sister.

Egged on by Harriet, Grace obediently loses her mind. Instead of sending her to an asylum, however, Harriet takes care of her at home. There's a reason for this, and all the other Wasps in the seaside town know what it is: fifteen years before, Harriet stole Grace's fiancé. Now, reason the townspeople, her guilt has made her sacrifice her own happiness in order to care for her crazy sister. Isn't that nice of poor Harriet?

At the climax of the story, we are hit with a Wasp double-whammo, proving that relatives are *twice* as bad as we have been led to believe. It is true that Harriet stole Grace's fiancé, which accounts for Harriet's guilt. But it is also true that Grace sneaked into the lighthouse on her sister's wedding night and murdered the bridegroom, accounting for Grace's greater guilt and explaining why she has so graciously permitted her sister to drive her nuts. After all, it's *only fair*.

The Wasp-brother plot? "The violent drama of two brothers!

Their rivalry! Their brutal, undying hatred for one another! The woman they were both determined to have!"

On the road to family hostility, brothers get an earlier start than sisters. When they were seven and eight, John hanged George from the neck until he was almost dead. A faithful family retainer cut him down just in time, but of course he said nothing to the parents about it. "Boys will be boys," he sighs, relieved that neither of his charges is a sissy. That's the important thing.

In case anybody misses the Wasp-estrangement angle, the brothers are drawn as differently as possible—you would never know they were even distantly related. One is tall and blond, the other is short and dark. One is smart, the other is dumb. One is a prig, and the other is a black sheep. The black sheep is the hero because he did the proper Wasp thing by running way from home at fourteen.

The black sheep shows up just as his new sister-in-law is taking a solitary walk (what else?) in the woods (where else?). The black sheep introduces himself. The bride demands, "What are you doing here?" because, after all, she's a good Wasp girl; the last person she expected to see anywhere near her husband's property is his brother. She promptly reports to her husband, who yells, "He was paid to stay in Capetown!"

The very best Wasp-brother plot requires the Civil War. One brother is in the Union army and the other in the Confederate. They meet face-to-face on the battlefield and open fire.

Ben Ames Williams used the Civil War brothers in *The Strange Woman*, but his best Wasp-family drama is *Leave Her to Heaven*. The heroine, Ellen, offers to teach her polio-afflicted brother-in-law to swim because she has decided to drown him. In the end of the story, she poisons herself at a family picnic—truly a Wasp way to go.

Taking our family attitudes as a whole, the biggest con job ever perpetrated on the American people has to be the Norman Rockwell Wasp. The *biggest* happy family in the world, they somehow all manage to squeeze in together at the same table. Everyone is impossibly happy and impossibly Wasp; with the exception of the turkey, they all have freckles, snub noses, and round faces, but the turkey is a Wasp, too—he's stuffed with cornbread. He is also properly cooked, not splitting open or falling apart, or put back together again after being dropped on the kitchen floor. There isn't a whiskey bottle in sight and nobody is saying, "My *God!*"

Because Norman Rockwell drew people who were so obviously *us*, Wasps tend to try to emulate his families at holiday time, resulting in what psychiatry calls the Thanksgiving psychosis and the Christmas psychosis. We feel duty-bound to gather together and ask the Lord's blessing, but sooner or later we crack under the strain of family solidarity. From then on in, it's hark the herald angels *sink*.

The same thing happens when Wasp sisters read *Little Women*. For about three weeks, they try their best to be sweet and close and dear until, finally, somebody cracks. For that matter, the original little women cracked occasionally, too. Amy stole Jo's boyfriend.

The kith and kin situation is, of course, quite different in the South. War, hunger, poverty, Reconstruction, years of criticism, and consequent defensive psychology have made Southern families stick together in ways that all Americans are familiar with from the many books and movies about the region.

Less familiar are some of the startling remarks Southerners come out with on the subject of kinship. The uninitiated Yankee is invariably floored by that seeming allusion to total exsanguination, "She doesn't have any blood." It sounds like the Black Dahlia murder case but it isn't. It simply means that she . . . well, that she doesn't have any blood. Good blood, blue blood, old blood—that kind of blood. "She doesn't have any ancestors" has nothing to do with successful extrauterine experiments. Everybody has progenitors but ancestors are deader. A social climber in *The View from Pompey's Head* quickly found out how important ancestors were—namely, they had their portraits painted: "Kit's being the prettiest girl her age was not enough. Truly to dazzle, her radiance had to be looked down upon by portraits from the wall."

"My people" is a posher way of saying the more commonplace "my family." It originated in slave days when beloved servants were considered, and considered themselves, part of the family. It is an especially popular locution in Virginia because it has such a baronial ring, and it can be used to imply that you are related to everybody who is anybody in the entire state.

"He's family" does not necessarily mean he is a member of the speaker's family. It refers to descendants of the nation's original founders, people who either belong to official groups like First Families of Whatever, or who are simply recognized without being organized.

At the first scent of a visit from a relative, Southerners always say, "We'll *make* room." Even flaky relatives are welcome. When Cousin Eulalie, who is a little bit funny, stops by for a cup of coffee and stays a week, the family will somehow make room for her. If there is no place to put her but the living room floor she won't mind; she's having the change of life and can't sleep anyway. The Southern family's vast experience in making room might help explain why the New South has been able to make a number of political accommodations that came as a pleasant surprise to the rest of the country. Cousin Eulalie is, after all, excellent training in the art of coping.

When the pioneers were asked why they wanted to push farther and farther west, they replied, "Because it's there." A remarkable vagueness lurks under that attractive swagger. Given Wasp family attitudes, they probably meant, "We can't stand another Christmas with Uncle Hiram and that damn bunch in Erie."

Now that the frontier is closed, thoughtful Wasp corporations have provided us with an updated version of the old escape hatch. Executives are transferred to Fresno "because the new office is there." Casual and regular uprooting of employees is now a fact of life in America. It has been to the Wasp's advantage that he generally manages to cope quite well with a nation of strangers. He may not care about the kinsmen he has left behind, but, after all, *neighborliness* was a quality the pioneers had to develop for their own survival. Today's Wasp makes a very nice neighbor as a rule; he is pleasant and helpful without being sticky.

In keeping with our detachment, there is a certain type of shallow Wasp who makes an excellent fair-weather friend. In this day of intense all-absorbing conversations about relationships . . . commitment . . . viable alternatives, a friend who refuses to talk about anything unpleasant—or even interesting—can be refreshing. Eloise and Dicky are good with the amusing mini-drama: "You'll never guess what happened when I got my tennis racket restrung!" Whatever you do, don't depend on Eloise and

Dicky for anything important; simply enjoy them, realizing that they are what they are and will never be any different. They stand like stone walls against the onslaughts of all crusaders and drive the dedicated crazy. Intended by the Almighty to spend their time tea-dancing at the Copley-Plaza in 1925, Eloise and Dicky feel out of step in today's world and are happy to repay, in their own tinny coin, anyone who does not hate them for being selfish. Use them as social directors for your cocktail parties provided your guests are interested in light-hearted chatter, but keep them away from the political analyst—they still don't know where Biafra is.

In *Lonely in America*, Suzanne Gordon writes, "Couples in America are very reluctant to have single men or women as close friends." But that is not true of a certain kind of Wasp couple. Usually small-town or rural people, and often Westerners, the Wasp adoptive couple are a breezy, brother-and-sister sort of team with little or no sexual awareness between them. The wife is absolutely free of jealousy and usually initiates the friendship. They will adopt a younger woman; take her fishing and skeet shooting and help her repair anything. ("Harry! Go fix her tire!") Quite often she is a happy substitute for a child of their own with whom they did not get along, but mostly they enjoy her, because as a stranger, she is safe. She is not a hostage to fortune, even though they spend money on her. Her charm is that she is *not* their child.

8

THE BEACHCOMBER WASP
or
How Rock Hunter Spoils Success

In addition to the upper-class Wasps, there are also many, many poor Wasps with no connections whatsoever. There are also scum-of-the-earth Wasps. The buggering mountaineers in *Deliverance* were from a section of the country known for its pure unadulterated Anglo-Saxon blood. Like the monarchs of old Europe, crackers and hillbillies intermarry until they produce aberrations that would make European royalty's hemophilia seem like a dashing conversation piece. The folks to whom "I'm My Own Grandpa" was dedicated are all Wasps with yellow hair and eyes like an October sky, except that they may be crossed.

We really can be appalling, but no one wants to believe it. According to an unshakable ethnic myth, every Wasp father is a bank president. This being the case, it follows that every Wasp graduate has a lifetime niche waiting for him as soon as he sleeps off his graduation-night drunk. He "goes into the bank" and presumably never comes out again once the solid steel doors slam behind him.

If by some twist of Fate our fathers do not own banks, ethnics assume we can invoke our infamous "old boy network" to get a job in somebody's father's law firm. Curtis, Carter, Rawlings, Wakefield, Masterson, Stone, Simpson & Turner is a temple of fair employment practices: Carter married Miss Curtis, who roomed with Miss Rawlings at Vassar, and Wakefield recruited the rest at the Princeton Club. As the "real Americans," our membership in the button-down battalion is supposedly assured; we cannot avoid success because we were enrolled in life at birth.

In actual fact, we produce more than our share of bums. Never having been pursued by the furies of bigotry, we fear failure less than other Americans. Consequently, many of us have a casual attitude toward success. We do not worry what *They* will think of us if we produce too many failures—after all, *we* are They. Knowing that he cannot give anybody a bad name except himself, the Wasp feels free to sink into happy sloth and do what he really wants to do. Like the honor student gone wild, the "real American" can afford to say the hell with it and become a beachcomber.

The Wasp beachcomber comes in several different types. The most familiar, long ago turned into a cliché by the casting office, is the playboy-black sheep son of a self-made tycoon. Another is Ashley Wilkes, who went through life in a genteel daze because he was too used to being a Wilkes to develop what Scarlett called "gumption." A third is the middle-class son who becomes a professional roughneck; "Peck's bad boy" as he is sometimes called, he resembles Tom Jordache in *Rich Man, Poor Man*. But the foremost Wasp beachcomber is that devotee of the bat-brained scheme, Rock Hunter.

Rock is the man in the commuters' club car who suddenly decides, somewhere between Irvington-on-Hudson and Tarrytown, to quit his job, pack up his family, and go seek the simple life. Rock is easy to spot; a glass in one hand and a pencil in the other, he is madly scribbling figures on the back of an envelope to see what he can liquidate fast. The notations on Rock's envelope would bring on a stroke in the ethnic wife. Never one to leave any bridge unburned, here is what Rock has jotted down:

> House—$20,000 equity
> Silver and wedding gifts—$7,000
> Faith's engagement ring—$1,500
> Faith's mink—$5,000

Faith doesn't know it yet, but she was well-named.

It all started the previous summer when the Hunters vacationed in Maine and Rock saw the lighthouse. Perhaps it is true that our island heritage has put salt in our blood, because the mere sight of a lighthouse can set a Wasp man off and turn a New England vacation into a nightmare of great expectations. He decides, on the spur of the moment, that he wants to live in one.

Suddenly, waving lanterns at boats becomes his idea of satisfying, creative work.

Fortunately, lighthouse-keeping has been taken over by the Coast Guard, but the Hunters are not yet safely out of the North Woods. Rock is certain to strike up a friendship with some of those Wasp octogenarians who populate New England vacation spots. One conversation too many with those crackerbarrel philosophers will push a Wasp husband over the edge. Eben Perkins and Jared Winslow have been sitting on the pier for the last forty years, ever since they threw over multi-million-dollar businesses to come up to Merde du Loup and mend lobster pots for a living. They need no encouragement to sing the praises of the simple life, nor to relate the fate of the doctor who told them back in 1947 that they only had a year to live. In 1948 the doctor dropped dead.

"Heart," says Perkins, tapping his chest.

"Ayeh," says Winslow. "Work killed him. Only live once, might as well live right."

"Dern tootin'," says Perkins.

Faith is now in for what Wasp husbands like to call a surprise. Full of boyish enthusiasm—that endearing quality possessed in abundance by our men—Rock informs her that he is quitting his job, dumping his stock shares, selling the house, and auctioning off their furniture. "Honey, we're going into the lobster business!"

Note the Wasp *we*. Not for us the harsh patriarchy with a stern papa ruling the roost. We are hung up on fair play; our marriages are equal partnerships. By calling his wild scheme a joint venture, Rock is offering to match his wife chilblain for chilblain; together they will stand, shoulder to shoulder, gazing down a long vista of empty lobster pots; and the deed that will be handed to the sheriff at the bankruptcy sale will read *Rock Hunter et Ux*.

Faith could put a stop to this nonsense before it ever got under way if only she would do what any sensible non-Wasp woman would do under the same circumstances: scream, have a migraine, or point out that people who mend lobster pots stand an excellent chance of losing an eye. She could, but she never does, because she's a luv, she is. She is Mollie Pitcher sticking by her man even if it means sending her children to school along roads marked *Beware Charging Moose*.

Faith will chance it because in her world, the husband comes first. Where her husband's work is concerned, Faith received the same admonition from her mother as Betty MacDonald did: "If you marry a shoe clerk, don't complain that he does not have the income of a doctor; be grateful that he keeps regular hours. If you marry a doctor, don't complain about his irregular hours. Be grateful that he makes such good money."

In other words, DON'T NAG. This is the Wasp woman's first commandment, and she never forgets it. She does not have the faintest idea how to stem the tide of male madness, and she is helpless when it comes to controlling men with guilt. Determined to be what Wasp men call "a good sport," she is her own worst enemy.

If she is lucky, she can write a best-seller like *The Egg and I*, providing she doesn't go insane from meeting mountain lions on the front porch and bats in the outhouse. The biggest surprise that awaits her is the change that comes over Rock. Easily pleased in civilization, the moment he hits the wilds he becomes a martinet. Suddenly he wants home-baked bread, butter fresh from the churn, and a spanking white wash flapping on the line—what he calls "getting back to the basics." His idea of good clean living is now a woman who ages ten years in six months.

If Rock Hunter does not succumb to the New England madness, his wife would be wise to keep an eye out for the country-newspaper syndrome. Buying a little weekly in Wyoming is the dream of ad men, PR men, and communications executives. A sure sign that a country editor is in the making are those middle-of-the-night perusals of the Atlas. Maps are a danger signal in the Wasp home; Wasp boys like to send away to Gulf and Esso for free maps and spend hours staring at them as they make imaginary getaways. Faith knows something is brewing when she discovers that the spine of the Atlas is broken so that at the slightest touch it falls open to Wyoming.

When Rock's nocturnal prowling awakens her, we have a replay of the famous togetherness scene from countless Wasp novels and movies . . .

The camera comes in for a close-up of Faith in bed as she opens her eyes, turns her head, and looks thoughtfully at the rumpled pillow and the empty space beside her. She frowns thoughtfully. She bites her lip—thoughtfully—and gets up. Reaching for her pretty robe that is draped Waspily across the bottom of the bed, she puts it on because a Wasp woman never runs around in her shift. Knowing Her Man is troubled, she Goes To Him.

Rock is standing out in the yard with his fists balled in the pockets of his robe—meaning that he is mentally composing his letter of resignation. When he sees Faith, he smiles thoughtfully and puts his arm around her waist. She leans against him and waits in thoughtful silence until he is ready to speak, just as her mother always told her to do.

"You know . . . " he begins, then stops. Faith gets that nauseating look on her face that means Silent Understanding.

"I've been thinking . . ." Rock continues, then stops again.

His arm tightens around her waist. "That country weekly in Broken Bridle . . ."

"I know," Faith whispers thoughtfully.

He looks down at her tenderly. "Let's sell everything and go!"

"Yes, dear."

"You're sure you don't mind?"

Faith rests her head against his shoulder. "A man has to do what he has to do." She got that from her mother, too.

He tilts her chin up with his fingertips. "You're wonderful, you know that?"

The next weekend they stage that bargain-hunter's dream, the Wasp garage sale. Since Rock has decided that the family will live in a Rocky Mountain cabin without electricity, you can pick up a late-model Waring blender for fifty cents. Need a Halston evening gown? Got two bucks? The good sport won't need it where she's going. Infected with overconfidence from long years of being called the "real Americans" and envied by one and all, it never crosses a Wasp's mind that things might not work out as planned, and that he will need all those belongings again someday.

With the proceeds, such as they are, from their garage sale, the family now buys the things they will need in their new home. Overconfident people being impetuous, it never occurs to them that it is more sensible to wait until they get to Wyoming before buying lanterns, outdoor stoves, or whatever else is burning in their brains. Nothing will suit but a quick trip to the hardware store *right that minute*. The whole family is so swept up in child-like glee that they must buy all the new goodies in order to play with them first, and to hell with the extra U-Hauls they will have to hire to cart their coals to Newcastle.

They even step out of their Wasp character and enjoy a little intellectual activity during this preparatory period. Rock buys a copy of *How to Slaughter and Dress Your Own Beef* and reads it aloud.

The Wasp who does not kick over the traces permanently will always find a way to do so on a temporary basis. We are America's most enthusiastic vacation campers. Nothing delights us more than two weeks of mock homelessness and simulated disaster.

It begins with that hideous activity known as "getting an early start." For once, Mother has everything under control. She sets the alarm for five and actually gets up when it goes off. Husband oriented as always, she takes Dad his coffee in bed. He too is in fine fettle; pulling on his boots, which on this glorious morning he calls boondockers, he stamps out to the kitchen where Mother is frying the first round of the two hundred pre-dawn eggs that will be her destiny in the coming fortnight. When everyone has finished breakfast, she collects the dishes and washes them *immediately*—this, you see, is a very special day.

Dad says, "All right, men, we're shoving off," and Mother and the boys obediently fall in. They all crunch their way to the camper waiting in the yard, fully packed the night before with all the emergency goodies that, if they are lucky, they will get a chance to use. The first-aid kit, the snakebite kit (the boys can't wait to encounter their first rattler), the fold-up stretcher, the portable water purifier. The boys climb in the back with the dog and immediately have a mock sword fight with their twelve-blade camping knives. Mother pays no attention to them because she is too busy saying, "Yes, dear" to Dad. When he finishes issuing orders about road maps and sunglasses, he drives off, whistling "Home on the Range" in double time.

As soon as the sun is overhead, Dad makes everybody take a salt tablet. "Are we gonna have a sunstroke?" the boys ask eagerly. "Read your spider book," Dad orders. *American Spiders and How to Know Them* is a must on a Wasp camping trip. "Gee, I hope we see a black widow, don't you, Mom?" Of course she does: she's a grand girl.

They arrive at the Bar X Campsite, which is marked by a wood-burnt sign. All the signs at Bar X are wood-burnt, for no Wasp in a rustic mood would dream of touching pen and ink or paint and brush. The family feels immediately at home because the whole place is swarming with Wasps—a nest of us. Children eating Gainesburgers, dogs eating Eskimo pies, women frying eggs, men expertly building fires and casting reels—us in all our glory, spread out before you. There is nothing on Wall Street to equal it.

The owner-hosts of the Bar X Campsite are Bob and Sal Watson, a married couple in their fifties who look exactly alike. They call each other Mother and Daddy but refer to each other as "he" and "the old woman." Like so many Wasp couples of this type, they get along beautifully, but it is impossible to imagine them ever being in bed together. Their version of sexual union seems to be hooking a Winnebago trailer onto a rear bumper.

Bob Watson can do anything. If a mishap occurs, Sal shrugs calmly, looks around, and says, "Where is he? He can fix it for you." Bob Watson has never had a job he didn't love. Lumberjack, apple farmer, salmon fisherman, riding instructor, saddle maker, he has spent his life earning a living at the things most men would gladly do for free, on doctor's orders, to cure their hypertension. It's as if he retired when he dropped out of high school on his sixteenth birthday.

Mention any famous fire, flood, or other act of God and Bob Watson was caught in it. Disaster does not stalk him; he stalks disaster. He loves nothing better than a dangerous natural challenge, and he thrives on it. Or as the old woman puts it, "That big blow back in '49? He was there."

Each night around the camp fire, Bob Watson holds all the vacationing Wasps in thrall with stories about the many times he nearly lost his life. Expert in all forms of survival, his greatest *cachet* is his knowledge of—you guessed it—how to live on roots and berries. "He was lost for three weeks in the Canadian Yukon in the dead of winter," explains the old woman, who punctuates and paragraphs his somewhat rambling stories. By the time the children have heard a few Bob Watson serials, they are tearing the bark from the trees and eating it like candy. Their mothers seldom mind; it means fewer eggs to fry, and besides, if Bob Watson says it's edible, then it's edible.

At the end of the evening, when all the stories have been told and everyone is feeling cozy, the Watsons lead a sing-along. The most fascinating thing about Bob Watson is his expert guitar playing. He never misses a chord even though he is missing three fingers from his left hand. "He met a grizzly when he was a forest ranger," explains the old woman.

The Bob Watson ideal is behind the Wasp boy's favorite game, "The End of the World." Indulged in chiefly by little Wasps aged nine to twelve, it involves tents, mess kits, and elaborate fantasies of earthquakes and Martian invasions. Sometime in April as soon as the weather turns warm, Jimmy and Ken set up an outcry: they want to sleep in the yard. Mother being Mother, this is never hard to arrange. The boys take *all* their equipment—Wasp boys have no end of equipment—and set up their bivouac. The next morning, even Mother may get upset, for it is not unusual to look out the window and see a trench worthy of the Army Corps of Engineers. Digging holes and hiding in them is part and parcel of childhood, but Wasp boys are oddly compulsive about the amount of reality they infuse into these expeditions. Any old shovel will not do; it must be an olive-green collapsible GI shovel from the government surplus store—these lads are sticklers for the artifacts of real trouble. Real walkie-talkies, real flares, real stretchers, are carried up to the "lookout post" in the tree. And what, pray tell, are Jimmy and Ken looking for? Given a choice, they would prefer the gray funnel of an oncoming tornado, but if they live in the wrong part of the country they will settle for a good nor'easter or a decent flood.

Why are Wasps like that? It's the pioneer heritage; the charm of the unknown, the unsafe, the lure of nowhere, the need to strike out for the wilderness simply because "it's there."

The American pioneer's heritage, in turn, goes back to the Englishman's rurophilia. In *The English,* David Frost and Antony Jay tell us, "Every Englishman is a countryman at heart. However many years he may have lived in the city, he does not believe he really belongs there. . . . The country stands for something enduring and unchanging in a world where everything else seems to be going rapidly down hill."

Rurophilia crops up in the strangest places and at the strangest times—including murder trials. The psychiatrist who testified for the Crown in the trial of mass murderer John Reginald Christie described the defendant contemptuously as "an insignificant, old-womanish city man."

It can even be a decisive factor in political philosophy. The most famous Wasp rurophile of our times was Whittaker Chambers, whose obsessive belief in the political purity of country life runs through his autobiography, *Witness.*

"My old need for the land asserted itself. . . . That craving seized me like an infection that I could not throw off, and which made me physically ill. The slum in which we lived became unendurable to me—not just because it was a slum. Every other part of the city affected me in the same way. I felt that life was not worth living if it had to be lived away from the land."

One of the first things Chambers did after leaving the Communist party was to buy a dairy farm in Maryland. He came to feel that hard physical work and a rural environment were morally cleansing; conversely, he believed that Communism thrives on city living. The hiding place he chose for the microfilm evidence—the interior of a hollowed pumpkin—indicated more than a puckish streak in his personality. It was, I think, a country man's ultimate revenge on the urbane Hiss.

When New York City's financial crisis struck, hinterland Wasps nearly burst their seams with self-righteous glee. It *proved* that cities are wrong and that the provinces are right, by golly. No one can hate cities like a Wasp, and New York being the most citified city in the world, the reaction was inevitable. Some of the comments I heard from Westerners sounded like the passages in praise of country folk in George Eliot's rustic novels. In this one area, at least, Wasps still wield a hefty influence. In the last few years, everyone seems to be taking a leaf from the Wasp tree. The quest for a better "quality of life" has inspired people to pull up stakes, leave the big cities, and try to settle, if not in the country, then at least in small provincial cities like Cheyenne, Boise, and Concord, New Hampshire. They are now willing to take big salary cuts in exchange for fresh air and leisurely privileges like walking to work.

Despite our rurophilia, the hinterland Wasp can be an extravagant culture-vulture. When the Metropolitan Opera or big-city theater groups tour the backwaters, Wasps show up in droves, dressed in their best. They may or may not like opera or plays, it doesn't matter; unlike the New Yorker who ignores the culture to which he has long since grown accustomed, the provincial Wasp wants simply to *go*. Texans especially think nothing of driving a hundred miles to attend a performance of *La Traviata*.

At such times, the Wasp husband insists upon saying things like, "She looks pretty healthy to be dying of TB," but that is merely his own private tropism. He enjoys the performance far more than he usually admits.

A first cousin of the beachcomber is the late-blooming Wasp. Three famous examples of the breed were all in their forties when they finally hit pay dirt.

Samuel Butler was a jack of all trades, into music, art, architecture, and several other fields before he finally came up with his masterpiece, *The Way of All Flesh*.

James M. Cain spent many years trying to become an opera singer; then, in middle life, with hope nearly atrophied, he wrote the fabulously successful novel, *The Postman Always Rings Twice*. Now eighty-four, he is still writing.

The most interesting late-blooming Wasp was Sherwood Anderson. Long before anybody started nattering about changing life-styles, Anderson changed his with a vengeance. A highly successful paint manufacturer, he pulled one of our favorite stunts: walking off the job. According to his memoirs, he was in the middle of dictating a letter to his secretary when he decided he had had it. He got up, left his office, and walked down the railroad tracks toward Chicago with six dollars in his pocket. Anderson decorated his account with some d'Artagnan flourishes, leaving out some of the less romantic facts—he returned home and had a nervous breakdown before he officially entered Chicago's literary world—but the basic story is true.

Wasps have itchy feet and tenuous family ties, and the combination makes us selfish as well as impetuous. Anderson wanted to be a writer freed of all business and domestic responsibilities, so he split, even though he had a wife and several children. He did not doubt that somehow, some way, he could pull it off and do the kind of about-face that most men can only fantasize. Nor did the sudden reversal of fortune upset him. When he arrived in Chicago, he was forced to take a room in a motorman's flat and sleep on a cot in an overcrowded, poverty-stricken atmosphere after having lived the life of a very prosperous Midwestern businessman.

Being on a downspiral is virtually guaranteed to crack up less secure and less cavalier personalities; Anderson's neuroses were legion, but they did not affect his basic Wasp self-confidence and optimism. Nor was he troubled by the specter of eccentricity. The English have always adored certifiables, from Everyfamily's dotty old auntie to King George III. We cherish our charming nut cases and dine out on their exploits; Agatha Christie made a fortune writing about *le type anglais.*

More often than not, however, the late-blooming Wasp never blooms at all. We are the people who provide tenants for skid-row hotels full of old men born in the wrong century. We produce a certain type of primitive male who is superb at building civilizations but totally helpless when it comes to living in them. Impatient and simplistic, they see everything in black and white; action followed by reaction with no cogitation in between.

The skid-row hotel appears more and more frequently as you travel west. In the Far West, not surprisingly, there seems to be one on every downtown street. Old men stare blankly out windows whose sills are lined with cans of orange juice and cartons of milk. Whenever a death occurs in such hotels, the name in the paper is nearly always a Wasp one—or an Indian one. The descendants of men who fought each other over the land cannot survive in cities.

The Wasp Failure Freak? He's out there somewhere, and, under the circumstances, he is never hard to find. Unlike the Serenity Wasp, who is willing to work for a living and is a dependable if not an inspired employee, the Failure Freak is a bit of a psychopath. He is the boy who quits college in the second semester of his senior year to become a *real* beachcomber. He has been destroyed by the Wasp stereotype of dull, plodding success. In the fifties I went to school with several such young men; they ranted continually about gray flannel suits and carried Yugoslavian freighter schedules with them at all times. Today the Failure Freak is the pseudo-ecologist who pretends concern for the environment so that he can break the family custom of going to law school, and go to a commune instead.

Unlike the Wasp scions in the past who wanted to join the French foreign legion, the bona fide Failure Freak does not want adventure because it would threaten his pathological need for absolute peace and quiet. All he wants is a life completely free of worry and excitement.

The most extreme example of this type is Carry Nation's husband. David Nation, nicknamed "Stag Nation" by reporters covering his wife, would have gone unnoticed as the only living man in a morgue. On the Kansas-Texas frontier his torpidity was positively eery. A lawyer by training, his idea of building up a practice was to stand motionless on the main street of Holden, Kansas, waiting for clients to come up and solicit his services.

Since few people wish to be represented by a statue, David's practice did not grow. He decided to enter the ministry, a decision that resulted in what Robert Lewis Taylor calls "one of theology's bleakest chapters since the days of Peter the Hermit."

Willing to endure anything to avoid effort, David submitted totally to his wife, and given her unsubtle methods, his ministry was doomed to failure. Wrote Taylor:

> Carry had undertaken to choose his text, implementing it with wrathful and bloodcurdling anecdotes—principally involving liquor, tobacco and sex. . . . She seated herself conspiculously in the front row. . . . Nation rarely got out a sentence without some noisy and helpful assist from Carry. If he seemed to be speaking slowly, she boomed from the pews, "Speed it up, David. You're dragging." She told him to raise his voice, lower his voice, clear his throat, blow his nose, clutch his lapel, walk to the right, kneel briefly, pull his beard and make gestures such as "Stop right there and point at the Heavens!" . . . When Carry suspected that he was winding down, she bawled, "That will be all for today, David"; then she hied herself to the rostrum, banged shut his Bible, and led him out. . . .[1]

Ostensibly the family breadwinner, David Nation avoided the strains in this task by failing quickly and conspicuously at everything he set his hand to. Just as he was preparing to sit motionless at home and spend the rest of his life enjoying complete freedom from tension, Carry came home covered with blood and broken glass, hatchet in hand and sheriff hot on her trail. For the next two

---

[1] *Vessel of Wrath: The Life and Times of Carry Nation.*

years, until he divorced her, David Nation's life was a nightmare of edged weapons, shrieking women, murder threats, lynch mobs, jail, beatings, and international fame.

Carry's first husband, Dr. Gloyd, was the lush of her life. He provided her with her cause, but it was surely David Nation who inspired her methods. Women married to Wasp Failure Freaks invariably develop a taste for action.

America's most famous Wasp who didn't try harder was Calvin Coolidge, the man who got everything without trying. As William Allen White put it, his greatest gift was "God-given inertia."

Often called the luckiest man in America, Coolidge never tried to win and so never lost. His political victories were matched by personal ones. With no money, no looks, and certainly no personality going for him, he won as a wife a woman who became the most charming and vivacious First Lady since Dolley Madison. Grace Goodhue was knee-deep in suitors when she met Calvin, but he got her because, said a relative, "He out-sat everybody else."

He had a genius for moseying into those unique political limelights that the most aggressive PR man could not in a million years create. For instance, he just happened to be governor of Massachusetts during the Boston police strike. His famous telegram to Samuel Gompers, "There is no right to strike against the public safety by anyone, in any place, at any time," solved nothing, but its tone of Olympian self-confidence convinced the nation that Coolidge had single-handedly rescued every American from anarchy and bolshevism.

The telegram led to the Vice Presidential spot on the Harding ticket, prompting a newsman who had followed Coolidge's career to predict that Harding would either be assassinated or die in office—"Because Calvin Coolidge is the luckiest man in the world." Two years later, Harding died.

Coolidge got word of the President's death while vacationing at his father's remote Vermont farm. Advised that he must be sworn in as soon as possible, he turned to his father and calmly asked, "Are you still a notary?" The scene that followed is one of the most beloved in American history, one that enabled Coolidge to out-log-cabin Abe Lincoln in one effortless stroke.

In the White House, Coolidge took a nap after lunch no matter what happened, and enjoyed additional relaxation by sitting on the front porch and watching the streetcars go by. He not only got away with remarks that no one else would dare utter, like "When more and more people are thrown out of work, unemployment results," he was lauded for them. Americans called such Calvinistic pearls "plain talk . . . common sense . . . getting to the heart of the matter."

His utter disinterest in what anybody thought of him was best described by Edward Lowry, who saw him at a party:

"He didn't seem ill at ease or embarrassed or tongue-tied. He was just still. Silent upon a peak at Darien is no word for it. He gave no appearance of being about to say something presently. He was an absolute calm. *Old Ironsides* at anchor lay in the harbor of Mahon, the waves to sleep had gone. Not a leaf stirring . . ."

Coolidge's final effortless victory was his decampment from the White House just in time to avoid being blamed for the Depression. Jobless Americans called their tar paper shacks Hoovervilles instead of Coolidgevilles. From 1928 till his death in 1933, Calvin bestirred himself enough to write a syndicated column in which he calmly discussed such topics as economic theory.

Calvin Coolidge embodied all the Wasp virtues—and one of our biggest faults. Feeling that he could do no wrong, he did not bother to do anything much at all.

9

ANTI-INTELLECTUALISM

or

My Father's Dumber Than Your Father

"Books muddle me," said Henry Ford, who refused to let his son Edsel go to college. I could fill the rest of this book with comparable Wasp quotations but I will limit myself to these sterling examples:

Alexander Pope: "Scholars are forever reading, never to be read."

Caroline Bird: "Excessive experience with books can cut people off from reality."

My grandmother: "If your eyes fall out from all that reading, don't come crying to me."

Wasp anti-intellectualism takes several different routes, but they all lead to Canterbury. What today's Wasp contemptuously dismisses as "sitting around and thinking" also exasperated his late medieval forebears. The rise of scholasticism was one of the principal causes of the Protestant Reformation. Monastic scholars "sat around and thought" about matters that were supposed to be beyond rational intellect and logic. Revealed faith, by definition, did not need to be proved by the incessant arguing and debating that church pedants indulged in. The intellectual methods of the medieval church were self-destructive methods. Attempting to penetrate and clarify infallible dogma is a contradiction in terms, or as the blunt Englishman would say, "If it's infallible, then button your lip." Intellectual life, dominated by the church, degenerated into quibbling and hair-splitting about how many angels can dance on the head of a pin. By making faith the object of thought, the scholastic church ironically encouraged the spirit of free inquiry that led to Protestantism. Distaste for learned magpies has been an identifying mark of the Protestant ever since.

Protestantism took the contemplation out of Christianity and replaced it with industriousness. The bedrock of our theology is the belief that God helps those who help themselves, and the only way to help yourself is to work. God's face shines upon anybody who can make money, and failure to rake it in is *ipso facto* proof of sloth, one of the Seven Deadlies. We cannot separate virtue from hard work, which is why the descendents of Yankee missionaries-turned-entrepreneurs who went to Hawaii to do good ended up doing well.

The best time to see Protestantism in full flower is not in church but on report-card day in a Wasp home. When Gail Parent's hero David Meyer brought home all A's, he was praised as "a regular Einstein." When the Wasp child brings home all A's, he is paid off in cold cash, so much for each A. The Jewish parent cares about what his child has actually *learned.* The Wasp parent is concerned with how hard his child worked. Therefore, report-card day is really payday.

Comparing our loot was standard practice for my classmates and me on day-after-report-card day. I got a dollar for every B and three dollars for every A, and considered myself gainfully employed; school was my "job."

Praise was something else. My parents said, "That's nice," and Granny said, "A studious woman and a crowing hen always come to a tragic end." Nobody ever spent the proverbial "week on the telephone" bragging about me, and I was never nagged about grades unless you want to count my mother's admonition the day I entered kindergarten: "I don't care if you're not the smartest one in the class as long as you're not the dumbest."

Wasp parents nag about other things. Committed to practical (i.e., $) knowledge and harboring a fundamental distrust of pure scholarship, they are constantly on the lookout for "horse sense." This quality, as we are so fond of saying, cannot be taught; you are either born with it or you are not. The greatest exponent of horse sense in our family was my grandmother, whose hobby, if she could be said to have had one, was marrying men of substance who "only went to the eighth grade." This is a favorite Wasp boast; bragging about how dumb you are is the mark of the successful self-made man. Granny bragged so much about her three deceased husbands that I decided functional illiterates must be the only good providers around—they left women "well fixed." Conversely, she felt there was something inherently wrong with people who had what she called "too much" education; so whenever I did something unthinking like peeling potatoes toward me, she would sigh, "You're brilliant, but you're not very bright."

My mother never checked my homework, but she kept abreast of my horse sense by firing riddles at me, her favorite being, "Which weighs more, a pound of lead or a pound of feathers?" The correct answer thrilled her more than the four-year scholarship I later won.

Wasp parents also nag about good attendance and punctuality. At my high school graduation, I received a number of academic prizes, but the prize that pleased my family most was my perfect-attendance medal. The Wasp ideal is, "If you can't be smart, at least you can be *there.*" Never being absent or late is Protestant training for later life; teacher is a stand-in for the future boss who will dock your pay if you don't watch out.

Otherwise, teachers are villains in Waspland. We have done everything possible to denigrate them in our literature and popular entertainment. From the ghouls in Dickens and Charlotte Brontë, to Ichabod Crane, to the sexually frustrated, spindle-shanked Miss Sidney in William Inge's *Picnic*, we have drawn teachers as loathesome, utterly ridiculous, and inadequate in all ways. And, of course, skinny, should anyone miss the point of their poverty.

In the Wasp mind, it is adults who make money, have money, spend money; children represent liabilities, with red ink smeared on their faces like strawberry jam. Anyone who chooses to make his living from children is simply deficient in common sense and no different from the person who buys a hole in the ground and calls it a gold mine. Moreover, since children are paupers by definition, the combination of children and teachers amounts to a conspiracy of the have-nots. Danger lurks here as it does in any conspiracy of have-nots. The fear is never articulated as such, but it emerges from the Wasp subconscious in that traditional put-down, "If they're so smart, how come they're not rich?" My grandmother went one better. Speaking *ex cathedra* as usual, she proclaimed, "They're nothing but servants."

We believe that teachers are people who wish to be important, but who fear that no one but children will find them so.

We also feel that teachers are timid people with an underlying bullying nature who must arrange matters so that their victims are certain to be physically smaller. This makes teachers offenders against fair play—an even greater sin than timidity. Today's teachers have unions and tend to be militant rather than timid, but the Wasp has an answer for that, too. Militant teachers are "on their high horse." How dare they *not* be timid? After all, they're *only* teachers. It's their *duty* to refuse to strike because they are supposed to be dedicated. However, the most scorned teacher is the most dedicated one because, in Waspland, dedication to lofty ideals instead of lofty salaries is proof of impracticality.

It gets even worse. Many Wasps feel there is something strange about an adult who chooses to be around children so much. Don't teachers feel confident of their ability to cope with their contemporaries, and if not, why? Are they weak? Spineless? If so, you can't trust them. In England, choosing the company of children carries even more ominous overtones. As Evelyn Waugh made plain in *Decline and Fall*, pedagogy and pedophilia go together like tea and crumpets. As the expelled hero leaves Oxford, the gatekeeper says, "Sent down for indecent behavior, were you? Expect you'll become a schoolmaster, eh wot?"

It would appear that Wasps hate teachers. We do. On the other hand, we do not, for our pitiless contempt is balanced by our Miss Dove syndrome.

Miss Dove is the *one* teacher in every Wasp's life to whom he owes everything. However, she must be a certain kind of teacher; her forte must be character building, not intellectual training, which is why she is nearly always an elementary-school teacher. The original Miss Dove in Frances Gray Patton's novel was a fiend on geography but her real fame rested on her reputation as a martinet; specifically, her ironclad rule against excusing pupils who wanted a drink of water. Thanks to her irrational war on thirst, one of her little boys grew up to become a hero in a real war. Shipwrecked in the Pacific, he spent a record number of days on a raft without a drop to drink. He lived to tell the tale, attributing his staying power to Miss Dove: whenever he felt he would go mad from thirst, he pretended the raft was his old schoolroom and that the Japanese were Miss Dove. The comparisons, he felt, were remarkably apt.

Ironically, Wasps and teachers get along quite well together. For one thing, we support our PTA. The average Wasp is given to parliamentarianism and feels obligated to attend any meeting in the name of community service (read *running things*). Teachers appreciate Wasps because we do not make them feel uncomfortable by kowtowing to them as do many ethnic parents. My own teaching experience brought this home to me in no uncertain terms. After being embarrassed by a Polish grandmother thrice my age who called me ma'am and kept bobbing up and down in near-curtsies, I welcomed the Wasp family who invited me for a drink at the local gin mill after PTA. Given our attitudes toward children, Wasps feel that if anyone needs a drink, it's a teacher.

The best weapon of all in the Wasp/teacher truce is our lip service to education. We are perfectly capable of standing four-square behind just about anything with an utter lack of sincerity, simply because it's the "nice" or the "right" thing to do. Joining forces with the Jews who care are the Wasps who don't care. Our yes votes on high-priced suburban school bond issues are frequently motivated by a modern, democratized form of noblesse oblige: "people like us" do not turn down school bond issues.

On the other hand, in Waspdom's lower echelons, schools are the first "luxury" to go during hard times. North Bend, Oregon's schools closed down lock, stock, and barrel last year when voters simply refused to tax themselves anymore. From time to time in the news we hear of the pattern repeating itself on a less dramatic scale as voters get their backs up and relieve their economic frustrations on the schools. Like North Bend, such localities are predominantly Wasp.

It is entirely possible for the intellectually inclined Wasp child to develop a guilt complex about his tastes. The casting office has used this situation many times in movies about the sensitive scholarly son at loggerheads with his self-make father, or the learned daughter at odds with her dazzling mother or sister. Like Duncan Calderwood in Irwin Shaw's *Rich Man, Poor Man*, the Wasp father says things like, "The world belongs to the meat

eaters" when he discovers that his son wants to teach. Any story
about Wasp pioneering is certain to contain one of those rich
patriarchs universally referred to as "the King" who engages in a
bitter struggle to break his youngest son's habit of writing poetry.
In Peter Gilman's novel *Diamondhead*, "King" Howland felt that
once a man had read *Huckleberry Finn* and the Bible, his literary
education was completed. "Not that I have anything against reading things," he explained, "except that it makes a person unhappy
and unfit for work." Such men also believe that books destroy the
nervous system and lead to sexual impotence.

No Wasp can escape the damaging effects of our anti-intellectualism entirely. We all grow up hearing snide remarks
about "bookworms" and "greasy grinds" and the unwisdom of
being a "brain." Even the brilliant Mrs. Davison in *The Group* was
dead set against Vassar girls making Phi Bete in the junior year,
telling her equally brilliant daughter Helena that premature Phi
Betes "smelled of the lamp."

My own vague guilt feelings began in 1943 when I skipped the
third grade, prompting Granny to predict, in one of her better
mixed metaphors, "When she gets to high school, her bust will be
a year smaller than the other girls'." (Her own cup size was DAR so
she worried about these matters.)

When I took French and got straight A's in it, she implied that I
was guilty of treason at worst, and insufferable mannerism at best:
"I don't know why you're taking French. Who are you going to
talk to? I don't see any Frenchmen around here, and if I did I
wouldn't let them set foot in this door. They can't win a war
without our help because they sit over there jabbering in French
until it's too late."

When I acquired a copy of Racine in a very smudgy French
imprint, she warned me not to read it if I had the slightest cut on
my finger: "The ink will get into your bloodstream and travel all
through your body, and when it reaches your heart, you'll die."
Only Granny could reduce the flower of classical drama to the
status of an air bubble.

When the subject of college came up, I asked my father if I
could go and he replied, "Of course you can go if you want to." My
mother said her usual, "That would be nice," and Granny said, "I
never thought my only granddaughter would be a bluestocking."

But wonder of wonders, when I won a scholarship, all three members of my cheering section went into Wasp ecstasies: "That'll save money!" In Waspland, if it's free it can't be all bad.

I made the dean's list throughout college, and on each "report-card day" I was rewarded in the manner to which I had grown accustomed: a dollar for every B and three dollars for every A. But when I graduated from college in 1957 and found no employment doors open to me but the one to the secretarial pool, I blamed college and wallowed in guilt for having gone. A bigotry-wise ethnic would have blamed the unfairness of the system—in this case, the anti-feminism then rife in the business world—but being a Wasp, it never occurred to me that I could be undesirable simply because I was what I was. Education, which I had been programmed to scorn, seemed to be the obvious villain; I had grown up hearing about "educated fools" who could not make money, and now I was one, too. I couldn't get a good job, so it *must* be the fault of college.

There was nothing to do except go back to college, so I won a graduate fellowship—which made me even guiltier, especially after Granny defined graduate students as "people who go through school twice." The only way I could do penance was to mess up in graduate school, so I did. I continued to get all A's and B's but I developed a block about my thesis. Many people never finish their theses, but I didn't even start mine. My sole effort in behalf of original scholarship was buying a pack of three-by-five cards from which I never even removed the cellophane.

Ironically, it was this act of academic non-writing that led me into professional writing. Needing a rationalization for my wasted year, I began to write and sell true confessions, smugly telling my professors, "Why should I write for free for the university when I can get paid for writing?"

It was a neat Wasp sleight-of-mind. In one fell swoop I was able to honor my father and my mother—and the Queen Mum—by becoming anti-intellectual; and at the same time remain in school, pretending that the $250 McFadden checks were merely a more generous version of the academic payoffs I had received since the age of six.

When I returned home, I was inundated in forgiveness. I had a hard time getting my McFadden checks to the bank because Granny liked to look at them. If she said it once she said it a hundred times: "I always knew you had good sense." My mother, discovering that I could write a salable confession in less than three hours, did some gleeful figuring on the back of an envelope and said, "Even bad women can't make money that fast." (She persisted in believing that they only charged two dollars.) As for my father, he took a copy of "Dear God, My Husband Thinks I'm a Slut" to work with him and spent the whole day bragging.

Not one of them ever inquired as to the whereabouts of the missing master's degree.

I was lucky compared with many Wasps. Being a girl helped because my scholarly tastes could be passed off as "accomplishments." It never hurts a man to have a wife who can engage his business partners in interesting conversation, etc. etc. I was also an only child, which saved me from unflattering comparisons with a cheerleader sister. My greatest asset was my father. He spoiled me so shamelessly in so many other areas of life that I never could feel very guilty very long about anything.

The male Wasp is the real victim of our anti-intellectualism. His family, especially his father, rags him unmercifully, using that now-famous quip, "He's got more degrees than a thermometer," which was first uttered by Helen Hayes in the 1950 movie, *My Son John*. Although the family in the movie were Catholic, Wasps identified with them and gleefully adopted the line as their own.

Our male intellectuals suffer from a persecution complex that Jewish intellectuals, for all their other persecution complexes, are not troubled with. The Jewish intellectual is secure in the knowledge that he has fulfilled his people's dream of scholarly excellence. The Wasp intellectual is haunted by the knowledge that he has failed his people by being hopelessly impractical. He feels like the biggest Protestant pain in the ass since Martin Luther's constipation.

Forever smarting under our happy-golf-player image, he becomes a most unpleasant intellectual, embarked on a holy crusade to out-couth everybody regardless of race, color, creed, or national origin. His model is what he *thinks* the Jewish intellectual is like. He never grasps the fact, however, that the Jewish intellectual can relax and kick up his heels in the hora at a family wedding, confident that all and sundry not only love him, but love him *more* for his scholarly bent. The Wasp can never relax his embattled and embittered stance, and if he goes to a family wedding, he knows that somebody is certain to poke fun at him; since Wasps drink rather than dance at weddings, his presence can only lead to trouble, so he usually stays away.

As he scrambles eggs in his wok, he talks about his latest "agonizing" decision and the most recent "awesome responsibility" he has taken on. He never goes to movies but to films; he never listens to the radio but to FM. The more obscure something is, the better he likes it. In music, he loathes any work that contains what other Wasps call "good parts." Nothing will do but the works of that seventeenth-century nonentity, Pierre de Bock-wurst Marginelli, played on the mighty zither. Should you confuse this composer with his son, Pierre de Bockwurst Marginelli-Vargas (the illegitimate epileptic), the intellectual Wasp will slap your wrist with his chopsticks.

Nor does he really enjoy his scholarly tastes, because the part of him that feels compelled to identify with his father is *anti*-intellectual. He sneaks detective stories and then feels guilty for having "wasted time" or "cheated." He is tortured by a gnawing conviction that he must "keep up" with every single event in the intellectual world. Being informed can turn into a house that Jack built: "This is the *Times* with the magazine and the Section Four behind the opera fold-out between the book reviews on top of the crossword puzzle that's sitting on the *Newsweek* that I've *got* to read."

He is subject to a vicious hatred for his own people that is bound to lead, as such collective hatreds do, to self-hatred. He will accuse Wasps of any and all of the world's evils; to hear his analysis of the ecology problem, you would think Wasps are the only people who ever chopped down a tree. At this point in the discussion, he likes to quote Herman Melville:

> The Anglo-Saxons, lacking grace
> To win the love of any race;
> Who in the name of Christ and Trade
> Deflower the world's last sylvan glade.

The Wasp version of machismo being that of the rough-and-ready man's man rather than that of the Don Juan, the intellectual tends to feel that his tastes contribute to a general febrility so that he is torn between hatred and envious admiration for ruthless masculinity.

The Anglo-Irish intellectual, George Bernard Shaw, manifested this conflict during the Jack the Ripper murders. For several years before the 1888 crimes, reformers had been trying without much success to get the government to do something about the squalid conditions in London's East End. Literally with one slash of the knife, the Ripper succeeded where the earnest theorists had failed. Suddenly everyone, including Queen Victoria herself, was agitating for social reform, new housing, and a war on vice.

The Ripper had called attention to East End conditions in the most manly way—with brutal violence. Shaw felt impotent; in a letter to the editor of the London *Star*, he could not conceal his contempt for his side's softness:

> Whilst we conventional social democrats were wasting our time on education and agitation and organization, some independent genius has taken the matter in hand, and by *simply* murdering and disemboweling four women, converted the propertied press to an inept sort of communism [my italics].

The Wasp intellectual male, like Sir Walter Scott, is torn between an instinct for physical action and the requirements of life in an unchivalric technological world. Said David Daiches in his introduction to *The Heart of Midlothian:* "Scott's head urged the necessity of coming to terms with progress, with commercial civilization, with the nonheroic modern world; but his heart yearned for the 'crowded hour of glorious life' which only the old way of life could provide."

Even among truly intellectual Wasps, there is a tendency to denigrate intellectualism and refer to oneself as merely "cerebral." Our writers are known for saying, like Somerset Maugham, that their sole aim is to tell a good story. One of Maugham's best stories, "The Verger," is about a man who made a fortune despite the fact that he could not read or write.

Erskine Caldwell takes a different and somewhat backhanded tack; in his memoir, *Call It Experience,* he states that he reads few books, adding, "Many years ago I divided the population into two parts; those who read and those who write. I wished to belong to the latter category."

Wasp writers' guilt is strongest among Southern male novelists who seem to feel that writing is "woman's work" because it is done indoors in the daytime. Wasp writers in general are plagued by the inherent conflict between Protestant industriousness and the writer's habits: sitting home all day tapping on a typewriter when honest hard-working people are out earning their daily bread by the sweat of their brows, an attitude that explains why I go around apologizing for my occupation. I have apologized to the census taker, American Express, Master Charge, Bank Americard, and the lady at the cleaners.

Closet intellectuals abound in Waspland. Typical of the breed was—are you ready for this?—Calvin Coolidge. Said John Spargo of him, "His greatest strength is his lack of intellectual or other distinction separating him too far from the average man." Yet a look at Coolidge's life reveals that he graduated cum laude from Amherst at a time when college curricula were far tougher than they are today. His major was classics, he read Greek, and amused himself in the evenings by translating Cicero and Dante's *Inferno*. [1]

The Southern self-taught military historian has a mind-boggling wealth of knowledge, though he tends to be an *idiot savant*. Often a good ole boy, he can hold forth like Bama Dillert in *Some Came Running* on a detailed analysis of the campaigns of Nathan Bedford Forrest that no history professor could top. He owns a fortune in rare old books and could easily make his living as a technical adviser for Civil War movies.

The Moby Dick intellectual is the Wasp man who loves the sea, as many Wasp men do. My father belonged to that category; he had read Melville seventeen times, Dana twenty times, and bought every biography of Lord Nelson in existence. (He skipped the parts about Lady Hamilton.)

But our most famous closet intellectual is the patriotic-society lady genealogist who is the world's champion researcher. She can find anything under the sun in any library, archives, or court-house in the land. Ask her how many bales of cotton were stored in England by Southern blockaders in June 1862, and she will head like a bird dog to the proper dusty tome and have the facts at her fingertips in a trice.

---

[1] Jules Abels, *In the Time of Silent Cal.*

Would you believe? Granny.

Regardless of our anti-intellectualism—probably because of it—Wasps are America's foremost alma mater freaks. As alumni offices know, the Wasp cares. Not only will he part with money, but he is always ready to hoist a tankard and sing "Hail to Thee, Old Fingerhut, We Thy Sons Are Ever True."

Like our love affair with breakfast, our love affair with school is English in origin. As Robin Maugham wrote in his novel, *The Link: A Victorian Mystery:*

" . . . Eton was a way of life, for in a sense Etonians never left Eton, they merely changed into being old Etonians. One could see it in their enthusiastic attendance at cricket matches or at Founder's Day or on the Fourth of June. One could read it in the tedious books of sentimental reminiscences which were bought so eagerly."

Learning something in college may not be for us; our forte is *going* to college. We may hate books but we love school.

That a connection could exist between this attitude and America's excess of college graduates without Caroline Bird finding out about it is in itself a phenomenon. Nevertheless, we are the folks who made college synonymous with fun, the same folks who gave you those judas goats of the sheepskin psychosis, Joe College and Betty Coed, whose antics were lovingly recorded by the Waspiest non-Wasp of all time, F. Scott Fitzgerald.

In the twenties, ethnic students made grades while Wasp students made whoopee. Thanks to us, "collegiate" entered the language and became the most overworked adjective in American English. It had nothing to do with what went on inside a classroom; it referred to Wasps who cut class to ride around in jalopies inscribed with *This Is the Mayflower, Many a Little Puritan Has Come Across in It,* singing "Who Paid the Rent for Mrs. Rip Van Winkle While Mr. Rip Van Winkle Was Asleep?"

With that Wasp knack for making themselves enviable for no really good reason, Joe and Betty snake-danced their way into the national imagination and thence into movies and ads. Soon nobody spoke of college alone; it was always "carefree college days," and *grass* became *campus.* Anybody who really wanted to practice the pursuit of happiness *had* to go to college.

When the Depression came along, life changed but Wasps did

not. We remained ever ready to set bad examples that would grow into national obsessions. The Great Wasp Collegiate Student went underground for a while, only to surface in the quiet fifties as the personification of yet another enviable American Dream that also required a college education. Now it was necessary to be *serious*, so we replaced Joe College and Betty Coed with a pair who represented uncomplicated mental health, good social adjustment, and earnest purpose. I refer to those twin banes of my college years, the Big Man on Campus and the Great Girl.

Todd Armstrong was a student council major with a minor in prom committee who spent his entire college "career" running back and forth between the union building and the gym. His favorite word was "hi" and his favorite sentence was "I gotta meeting."

Joe College never read a book or even pretended to, but Todd Armstrong, being solid and well rounded, had. His copy of *Plot Outlines of 100 Famous Novels* was threadbare. Reading whole novels did not fit into his busy schedule but he wanted to make sure he had what the careful fifties called a broad, general education, so he cheated a little at everything. He got a straight, like his teeth, two-point-five average, or C plus, and a crooked, like his grin, outlook on life.

Todd's slightly-better-than-average academic record did double duty for him. It told the talent scouts from big companies who sniffed around during Career Week that Todd was so overloaded with extracurricular activities that he was an expert at manipulating people. At the same time, it provided him with a devilish sexual reputation, for a bright young man—and he was bright —who could do no better than C plus must have spent most of his time boning up on cocksmanship.

Todd needed this assist very much, for despite his good looks and expert kissing, he was a grim, even frightening cavalier who left women unsatisfied.

Sex with a man who has his shoulder to the wheel, his ear to the ground, his finger on the pulse, and his eye on the main chance is an unsatisfactory business. In such a contortion as that, he couldn't possibly do anything but kiss. Kissing was Todd's sole form of lovemaking, and he could go on for hours with no visible means of support for his reputation as a ladies' man. He had other ways of making a girl feel like a wanton, however. Whenever she responded too warmly, he always drew away with a friendly showstopper: "Hey, whoa!" which really meant, "If I get you preggers it'll ruin my career. I can't get serious now!"

Todd prefered a girl with a C plus libido. His favorite girl was loads of fun, really a great girl, always good for a laugh, I mean she's got a terrific sense of humor, you know what I mean? But God help her if she was witty. Matching Todd knock-knock joke for knock-knock joke was one thing, but if she was prone to puns, irony, acerbic slices, or deadpan quips, he got that put-it-out-of-your-mind look on his face that Catholics get when somebody mentions reincarnation and then spread it all over campus that she was weird.

Being weird on a Waspy fifties campus was easy to manage. Basically it meant not being exactly like Todd Armstrong. Carrying too many books, especially in any kind of container ("the drip with the briefcase") was sure to do it. Being *really* weird—a specialty of mine—meant an inability to throw off the mood of a movie like *Wuthering Heights* the moment you set foot out of the theater. If this happened, Todd Armstrong waved his hand in front of your face and said, "Hey, snap out of it! Hey, you're a thousand miles away! Hey, you're deep!"

Tap Todd Armstrong and you get a firm baritone echo.

Mary Beth Butterfield's motto was "Todd! Todd! You're more myself than I am!"

Mary Beth was a great girl, I mean a really great girl. Except when she was kissing Todd, her mouth was always open. She smiled so much her teeth were always dry and cold, and she had so much school spirit that she stayed hoarse from November to February.

Mary Beth Butterfield had cornered the market on "leadership," meaning that she had so many extracurricular activities that the printer couldn't set the yearbook. Her major was sociology, which she called Soc, or, heaven help us, education—the only subjects in which she could keep up her perennial grade of B minus and still have time for all her activities.

Everything about Mary Beth was a B minus: her complexion, her father's salary, her bust—a B cup is a little roomy on her—and her brain. Uncerebral in the extreme but as smart as the proverbial whip, she belonged to one of those female honor societies with a name like Valkyries or Amazons. According to their charters the most important requirement for membership is "service to the school," but in actual fact it is a photographic memory. It is the only way the Mary Beth Butterfields of Waspland can survive. After spending an entire semester knee-deep in crepe paper and raffle tickets, Mary Beth locked herself in her room the night before finals, turned on the radio, and memorized the entire textbook. When she came to typical sociologisms like "Riots and insurrections are a sign that the people are discontented," she memorized those, too.

She also made things easier for herself by signing up for classes with professors who gave nothing but multiple-choice tests. A whiz at them, her expertise spilled over into her general conversation in unsettling ways. Say "Sartre" and Mary Beth would immediately reply, "Ummm, existentialism." This is how she got her reputation for being well-rounded.

Mary Beth's dorm was the noisiest on campus. When she was not banging gavels, she was indulging in an updated version of the nineteenth-century mission of mercy so popular with gentlewomen who gave of themselves unstintingly to everybody except their husbands. If you heard a tap-tap-tap at your door followed by a rattle of coins, you knew it was Mary Beth with a Nescafé jar, collecting for Mentally Retarded Orphaned Victims of the Tsetse Fly.

She prided herself on being friendly and specialized in what she called "bringing people out of their shells." There was no way to escape the group sings, square dance lessons, or marathon games of charades that our dynamo virgin organized the moment she found someone reading *The Education of Henry Adams*.

Mary Beth was president of that scrubbed and shining self-police state known as the Girls' Honor Council. Whenever you did something wrong, you did not have to appear before the dean of women, you had to appear before Mary Beth, which was worse.

Mary Beth was assisted by five associate council members, also great girls; a gang of Sunday school thugees who looked as if they had spent one year too many in the 4-H Club. Their job was to look at the offender with that expression of harsh pity that Christianity calls loving thine enemy while Mary Beth said in earnest tones, "I know you want to do better, and we're here to help you."

Gently, she told you that whenever a boy tries to pet, you

should distract him by suggesting that you toast marshmallows together. She recommended group dating because "there's safety in numbers," and she bragged about the many times she had turned the lights back on at frat house parties.

Despite Mary Beth's attitudes toward sex—or perhaps because of them—she is the type for whom books like *The Sensuous Woman* are written. The sexual content would threaten her but she would love the author's tone: "Golly, isn't this *fun?*" She is constitutionally incapable of enjoying sex in a bathtub but she would have a wonderful time making all that Jello and running back and forth from stove to tub with quivering pot after quivering pot. It would remind her of college—taffy pulls, apple ducking, and the hundred pounds of fudge she made in the sorority house kitchen for all those one-eyed mental defectives she sponsored every Christmas.

The twenties Wasp boola-boolaed his love for his school. Todd Armstrong transferred his to the company that hired him in his senior year. He was never really a college student at all, but a junior executive in a four-year training program. His college "career" was literally a career. His alma mater loyalty became corporation loyalty; as an exalted "member of the team" he became the model college-grad-turned-executive that all Americans were supposed to envy and emulate. Once again, Wasps had shown America the catbird seat, and once again you needed a college degree to sit down.

The problems began when our Todd Armstrongs came to believe their own propaganda. Corporation loyalty is not so bad unless the corporation you work for happens to be the executive branch of the government. Watergate was full of handsome, charming Todd Armstrongs, and their boss was the drip with the briefcase. It is possible that Richard Nixon's lifelong problems with gaucherie were exacerbated by the presence of Waspy Big Men on Campus like Dwight Chapin and Jeb Stuart Magruder, causing him to feel even more insecure and hence more desperate to be reelected at any cost.

With Mary Beth Butterfield posing as the ideal female college graduate, it is no wonder that we ended up with a feminine mystique and a women's liberation movement. The suburbs filled up with "Ummm, Sartre" scholars who could not understand why they felt so ineffectual, useless, and stupid. Clutching their something-to-fall-back-on liberal arts degrees, they simply fell back on their backs, brooding over their growing sense of inadequacy every time they had a B-minus orgasm. They tried to be wife, mother, mistress, housekeeper, chef, chauffeur, and accountant with the same cheery, I'm-never-tired volunteerism that Mary Beth Butterfield brought to *Le Cercle Français* and the Canterbury Club—and wallowed in guilt when they found they could not keep up the pace or the interest.

Happily for the rest of us, Todd Armstrong and Mary Beth Butterfield tend to marry each other. It would be nice if they choked on each other *in medias soixante-neuf* but unfortunately they never will. Despite their fondness for platitudes like, "Anything two people do together is right as long as they're in love," Mary Beth and Todd would not dream of indulging in such activities. By *activities* they mean something else altogether: something involving a lot more than two people, and which is approved of by the world. Their target is what another Wasp ungrammatically called "normalcy," and they are right on every time. They are never really a couple in the true sense of the word except when Todd takes Mary Beth to the final-approval job interview, the one where they want to take a look at the wife before they hire him. There is a large collection of big-wig executives present, which makes them both feel secure and confident—"There's safety in numbers," as Mary Beth used to tell the accused at the honor council meeting.

Thanks to Mary Beth, Todd always gets the job, for she matches perfectly the stereotype of the healthy, normal, well-rounded Wasp coed of song, story, and movie. The reason she matches it is because she *is* it. Wasps are so thoroughly stereotyped that some of us spend our lives doing imitations of ourselves. The executives take one look at Mary Beth and relax; they know that she will never embarrass the corporation, never become the Emma Bovary of Corning Glass, because she's a great girl, I mean a really great girl, you know what I mean? Terrific sense of humor, and so well rounded. Ummm, Sartre.

10

HOT/COLD WASPS
or
Sex vs. Self-Sufficiency

Resentment of sexual desire is the underground stream that flows through the Wasp personality. It is the motivating force behind much of our best-known behavior, from the quaint to the maddening and on through to the noxious.

Our distrust of sex comes through loud and clear in the literary genre that we dominate. Anglo-Saxons are the undisputed masters of the murder mystery, as well as its most enthusiastic readers. The first rule of classic mystery writing is: never clutter up your murder with sex. It must be a *nice* murder, an intellectual puzzle devoid of passion. A husband may murder his wife for her adulterous behavior, but the writer must not detail that behavior. It is permissible to describe her stiff body in the boudoir, but not her moving body. If she is found with her heels up, she must be in *rigor mortis*, not *flagrante delicto*. Break those rules and you will disappoint your reader and ruin his fun. He wants murder, not mush.

Blithe acceptance of violence and a corresponding stuffiness about sex is what upsets critics of "our Anglo-Saxon morality" most and leads to accusations of hypocrisy. It is a careless and shallow accusation; the source of our priorities goes much deeper. The Anglo-Saxon does not love murder, only what it symbolizes. Namely, oneness acting alone to end troublesome emotional entanglements. It goes without saying that the murderer does not need people. The sensualist does. Thus sex threatens self-sufficiency as a good clean kill preserves it.

The Wasp's quest for self-sufficiency knows no end. One of our favorite anti-sex training measures is the deliberate cultivation of bodily discomfort. As the tourist quickly discovers, England is the land of stoic endurance; there is always something to do without. Turning up the heat in most English houses, or to be more precise, turning it *on,* simply isn't done. Doing without heat is a symbolic way of doing without sex. The object is to prove your hardihood by winning the Order of the Cold Bath.

Subconsciously, the Wasp welcomes emergencies like the energy shortage. The evident pleasure on Richard Nixon's face when he announced that the White House thermostat would be kept at 68° is a case in point. An energy shortage provides us with a perfect excuse to practice self-discipline and do battle with soft pleasures at every turn.

Nobody can diet like a Wasp. We stick to diets and actually lose weight thanks to our innate admiration for abstemious habits. We also admire exhausting habits, like taking long, purposeless walks. Two of our most telling euphemisms are "walking it off," referring to the banishment of unwelcome emotions, and "a good stretch of the legs," which is also an apt description of sexual intercourse.

Legendary walks are an olde Englishe sport. David Copperfield walked from London to Dover, and Lassie walked four hundred miles from Scotland to Yorkshire. The first line in *Jane Eyre* is "There was no possibility of taking a walk that day." That sentence immediately tells the reader what kind of story to expect: a sexual tragedy. If only Jane could have gone tramping over the moors, she would not have been propositioned, she would not have discovered the crazy wife in the attic, and she would not have ended up married to a blind man.

Victorians stretched their legs without surcease on their endless walking tours of the Lake District, lovingly recording their every step in privately published journals called *My Gleanings.* One of the greatest Victorian walkers was Sir Charles Dilke. His biographer, Roy Jenkins, wrote, "Dilke thought a thirty-mile walk the most agreeable way of passing a quiet Sunday afternoon, and he was known on occasion to walk from Cambridge to London during the day, attend a dinner in the evening, and walk back during the night," a stretch of the legs totaling about eighty miles.

Dilke's obsessive walking makes sense when we consider his other favorite sport. A notorious satyr, he was named corespondent in a perversion-packed divorce case that rocked England in the eighties. It seems fairly clear that Dilke sought escape from guilt and lust in his record walks. To the sex-resenting Wasp, walking is like baptism: if you walk far enough for no reason whatsoever, all your sins are wiped out and you will be too tired to commit any more.

The contemporary American Wasp operates on the same principle. Somehow he always manages to bring up the subject of walking in the lectures he delivers to his fractious offspring. Johnny's latest crime may have nothing to do with walking or not walking, but his father will harp on it anyway, bragging about how far he had to walk to school when he was Johnny's age. Whether he actually did or not is beside the point; what is at stake is that brand of masculine purity that Victorian headmasters called "muscular Christianity." It boils down to a good stretch of the character: walk or rot.

The Wasp need to deny sexual desire makes us belittle *any* kind of physical distress. "Aw, hell, it's just a scratch," says John Wayne as he looks down at the hole in his stomach. Biting the bullet is a cherished ideal, and no Western is complete without the wound-cauterizing scene. A seamy-faced, tobacco-chewing, alcoholic desperado pokes his grimy fingers into the hero's wound and says, "This here bullet's got to come out. Gimme a knife!" After he digs it out, he barks in his best wagonside manner, "I got to cauterize this here wound. Gimme the brandin' iron!" When the red-hot poker touches the open wound, the hero says nothing. Afterward, he says, "That wasn't so bad."

Like sex, doctors threaten Anglo-Saxon self-sufficiency, so we respond by hating them. Instead, we doctor ourselves. For years, movie Wasps have been slicing and sucking their own snakebites, delivering their own babies in jouncing covered wagons in the midst of Indian attacks, yanking arrows out of their own shoulders, and performing do-it-youself major surgery. The dauntless trooper looks down at his exposed femur and confidently decides to set it himself, using his cavalry saber and his yellow neckerchief.

Real-life Wasps are almost as far gone into medicinal megalomania. Whiskey or salt will cure anything, and no matter what is wrong with you, "a good cleaning out" can't do any harm. The hell-for-leather purge was a favorite endurance test of Victorians; patent medicines containing strychnine, henbane, and even prussic acid were sold freely over the counter, but the prize surely goes to the British colonial army in India, whose favorite laxative was a spoonful of gunpowder in a cuppa 'ot tea.

Several classic English murders could not have occurred without our hobby of dosing ourselves. In *Regina* v. *Mrs. Florence Maybrick* (1886) the deceased, husband James, had heard about the marvelous stamina possessed by Swiss mountain climbers, who attributed their athletic prowess to arsenic. James decided that it might do the same for him, so he bought some. Operating on the Wasp theory that more is more, he increased his dose until he became an arsenic junkie.

When James died suddenly of arsenic poisoning, it seemed clear that he had accidentally poisoned himself, but then a maid told the police that Mrs. Maybrick had bought fly paper and soaked the arsenic from it to use as a facial astringent—a beauty aid favored by Victorian ladies. The prosecution reasoned that Mrs. Maybrick had wanted to poison James but had needed pure arsenic, since he had built up such a tolerance for the compounds in his medicine. She was convicted, but not for collecting arsenic. That sort of thing would never upset a Wasp jury much. What did upset them was the fact that she had a lover. Taking their cue from the judge (Mr. Justice Stephen, Virginia Woolf's cousin), who called Mrs. Maybrick "that wicked, wicked woman," they sent her up. Her execution was stayed on the grounds that the judge's unabashed prejudice constituted a mistrial. She never got a new trial, and she languished in prison until 1904, when the new monarch, Edward VII, intervened personally on her behalf. Edward later admitted to friends and to the Home Secretary that his mother, Queen Victoria, hated Mrs. Maybrick so much that she would not permit her name to be mentioned. The Queen was bothered by the same thing that bothered judge and jury: not murder, but adultery.

Two years later, in *Regina* v. *Mrs. Adelaide Bartlett*, the deceased, husband Edwin, found a loose pill in a bureau drawer. He had no idea what it contained or where it had come from, nor did he bother to inquire. Thinking it might help his toothache, he took it, as he later admitted to the doctor.

His pharmaceutical arrogance was surpassed by his wife's, for shortly thereafter, Mrs. Bartlett did something that cast grave suspicion upon her. Edwin had been suffering from insomnia, and so she decided to cure him herself. She bought a pint of chloroform—also available over the counter in any drugstore.

The police coroner later testified that when he opened Edwin Bartlett's stomach during the postmortem, the smell of chloroform was so strong that it nearly knocked him out.

Mrs. Bartlett was acquitted by twelve Wasp good men and true, who had no difficulty buying the defense's contention that Edwin, in a rerun of the pill incident, must have seen the chloroform bottle and, without bothering to ask what it was, had taken a swig for good measure.

Resentment of sexual desires makes many Wasp men notorious seekers after lust substitutes. Crises, for example. Richard Nixon's analysis of the stages of a crisis[1] sounds remarkably like the description of foreplay, consummation, and afterglow found in the average sex manual.

First, there is confidence, which "depends in great part on adequacy of preparation . . . "

Coolness, or what Nixon calls serenity, corresponds to an absence of what Masters and Johnson call performance anxiety.

Courage, or more precisely, lack of fear, and an ability to concentrate on "winning the battle."

Experience helps a man understand and accept those crisis signals: " . . . his muscles tense up, his breathing comes faster, his nerves tingle, his stomach churns . . . "

When a man approaches the end of the battle, he tells himself, " 'Just as soon as this is over I'll feel great.' But except for a brief period of exhilaration if the fight ended in victory, he will then begin to feel the full effects of what he has been through. He may even be *physically sore and mentally depressed*. . . . He is just too *spent* emotionally, physically and mentally to enjoy the fruits of victory he so eagerly anticipated."

Aftermath is the most dangerous part of a crisis. "It is then, with *all his resources spent and his guard down*, that an individual must watch out for dulled reactions and faulty judgment," says Nixon. (To the sexually oriented man, this is the moment when women spring something, or start digging for an "I love you" or a proposal of marriage.)

[1] Richard M. Nixon, *Six Crises*.

Winding up his comments, Nixon waxes ecstatic and uses some very yeasty language. "A man who has never lost himself in a cause bigger than himself has missed one of life's *mountaintop experiences*. Only in losing himself does he find himself. . . . Crisis can indeed be agony. But it is the *exquisite agony* which a man might not want to experience again—yet would not for the world have missed" [my italics].

Bona fide crises of such Olympian proportions being hard to come by for the average man, some Wasps eschew sex for work. The Wasp workaholic is the bulwark of novels and movies about crumbling suburban marriages: "The children were always asleep by the time you got home." Children in workaholic dramas are always asleep, but Mrs. Workaholic is an insomniac owing to a ceaseless pelvic itch that is never satisfied. Bold as brass because of her sexual frustrations, she is a female rapist who is perpetually saying things that would make Mirabel Morgan's "I crave your body" sound like a maidenly simper. But no matter what she says, she always gets the same reply: "Not tonight, honey, I'm bushed."

The busy drone having been a Protestant ideal since John Winthrop declared profit to be a sign of God's grace, the Wasp workaholic can enjoy sex only when it is somehow connected with his job. The best connection is, of course, that eternal loser, the "office wife." Another ploy of the workaholic is juggling his expense account so that he can take along a female traveling companion on a business trip. He will labor like Hercules over bills, receipts, and genteel forgeries, exhausting himself with *that* work before he ever gets near a bed. It would be much easier to pay the lady's expenses himself, or hire a better lay from the local madam after he arrives, but such commonsense alternatives threaten him. He doesn't *want* sin made easy, he wants sin in triplicate. Sex bears more resemblance to work when records of it can be Xeroxed and filed.

The workaholic labors just as hard over a hometown affair. For him the fun lies not in the sex but in the efforts such covert activity requires: getting a room, borrowing an apartment, figuring out a set of signals, bribing doormen, and synchronizing watches with his lady love like Wasp pilots in flying-ace movies, so that they will be sure to leave the office at different times.

Women's magazines are unflagging in their naive belief that the workaholic can be made sexier and more romantic if his wife will only help him "unwind" when he drags himself home. Hence that perennial piece of advice, "Meet him at the door in a black lace nightgown, with a pitcher of martinis." Despite the fact that "unwind" is the workaholic's favorite word, it is the very last thing he wants to do because to him, the only good sex is worksex. Easily potent on his lunch hour, he wilts the moment he sets foot in his suburban door. He is never really happy except when he is at work, for his office represents the detachment that he craves. It is an asylum for emotion, a Protestant monastery in which the coffee-wagon bell and the telephone measure his liturgical day.

He loves his office because it is so Waspy. The Wasp office, says Michael Korda, is noted for its "rigidity, fixed hierarchies and a lack of flexibility. . . . Non-Wasp organizations tend to be run like families." In the Wasp office, says Korda, it is easier to get along by following rules and regulations and forming committees. But in the non-Wasp office, "it is more effective to behave like a member of the family—drama, tears, rage, and an appeal to justice are likely to be more effective, whereas forming a committee would seem like a hostile and treacherous act."

The workaholic dislikes his home precisely because it can so easily turn into a non-Wasp office; an arena for drama, tears, and rage. Home is where upsetting emotions erupt, but his office is run along hierarchical lines designed to prevent such emotional eruptions. Associating his office with emotional safety makes it the only place where he can permit sexual desire to flourish. Work-related sex becomes part of the fixed hierarchies (socially inferior but sexually available secretaries) that shield him from emotion. He can subject his worksex to the inflexible rules and regulations he lives by (lunch hour is from one to three), thereby fitting it into his schedule.

Every cloud has a silver lining, however. In her novel *The Goddess Hangup*, Joyce Elbert observes, " . . . I have gone to bed with any number of both Jewish and Protestant men and invariably the same sexual rule seems to apply. Jewish men have an absolutely frenzied need to be gone down on, and Protestant men have the same need to go down on you. Don't ask me why."

I don't know about Jewish men but I can answer the other half of Miss Elbert's query. No undertaker will ever have to put a smile on the face of the woman who traffics with Wasp workaholics. Cunnilingus being the quickest and most effective way to produce female orgasm, the Protestant man uses it as a fail-safe means to get it over with, shut the lady up, and go to sleep so that he can get up and go to work in the morning.

In *The Collector,* John Fowles speaks of "that stupid, clumsy, frightened-of-being-soft English male cruelty." The problem was exported to America, but being a folksier country, we have produced a rather endearing version of the breed: the laconic lover of yep-and-nope fame.

Usually a New Englander or a Westerner and only rarely a Southerner (they're much too garrulous), Oliver Stone wears starched white shirts, vests, and a pocket watch. The back of his neck is West Point smooth from the barber's clippers, and he just might shave with a straight edge at home. If he does, he never cuts himself.

Lavish compliments are not Oliver's way. When his secretary hands him his letters he gives her a deadpan stare and says, "You don't *look* like a mailman." If he is in an anachronistic mood, which he often is because he is congenitally old-fashioned, he might say, "If I may make so bold, you don't look half bad today." If the recipient of these extravaganzas is a Wasp herself she will understand and correctly deduce that he is teetering on the very abyss of venery. If she is a non-Wasp, she may go mad.

Oliver's girlfriend has many crosses to bear. At parties, women are always taking her into the kitchen for heart-to-heart talks that begin, "Do you really think you should go on seeing him?" While the kitchen summit is in progress, Oliver is in the living room taking the wind out of yet another woman's sails. A self-proclaimed swinger on her seventh whiskey sour musses his neat hair and brags about her multi-orgasmic capacities. "I have one right after another! Five, ten, twenty! I can't control myself, I just scream and come and scream and come!"

"Any epilepsy in your family?" Oliver asks, then takes out his little black comb and carefully rearranges his hair.

Oliver never calls women honey or darling, preferring endearments like Little Iodine or Sweet Pea, unless he invents a nickname based on her last name. Early in the courtship stage Miss MacAllister becomes Mac, Miss Buchanan becomes Bucky, and Miss West becomes Westy.

He is likely to be opposed to Women's Liberation, in the upper-case sense, but he is surprisingly supportive of a *particular* woman's ambitions. Protestantism having been founded on individualism, he will sanction in one woman what he opposes in a group—which he unfailingly calls "a gaggle of females." When *his* woman sets out to do something, he will boost her morale and jolly her along when the going gets tough. He may make her feel a little like a platoon ("Crest the ridge . . . fire when ready . . . give 'em both barrels . . .") but it *is* encouragement and he *does* mean it.

If Oliver sticks around for any length of time, his girlfriend can assume that though he never says it he likes her and she is secure. He cannot be bothered bolstering shaky egos; the woman who craves constant reassurances, the woman who needs to be called once a day merely to remain alive, will have a nervous breakdown if she ties up with Oliver Stone. The fact that she has been in analysis for ten years will not only fail to rouse his compassion, it will rouse his utter contempt. Insecurity and Wasp emotional reserve are hopelessly incompatible; Oliver will not gab on the telephone, and the woman who waits for him to call simply to say he loves her will wait forever. He considers the telephone an instrument of communication and nothing more; his standard greeting is a toneless "It's me." Once he has transacted his business, no matter how much in love he is, he will say, "All right. Behave yourself. 'Bye."

He is inclined to criticize all *outré* fashions with a withering, "What's *that?*" Old-fashioned to the end, he wants every woman to look like the girl on the nineteenth-century candy box, trailing ribbons from her leghorn hat. Flinty soul that he is, he loved *The Great Gatsby* for the hats Mia Farrow wore, yet his gifts to women run to things like a new garbage can or a handbag that looks like WAC surplus. He will sit up till three in the morning to catch an Alice Faye movie, and the songs he whistles while shaving —unfailing clues to a man's personality—run to numbers like "My Gal Sal."

A woman need not starve herself to attract Oliver, for among his many anachronistic tastes is *fin de siècle* proportions. Other men comment on a woman's *figure*, but Oliver calls it a *shape*. He likes a woman with "a good rump on her," and his pet name for breasts is that James M. Cain favorite, "the dairy." A dieting woman irritates him, not only because he thinks she looks "just fine" the way she is, but because his innate sense of fair play decrees that he cannot eat anything tempting in front of her. The upshot of this bizarre exercise in thoughtfulness: he will eat exactly what she eats, and then spend the rest of the evening grumbling.

Secure himself, he is not jealous. Any woman who has ever been involved with the sort of man who counts dents in vaginal jelly tubes is bound to appreciate Oliver Stone. His obsessive regard for privacy prevents him from showing any affection to a woman in public, leading many of her friends to think him dangerously repressed, but it also safeguards her against off-limits snooping on his part. If he asks her for change for the parking meter and she indicates her handbag lying on the desk, he will bring it to her instead of rummaging in it himself as so many men feel free to do once they have slept with a woman.

It is extremely easy to get on Oliver's nerves because he insists upon calm and order. The woman who does not know the difference between sound and noise is his nemesis. Usually a woman who cannot bear to be alone—Oliver loves to be alone—she plays the phonograph, the radio, and the TV all at once, and talks over all of them. If that ever happens, the usually clamlike Oliver will roar at the top of his lungs and stamp out, never to return.

He is scrupulously neat. A little dirt doesn't bother him, but he likes to fold things. Intoning "Outward disorder is a sign of inner chaos," he will roll up his girlfriend's underpants GI style; he will even fold bras.

In the realm of sex, he is good at anything below the neck but he is not much of a kisser—it seems to strike him as foppish. He more than compensates for his frigid public persona when he gets you alone. He is not only willing but eager, albeit in a grim way, and his staying power is extraordinary. He copulates with silent ferocity; afterwards, he pats you on the thigh, says, "Pass the cigarettes," and places the ashtray on your stomach.

Oliver is potent because he does not exhaust himself during the clothes-on courtship stage as the Latin lover does. To him, wooing is tactile, not verbal, and it belongs in a bed. He does not attempt poetry except for ribald limericks, which Wasp women enjoy more anyway, and he does not puncture his fingers doing the tiresome single-rose number. He will, however, do a parody of it. Using practical jokes as a sign of affection is a trick of his; if he reads something mushy in a women's magazine about the single rose, Oliver will take the trouble to go out in the woods, chop down a small tree, drag it into the house, and lay it at his lady's feet. Then, with a straight face, he will pretend that it is not there: "What tree?"

His honorable proposals tend to kick off with "Well . . ." or with that most portentous of all Wasp openers, "Oh, by the way . . ." To give himself a graceful exit and cover his hurt in case the lady says no, he will pretend that his proposal is a joke, refusing to be serious until he has forced her to say, "Do you mean you want to marry me?" To make absolutely sure that such tender moments are infused with enough comedy to quash those ever threatening emotions, he likes to propose on merry-go-rounds, during half-time at football games, or during a Tom and Jerry cartoon.

Oliver's real idea of a date is tramping all over the Gettysburg battlefield on either the hottest or the coldest day of the year, armed with maps, books, and binoculars. Like Winston Churchill, he may collect toy soldiers, so his lady friend must learn to effuse over a new Hessian and refrain from asking why the Life Guard is not wearing bathing trunks.

He also loves English-style pubs that feature those songs of passionless passion so beloved by Anglo-Saxons. We may fight the Irish on religious and political grounds, but we maintain a musical truce. Songs about fonts of virtue named Mary or Molly who die old maids because they waited too long for passage money from America that never came—that's Oliver Stone's idea of a love song. It must be sung at the top of the lungs, preferably off-key, and accompanied by lots of beer.

He will not set foot in Mexican restaurants because he lives in dread of limpid-eyed strolling musicians who pause at a couple's table to sing throbbing songs of the *poinciana-mañana-adios* school. Oliver Stone will pay them to *leave*. What's more, they know it—which is why they always pick the Oliver Stones.

The healthy Wasp makes a terrific one-night stand. We have the detachment necessary for a successful brief encounter, and we do not fall in love with passing ships. We know how to deliver a really superb hump with the greatest possible physical pleasure and the least possible social complications—a four-legged frolic, as the Cockneys call it. The coolness that gives us such a master touch with murder mysteries also enables us to go bump in the night in more pleasant ways.

The unhealthy Wasp is a prime candidate for that Anglo-Saxon specialty, *la nostalgie de la boue*, or slumming. Prowling the stews of London was a favorite activity of many eminent Victorians who could not accept their sexuality; Prime Minister Gladstone went looking for prostitutes and called it "social work," claiming that he wanted to reform them. The more the unhealthy Wasp believes that sex is a weakness, the more powerfully he will be drawn to tawdry partners whose opinion does not matter and whom he will never have to meet socially.

The most noxious recent example of sex-resentment gone wrong was John Reginald Christie, the Rillington Place strangler, who found sex so demeaning that he could enjoy it only with dead women.

Pride in hardihood, self-discipline, and the ability to endure physical distress marked Christie's earliest years. His father took the entire family for five-mile walks every Sunday afternoon. Said Christie, "We had to hold our shoulders back, swing our arms, and walk like Guardsmen."

Between 1940 and 1953, Christie murdered at least seven women. All the murders followed the same pattern. A firm believer in the niceties of life, the polite Christie first gave the women a cup of tea; then he killed them, copulated with them, clipped a sample of their pubic hair for his collection, and then buried them in or around his house. Most of them were prostitutes whom he sought out on his prowls through the slums of Notting Hill, but although he readily confessed to having murdered them, he refused to admit that he had ever been troubled much by sexual desire. When the Crown psychiatrist brought up the subject of masturbation, Christie stiffened with righteous wrath and said he thought it was a terrible practice and that he had never indulged in it. When the psychiatrist said he thought masturbation was harmless, Christie flew into a rage. Specific about how he had murdered the prostitutes, Christie persisted in lying about how he had made their acquaintance in the first place. He would not admit he had picked them up in pubs—he thought drinking and pub-going were shocking, too. He insisted that "it was the women who had made a nuisance of themselves, who had inflicted their unwanted attentions on the virtuous Christie, and it was he who had to put up with their drunkenness and rowing and otherwise unladylike behavior."[2] He insisted that they had im-

---

[2] Ludovic Kennedy, *Ten Rillington Place.*

portuned him, not the other way around and that he had replied, "I'm not like that. . . . It doesn't interest me. . . . I will not do that." Finally, according to Christie, he had had to murder them to protect his own chastity.

Christie lured his last victim to his house with her lover in tow. The couple had just been evicted from their flat and needed a place to sleep. Although Christie fully intended to murder the woman, he refused to let the couple occupy the same room because they were not married. The next day, after having forced the lovers to sleep apart in the interests of propriety, he waited until the man had left for work; then he strangled the woman, had intercourse with her corpse, and stuffed it into a kitchen cupboard with the two other prostitutes he had killed earlier.

There seems to be a streak of celibacy in the Wasp that may be related to our break with Roman Catholicism.

The Catholic has an outlet for this strange Christian yearning to deny sexuality. He can become a member of the celibate clergy himself, or he can experience vicariously the celibacy of the priests and nuns who have played a major role in his life since earliest childhood. He can "go away satisfied," as it were, by the unsatisfied sexuality of the celibates he has known.

Anglo-Saxon yearning for celibacy is often cleverly concealed. For all its throbbing passion, *Wuthering Heights* reeks of it. The morbid quest for the lover-self—"I *am* Heathcliff"—is the ultimate denial of duality despite its surface resemblance to what is today called "communicating." Not love but revulsion against love is the theme of the novel. Just as Cathy takes refuge from Heathcliff with the diffident Edgar Linton, the author takes refuge from *all* the characters, and from her readers as well, by placing herself at the furthest possible remove from the actual telling of the story. Like a cloistered abbess, Emily Brontë refuses to have anything to do with the fleshpots she has created. She tells the story neither as a first-person author nor as an omniscient one. Nor do her passionate characters tell it. It is told first by the epicene Lockwood and then by that favorite English type, the warm-hearted but sexless housekeeper. The author "keeps herself to herself," to use an old Wasp saying. Transcending mere solitude, the main characters and the author are in a perpetual search for oneness. The need to turn back in upon oneself is so great that Brontë created needless confusion by giving the second generation of characters the same names as the first.

The drinking, gambling, wenching rakes of Restoration and Regency times were closet celibates who used dissipation to avoid marital and family ties. Psychologically sterile to begin with, pox and circumstances finished them off. They ended their bachelor lives as raving lunatics, literally rotten before they ever reached their graves, leaving behind a legacy of romance that refuses to die. Our penchant for nicknames has a field day when we describe our boyish bucks. Lord William Throckmorton who died at twenty-two after chugalugging three gallons of ale while six naked women sat on him becomes "Bonnie Billy." No matter what prodigal waste of manhood Fucking Fitz committed, we excuse it with a shrug, a nostalgic smile, and that fond absolution, "He was just sowing his wild oats." The Anglo-Saxon attitude toward these clappy, lace-bedecked satyrs is nothing short of worshipful—the same sort of pride that Catholicism takes in its most psychotic hermits. Either way, it is pride in celibacy.

The contemporary Wasp mother does a pro-celibate number. If a Wasp girl wants to kill Mama, the best way to do it is to marry too soon. With a cry of "You're not dry behind the ears yet!" Mama turns into a keening matriarch. For once, she will give advice. And such advice. When it comes to denigrating the institution of matrimony, she is a match for St. Paul, except that her insults are unconscious.

"Do something interesting first," she advises. She means a career—not a job—in a nice office, but she will not say no to the Peace Corps, VISTA, or a reenactment of the battle of Poitiers. If she is really desperate she will even recommend professional studenthood. Get a master's, a doctorate, get two! Go to Oxford, Cambridge, the Sorbonne, or all three! Suddenly, she is an atypical Wasp: She likes eggheads.

If that does not work, she will say, "You're only young once . . . you have your whole life in front of you . . . sleep with him first and see what happens." In her distress, she might even turn literary, like my mother. She was not a reader and had very few quotations to hand, but what few she had she used freely, editing them at will. Hearing that I was planning to marry at twenty-one, she burst out, "These are your salad days—eat!"

She will also launch the "almost thirty" argument. Regardless of how old Mother was when she married, she will rewrite history shamelessly: "I was almost thirty when I married your father!" By the time the argument ends, she has convinced herself that she nearly withered on the vine.

For men, the rule is thirty or more. The subject of the thirtyish bridegroom crops up in novels about Anglo-Saxons from George Meredith to John O'Hara.

In Meredith's *The Ordeal of Richard Feverel,* the baronet rules, "He shall not marry until he is thirty!" to which the vicar replies, "He need not marry at all. Birth and death are natural accidents: Marriage we can avoid."

And in O'Hara's *Ten North Frederick,* Joe Chapin's mother "seldom lost an opportunity to point out that she had married his father when Ben Chapin was thirty-four. . . . A man of forty was still a young man. . . . She convinced her son that to marry before thirty was to take on burdensome responsibilities that could easily thwart a young lawyer's career, and unnecessarily at that, since a man had all his life in which to raise a family. . . . There was, she said, all the time in the world before getting serious."

11

COPING WITH THE WASPS IN YOUR LIFE
or
Any Ethnic Can!

Waspland's first rule is *Difficulties should be borne, not made.*

I have a friend who worked in Caracas. One day as he was passing a movie theater he saw a screaming crowd smashing the cashier's booth, ripping up posters, and throwing rocks at the marquee. As he stared with Wasp horror, the crowds captured the cashier, the manager, and a couple of ushers and began spitting on them.

A bystander told him what had happened: "The sound track, she broke. And the audience, they got mad."

Wasp embarrassment is totally incomprehensible to outsiders. You will simply have to take my word for it that one of the worst contretemps that can overtake a Wasp is being with someone who stamps, claps, or whistles when the sound track breaks. You are supposed to sit, frozen in polite endurance, and wait in patient silence for the projectionist to fix it.

We are painfully aware of other people's embarrassment. They may not even know they are supposed to be embarrassed until we start covering up for them. A good example is the way Mrs. Astor handled the soup-spilling incident. One of her guests accidentally tipped over his soup cup, so to make him feel better, Mrs. Astor deliberately overturned the entire tureen. Everyone agreed that it was very thoughtful of her. She made it possible for the whole table to ignore the question of spilled soup altogether.

Wasps are so obsessed with tact that we go through life with a seemingly gelid disregard for other people's *serious* distresses, although our intentions are of the best. Taylor Caldwell, who is

148

Waspy if not precisely Wasp in the religious sphere, exhibited this contradiction in her autobiography, *Growing Up Tough.* She fell down in the aisle of a plane and was mortified because everyone rushed to her aid. She felt it would have been kinder to ignore her and thus leave her with her dignity intact. By helping her up and fussing over her, they acknowledged that they had seen her fall. That was most assuredly tactless of them. It is comforting to be around a Wasp if you commit a minor *faux pas,* but if you tumble headfirst into a full oil drum, you may expect to drown with dignity intact. A Wasp will never let on that he saw your bare legs waving in the air.

And then there is pride. One reliable kind is moving-day pride, which turns the lackadaisical Wasp housewife into a Dutch fanatic. All the nobody-sees-it-anyway areas that she has avoided for three years are ripped up and dismantled for an all-out attack. Prying up the stove burners, she spends hours shoveling out the sea of congealed grease. The windows that never felt the touch of a human hand except when the children drew steam pictures are now saturated with ammonia. Why this sudden spurt of enthusiasm? "So the landlord will know that nice people lived here."

Asking for money, even when it is owed to you, destroys Wasp pride. We avoid it as long as possible, even when we are in actual want. Finally, when we can put it off no longer, we write offhand letters containing typically inscrutable ultimatums.

A few years ago when I wrote for a paperback company, writers' checks were delayed constantly. Three authors wrote to the publisher:

From Sid Silverman
$$$$$$$$$$$$$$$$$$????????????!!!!!!!!!!!

From Vince Vitucci
Look, I've got to have my check right away. I've got kids to feed.

From Florence King
Isn't it terrible how careless the post office is getting these days? So much mail is delayed or even lost that I have been concerned whether I have missed any recent letters from you. I do feel quite sure, however, that once again the

blame should be cast on the government and not on you,
for I know how prompt you are about answering your mail
and keeping abreast of even the most minor details. I shall
look forward to hearing from you in the very near future.

Guess who was the last to get paid?

Talking about money in the abstract sense is a favorite Wasp
pastime. How-to subjects—how to make it, invest it, endow it
—are perfectly acceptable. So too is talking about someone else's
money: "He is worth" a million dollars is a Wasp locution of long
standing, and its dehumanizing flavor does not offend us in the
least. But whatever you do, do not ask a Wasp how much he paid
for something. If you do, you will bring forth stammers, blushes,
incredulity, and pained hauteur. Direct, concrete discussions
about money wipe us out. If a person is a relative or a very old
friend, it is permissible to ask the price of a possession providing
you preface your question with an apologetic and highly rococo
preamble: "I know this is terrible, but would you mind very much
if I asked you . . ."

The proper Wasp reply? "Uh . . . I don't remember. I *think* it
was five hundred."

All of those quaint dodges serve the important purpose of
concealing the Wasp's real attitudes about money: namely, that it
is the most important thing in life, and furthermore, it buys
happiness.

Things that do not really matter, matter terribly to us;
picayune obsessions haunt us. A case in point is the right of a
member of the peerage to a silken rope for his hanging. If he does
not get it, the insult will wound him mortally. Furthermore, he
will protest. Huffing, "See here, I won't stand for this," at your
own execution is something that only a Wasp could pull off. It's
our kind of *hubris*.

Our lopsided priorities account for the large number of Wasps
in Bartlett's *Quotations*. Going out with a bang instead of a
whimper is dear to our hearts. We are positively queer for the
ballsy, last-minute remark; every one of us dreams of becoming
another Nathan Hale or Barbara Frietchie. Our concern for
panache can warp our attitudes toward larger aspects of morality,
so that, like Katherine Anne Porter's young heroines, we forget

what John Wilkes Booth *did* because we are so charmed by the way he did it: leaping to the stage like Douglas Fairbanks and shouting, *"Sic semper tyrannis!"*

"The little girls never doubted that it had happened in just that way, and the moral seemed to be that one should always have Latin, or at least a good classical poetry quotation, to depend upon in great or desperate moments."

When an older relative reminds the child narrator that nothing excuses murder, the ethical point escapes her entirely. She decided that "without the murder, there would have been no point in dressing up and leaping to the stage and shouting in Latin. So how could she disapprove of the deed?"[1]

The Wasp who keeps one eye on Bartlett's makes a poor verbal disputant. He does not keep his mind on the argument because he is trying to put together a ringing phrase that will echo down the centuries, or at least be repeated at cocktail parties for the next few weeks. Fond of the Churchillian roll that lends itself so well to words like "blight" and "perfidy," he ends up like Churchill at Potsdam, freaked out on his own oratory to the total exclusion of important matters at hand. As a result, one of the Wasp's biggest problems is repressed rage. By putting the cart before the horse in arguments, he gets so tangled up in his own syntax that he seldom expresses himself to his own satisfaction, and so exits from the fray with a knot of unarticulated anger in his stomach. Like Julian Gloag's very British protagonist in *A Sentence of Life*, "The source of revivifying anger was buried so deep within him that he could not draw upon it. Instead he would have to splash valiantly in the thin saucer of exasperation."

The more exasperated the Wasp becomes, the more pompous he sounds. Lapsing into phrases like, "Never have I witnessed a more disgraceful, if not malevolent—yes, malevolent—attack," he is soon hopelessly mired in an iambic pentameter snit, brought on by his malevolent attempt to make his argument scan before it even begins to make sense.

Talking and arguing are not our idea of a fight. Stereotyped as congenitally low-keyed, we only seem to be, thanks to our congenital hypocrisy. We are an essentially physical people, primitive beneath our surface cool. It is true that we gave the world par-

[1]Katherine Anne Porter, *Old Mortality*.

liamentary government, but we go back much further than that. Descended from one race of people who painted themselves blue and another who invented the battle axe, we know full well the murderous quality of our rage and it frightens us, and frightened people tend to become tongue-tied.

We are like Dickens' prim little spinster, Miss Pross, who had "a courage that Madame Defarge so little comprehended as to mistake for weakness." A few moments later, Madame Defarge learned a great deal about Wasps. Miss Pross, shouting her famous line, "You shan't get the better of me, I'm an Englishwoman!" hauled off and shot her.

Miss Pross got her Wasp rage out of her system. When most of us get mad, we have to resort to writing letters. Letters are our safety valve; whenever passion threatens, whether it be love or hate, we take to our desks.

An excellent example of Wasp fury is the Not Sent file. When thoroughly aroused, the Wasp writes such vicious, knock-down-drag-out letters that he gets everything out of his system before he ever reaches the mailbox. Having written himself out, he seals and stamps the letter, then falls exhausted into bed, drained. He sleeps deeply and peacefully in such a state of catharsis that he wakes up the next morning with second thoughts.

He burns with remorse, the kind associated with hangovers. His picky conscience torments him. To have felt such base emotions, and to have expressed them! Shame. Guilt. And, of course, he also fears for his own image, for the letter makes him seem un-Wasp and excitable. Horrors.

So he opens the envelope, steams off the stamps, puts the letter in his Not Sent file, and writes another—a calm, rational, fair-minded letter full of honest evaluations and lots of good sense.

My literary agent has a vast collection of lovely, soothing letters from me—and I have a desk full of curly, glueless stamps. He is constantly receiving my *second* letter. Written in the calm, smug light of a new Wasp day, it goes like this:

"I don't mind in the least doing those revisions. It's only fair that I redo the chapters because the entire misunderstanding was my fault. I must give the devil her due: she's a good editor even if we do have a slight personality conflict. She's not really so bad, and as I have said, the blame rightfully belongs on me."

Meanwhile, the time bomb continues ticking away because

nothing has really been settled regarding the problem that made the Wasp so mad in the first place. Soon the cathartic effect of the Not Sent letter starts to wear off, and the Wasp begins to brood anew. He works himself up to a full-blown guilt complex, castigating himself for being weak and compliant, for having backed down, for *not* having sent the first letter!

He goes into a rolling boil, stalking up and down the floor declaiming at the top of his lungs to his "enemies"—who he pretends are present—and takes swings at his palm with his fist (he pretends it is his enemy's jaw). There is nothing to do but write another convulsive letter to his literary agent:

"I lied when I said nothing was wrong. Everything is wrong! It wasn't my fault, it was hers! I hate her, I'd like to kill her! I want to get my hands on her! I hate her husband, I hate her child! I'm going to wipe the floor with her and knock her into the middle of next week!"

By the time this missive is finished and sealed up, the Wasp is once more drained of all anger, so he "sleeps on it"—a fine Wasp practice. The next day, more remorse, more curly stamps, another calm rewrite, and another addition to the Not Sent file.

This choleric rondo goes on for weeks until, one fine day, some little thing happens to tick the Wasp off. Usually, it is some minor household mishap like a stubbed toe, but it's enough . . .

Two days later, an astounded literary agent receives the *entire* Not Sent file, which stands a good three inches high and weighs somewhere in the vicinity of five pounds.

You may receive some dreadful letters from the Wasps in your life, but you will also receive some that you will save forever. Letters also bring out the tenderest side of our personality. Surely among the warmest words ever put to paper are those written by Calvin Coolidge shortly after his son's death, to a friend who had also lost his son: "To my friend, in recollection of his son, and my son, who by the grace of God have the privilege of being boys throughout eternity."

In *Lady L*, Romain Gary speaks of "that special English sophistication of the happy few, with its amoral and, in a way, terroristic sense of humor."

Anyone who associates with Wasps soon realizes that there is no rest for the witty. The English reputation for being funny must be preserved. Our gift for poking fun at ourselves makes for the congeniality often found between Wasps and Jews, for Jewish humor is also based on self-mockery. The similarity ends there, however, for Jewish humor is melancholy and ours is rollicking.

Our favorite comic situation is the hopelessly muddled confusion of the *Doctor in the House* variety. Anglo-Saxons have a careless streak born of our amused contempt for people who do things right, like French chefs. Foremost among the several dozen French traits that get on English nerves is their cold, humorless quest for perfection. That a French nobleman could shoot his maid for siphoning wine through a metal funnel and be acquitted on the grounds of justifiable homicide[1] leaves the Anglo-Saxon incredulous. The English hold that you can have much more fun doing things *wrong*, an outlook best summed up by a famous English joke: A customer asks the waiter for more gravy, and the waiter replies: "One lump or two?" It is said that this actually happened, and I for one believe it, because a genealogically strung-out friend of mine had a similar exchange in a Lancashire county records office.

Engaged in tracing her genealogy, like many of the older ladies of DAR proclivities, she informed the clerk that she was looking for her ancestors.

"I haven't seen them, madam. Have you tried left luggage?"

We are delightfully easygoing; you can count on it. Margaret Halsey roasted the English for their half-done jobs, half-cleaned homes, and half-broken equipment, but she was forced to admit that their good-natured attitude toward their own shortcomings made it all not only bearable, but fun. For the English don't just tolerate their faults, they cultivate them. Never have so many Wasps derived so much pleasure from screwing up. Any other people would have kept quiet about the Charge of the Light Brigade; the English immortalized it. We are not masochists, just very secure. We can afford to brag about our idiocies because history has been good to us, and we have been good to history.

The spirit of Crimea lives. The standard Wasp reaction to error is still "Oops!" followed by one of those cheery twinkling smiles that the traveler in England sees at every turn (the poker-faced stereotype is quite erroneous). According to a British author

---

[1] Sanche de Gramont, *The French*.

whose name, book title, and page references I have mislaid, the National Railways lost a train some years ago. It was supposed to be sitting in Victoria Station waiting for passengers but it was not there. Thanks to the miracle of the "wireless," which happened to be working at the moment, the authorities ascertained that the train was nowhere in the country. It had simply vanished—a conclusion that was greeted with peals of we're-all-right-Jack laughter. No one knew what to do, so they called in Scotland Yard. The inspectors arrived twinkling like Peter Pan, ready to enjoy the joke with everyone else. Such a good time was had by all that when the train was finally found, the issue of how it had gotten lost became secondary.

Knowing our capacity for rage, yet wholeheartedly committed to civilized behavior, Wasps realize that we need all the humor we can get. As Somerset Maugham explained our nature, "You are not angry with people when you laugh at them. Humour teaches tolerance, and the humorist, with a smile and perhaps a sigh, is more likely to shrug his shoulders than to condemn."

The moral issues involved in living together are not the Wasp's first concern. We may never get around to worrying about the moral issues, but we will worry a lot about the minor details of decorum. What will the mailman think? The grocer's delivery boy? The telephone man? For that matter, what will the burglar think? The opinions of all the people whose opinions should not matter, do matter. The Southern Wasp gets even more deeply mired in trivia. Should she use one of her engraved calling cards on the door? And if she does, would it *look right* to put her lover's name in ink underneath? Should he have calling cards of his own printed—the minimum order is five hundred—just so that he can have *one* to put on the door to match hers? What about Christmas cards? Would it *look right* to have both their names on them? Mother has accepted the news that her daughter is living in sin, but a *faux pas* involving cards would send her to her bed of pain.

The small, necessary lie trips up the Wasp. Years ago when my manuscripts sold sporadically, I ran out of money, encountered a writing block, and found that I had to go back to work. I had not worked for two years, so I needed a lie to account for the gap. I told my prospective employer that I had been married and just recently divorced—and promptly blushed maroon. What caused my sudden panic was not religious scruples or any sense of sin or failure, but the minor questions that popped into my head. How would I sign my name? Since I was lying, was it more proper to be Miss or Mrs.? What is the proper title for a divorcee who has never been married at all?

Age has done nothing for my Wasp trivia. A few weeks ago I received a new credit card and found that the store had used my middle initial, which I never use in my signature. Now I must sign Florence *V.* King the way it is on the card, thus implying that I have been divorced and that my maiden name begins with *V.* It actually bothers me because "people will think I'm divorced." This sort of fretting is 100-proof Southern Wasp, bottled in bond. Women's lib and Ms. can never quite vitiate it.

Does brand-name loyalty offend you? Better watch out, because your Wasp friends are likely to exhibit a hefty amount of it. Conditioned reflexes are not ethnically limited in this day of incessant television commercials, but Wasps harbor special fidelities that are tied up with "roots."

Feeling no need to prove our Americanism, many Wasps tend to be tepid in outward displays of patriotism. As with sex, the feeling is there but we are not ready to go public with it. Instead, we recruit patriotic surrogates from the dull, housekeeping side of life. I grew up hearing that some products are "as American as the flag." Among them were Campbell's soups, Cuticura soap, Arm & Hammer baking soda, Packer's tar shampoo, Old Dutch cleanser, and, of course, Morton's salt.

Devotion to Sears, Roebuck plays a large part in that phenomenon. Wasps who can afford to pay more regularly shop at Sears for certain "big" items. They would not dream of buying clothes there, but they head for Sears like a pack of bird dogs when they need washing machines, dryers, refrigerators—and beds. As far back as I can remember, the chant was, "I believe in buying a good bed. I believe in sleeping in a good bed. Sears has the best beds. Sears stands behind their beds!"

In Mary McCarthy's *Birds of America*, the teenage hero writes to his Wasp mother, "I think you liked Sears, Roebuck because it was traditional; your grandmother had 'always' bought lawn-mowers and sprinklers there. Sears, Roebuck, to you, was the 'old'

America where people had lawns and wore mail-order under-wear in the winter."

When I was a little girl I used to lie in bed imagining Mr. Sears was standing behind me. I thought of him as a kind of god. When I became a big girl, I still imagined he was there, except that he had turned into a voyeur.

You have probably heard that Wasps are never tacky, but we are. The most striking example of Wasp kitsch is the huge fanned-out handkerchief that our intrepidly friendly heartland waitress wears pinned to her shoulder. During a coast-to-coast auto trip a few years ago, I made an informal study of that phenomenon. As soon as we crossed the Hudson it began. We were waited on by our first Wasp handkerchief in Montclair, New Jersey. The next day, in Dayton, the handkerchief got bigger, fancier, and started to talk more. In Illinois, lace began to appear on the edges, and by Kansas the handkerchief was starched. But when we got to Colorado we saw the ultimate Wasp handkerchief: a foot in diameter, it blossomed out in astral glory around a rhinestone-studded pin. We heard the owner's voice but we never saw her.

If you love your Wasp friends, be prepared to love their dogs, cats, rabbits, and perhaps their foxes and raccoons, too. Our intense love for animals, unhampered by papist fretting over who does and does not have a soul, is one of the nicest things about us.

The first sight that greeted me when I disembarked in Dover from France was an RSPCA poster calling attention to inhumane French slaughtering methods: *Buttercup is an English calf. She is scheduled to die in a French abattoir . . .*

Leave it to the English to break the farmer's first rule and name an animal destined for the dinner table. Who could eat anyone named Buttercup? Whenever the French are under seige, they blithely eat anything to hand, including cats, dogs, and even the elephant from the zoo, as they did in the seige of 1870. The English would prefer to starve, or switch to vegetarianism.

In London a few days later, I saw the Gina Lollobrigida remake of *The Hunchback of Notre Dame.* The scene in which Esmeralda takes sanctuary in the church nearly caused a riot in the normally staid British audience. Nobody cared if Esmeralda made it to the church on time or not; what concerned the audience was whether

her pet goat, Dejali, who had also been accused of sorcery, would be killed by the mob.

As the church doors began to close behind Esmeralda, pandemonium broke out in the theater.

"The goat! Oh, crikey, wait for the goat!"

" 'Old the bloody door!"

"Mummy! Mummy!"

When Dejali slipped through in the nick of time, a collective sigh of relief shuddered through the auditorium. The mother with the hysterical children obviously considered this crisis equal to the Blitz: "All clear, luvs. You can come up now," she announced, whereupon Wendy and Peter emerged from under my seat.

The same reactions manifested themselves when I saw *Ship of Fools* and *Cabaret* in an all-Wasp suburb in that Waspiest of all states, Virginia. When the bulldog was thrown overboard by the two Spanish children in *Ship of Fools*, growls of rage rumbled through the viewers; when he was safely retrieved, applause broke out. The indignities committed against humanity in *Cabaret* were received in stoic silence, but when the storm troopers killed the heroine's fox terrier and left the bloody body on her doorstep, shudders and even gags could be heard, and several women wiped their eyes.

We are simply not "people people." Close emotional contact with our own species presents too many threats. Charming and exquisitely polite we may be, and fair-minded to an extreme, but we are not warm. The emotions that we repress must go somewhere, however, and animals are the lucky recipients. Besides, animals are the foremost practitioners of the fair play that we so revere. They eat only when hungry, mate only for the best and most natural reason, and kill only for food or in self-defense. No human being can make that claim, regardless of race, color, creed, or national origin.

One of the most trying problems awaiting you is the Wasp who gets off on *your* religion. Some Catholics turn Protestant and some Jews turn Christian, but the Wasp, almost by definition, is the most likely religious convert.

We harbor a secret envy of ethnic life, especially family life —what we are prone to call "color" when we envy Italians and "warmth" when we envy Jews. Longing for closer kinship ties and more emotional human ties in general, we turn to religions with "heart" as a means of overriding our natural reserve.

We are fascinated by the artifacts of Catholicism—which we call "all those little things they have"—and we tend to go wild in religious supply stores. To see a Wasp laden down with six rosaries, a dozen miraculous medals, St. Christopher dashboard statues, an Infant of Prague, ten phials of holy water, and a twelve-by-fifteen Sacred Heart, and paying for it all with an American Express card, is a sight no one should miss.

One of the most memorable Wasp converts I ever knew filled a shopping bag with such items and took them to a priest to have them blessed. She was about to unload it all when he stopped her and merely waved two fingers over the bulging bag. She gave him an indignant stare and demanded, "Is that all there is to it? How much do you charge to do it up right?"

When she got home, she shook her head sadly: "I thought it would be like Trooping the Colour," she sighed. To console herself, she hung her new crucifix over the bed, but when she hit her thumb with the hammer she reverted to type with a shockingly Saxon expletive.

A true Wasp, she never forgot her manners in the confession box, opening with "Good evening, how are you?"

Jewish men beware: The Wasp woman needs no encouragement whatsoever to sprout a full-blown Liz Taylor complex and become a Jew junkie.

Taylor finally gave up her Jewish fix to mainline Burton's Welshness, but the principle is the same: This kind of woman must drink in, absorb, digest, and store in her bone marrow the identifying quality of the men in her life. All she needs is one Jewish man, and before you know it, she'll be buying two iceboxes.

Such a Wasp is easy to spot. The signs are already visible while she is still in college. She is the girl who hangs around the foreign student center collecting admirers named Krishna and Jesus. One week after school starts she can be found practicing sari-draping; by midterms, she has switched her major to Spanish and is ordering extra-hot tacos at the drive-in. A month later, somebody named Stavros shows up, and suddenly she is ready to roll *herself* in a grape leaf.

The real fun begins when she graduates and moves to New

York. You invite her to dinner and she arrives in a glow. "I met the most fascinating man last night," she sighs, then refuses to touch the beef Stroganoff you labored over. "Thou shalt not boil a kid in its mother's milk," she observes, filling up on salad. "You know, they're *right*."

The new man, of course, is Myron, who likes his shrimp cocktail as well as the next man, except now he can't eat it. Samantha won't let him. She becomes more orthodox than anyone Myron has ever known, except his Grandma Rubin in Brooklyn. Like Grandma, Samantha also uses Yiddish, but the similarity ends there; Grandma's Yiddish is excellent but Samantha, like the blotter she is, takes it all in and gets it all backward. *Tallis* means prayer shawl and *tuchus* means derrière, but Samantha never can remember which is which. She wants to buy a *menorah* to put candles in but asks for a *meshugeneh*, which means crazy. Blooper follows blooper until she tells Myron that she would like to name their first son Drek. She thinks it's Yiddish for Derek.

When the non-Catholic finds himself at a Catholic mass, his fear is always: "How will I know what to do?" When to stand, when to kneel, when to sit, what to do when the sanctus bell rings. The human spirit craves ritual; the more we have, the more secure we feel. We Wasps simplified church, but missing the ritual we had eliminated from religion, we created a social ritual that raises the same question in outsiders: "How will I know what to do?"

We indulge in no end of pompous circumstances. Ritual politeness is a Wasp specialty; we wield it over people's heads like a club. In *Our Hearts Were Young and Gay*, Cornelia Otis Skinner tells us how her mother used politeness to triumph over customs officials:

> An officer told her she wasn't allowed on board and some able-bodied seamen held out restraining arms. What happened to them was what happened to anyone on whom Mother shed her charm. She just smiled at them, and in her beautiful voice murmured a lot of charming jargon that made no sense whatsoever . . . about her child and a friend . . . at Bryn Mawr together . . . just outside Philadelphia. . . . They had lived there too but not recently . . . and they

were all going in a motor somewhere, but that was a surprise for the dear children . . . so brave, too, although she hadn't approved of their being alone in the first place. . . . And somehow she got up the gangplank and onto the boat. People just gave way, a trifle dazed.

The seeming reluctance to talk hard business is another Wasp ritual. The more urgent the subject to be discussed, the more casually it must be approached by sublime lateral routes. The archetypal Wasp business conference occurs in Hamilton Basso's novel, *The View from Pompey's Head*. The hero reflects:

> Here they were confronted by a problem of such grave importance that it demanded a special meeting which was going to make everybody late for lunch, and yet it was required of them, as if by the rules of some secret society, that they first talk about something else. Not that they imagined the problem would disappear in the meantime, or that it was not occupying the whole forefront of their attentions, or that they were trying to screw up courage enough to deal with it. It was simply a kind of ceremony, reflecting an ingrained set of attitudes.

It takes a bona fide Englishman to carry off a really thorny set of pompous circumstances. What Margaret Halsey called "the boneless quality of English conversation" reaches its zenith in *Rebecca*. The first wife's wrecked boat has been found in the bay with her body in it a year after her husband positively identified another corpse. Not only that, but he has just informed his second wife that he murdered her predecessor.

With this under her belt, the second wife goes into the dining room to greet her luncheon guest, the local magistrate, who has the power to make an arrest. She fears that the magistrate suspects the truth, which he does, and the magistrate knows that she knows that he knows. Suspended in this turgid state, they have one of the finest hours in the history of civilization. Their table talk covers London weather, a comparison of the relative comforts of Indian saris versus Western dresses in extreme heat, and a debate on whether the raspberries from the local farms have fewer "pips" than raspberries grown elsewhere.

Wasp ritual can drive non-Wasps literally mad, as we see in Pierre Boulle's novel *The Bridge Over the River Kwai.*

There being no such thing as "the fine English hand," the beauty of Colonel Nicholson's psychological destruction of Major Saito is that it was unintentional. He merely wanted to show the Japanese commander what good losers the British were.

We first meet Nicholson as he prepares to surrender to the enemy:

" . . . He had worked out in his head a ceremony which would bear the stamp of quiet dignity. After considerable thought he had decided, as a symbolic act of submission, to hand over the revolver which he wore on his hip to the enemy officer in charge of the surrender. He had rehearsed the gesture several times and had made certain of being able to take the holster off in one easy movement. He had put on his best uniform and had seen that his men tidied themselves up."

Wasps call this sort of thing "setting a good example"—a way to master one's masters by making them feel ashamed that they are not Anglo-Saxon, too. Used on an Oriental obsessed with saving face, who needed bad losers for his *amour propre*, the results were predictable:

"Faced with this gift, the astonished major first stepped back in alarm; then he appeared extremely embarrassed; finally he became convulsed by a long burst of savage laughter in which he was soon joined by his fellow officers. Colonel Nicholson simply shrugged his shoulders and assumed a haughty expression. . . ."

Saito did not know that he could have saved face by saying, "I cannot, in honor, accept the arms of such a brave man." He did not even know enough to say, "Good show!" The only way he knew to save face was to make Nicholson beg for mercy. But the more torture he applied, the more Wasp ritual he got:

"The British officers stood up and snapped to attention. The Colonel gave a regimental salute. Saito looked quite startled. He had arrived with the intention of asserting his authority, and here he was, already visibly conscious of his inferiority when faced with this ritual performed with a traditional and majestic sense of propriety."

By now poor Saito was ready for a straitjacket, but the worst was yet to come. He merely wanted a temporary bridge that would hold up long enough to transport Japanese wounded for the duration of the war; but Nicholson, pointing out that the timbers of London Bridge had lasted six hundred years, refused to let his men build a lesser structure.

The countdown began, but whatever happened, it was curtains for Saito. If the bridge was not finished in time he would have to commit hara-kiri; if it was finished in time he would still have to commit hara-kiri because it would mean British engineers had triumphed where his own Japanese engineers had failed, a fact recorded for all to see by Colonel Nicholson, who had insisted on that most ritualistic of concepts: a cornerstone. Preserved for posterity on the bridge that would last six hundred years were the words: *THIS BRIDGE WAS CONSTRUCTED BY SOLDIERS OF HIS MAJESTY'S ARMY.*

American Southerners match and occasionally surpass the British in their devotion to ritual. Some unseen force still moves women toward the door at the most casual Southern parties, to form a simulacrum of yesteryear's receiving line. Many Southern women still use unspoken pristine gestures to indicate how they expect men to treat them. Typical is my own idiosyncrasy: I will not sit at a bar, even when escorted. Unescorted, it is so unthinkable that comparisons to other unthinkable acts, such as trying to fly, are totally inadequate. I do, however, like to drink, and whenever I am staying in a hotel, I always avail myself of the cocktail lounge. I take a table alone, and expect men to "read" me and know that I do not wish to be picked up. The table is my "escort." The fact that I am drinking straight bourbon is *not* a green light to men; it is perfectly all right for a lady to drink herself to death as long as she does it at a table.

It is no accident that Southern women speak of importunate men as being "out of place." We are programmed to view life as a measured quadrille, and we fear that one false step will throw everything out of kilter. Wasp ritual is a complicated dance in which everyone is supposed to move in a preordained direction on signal, like the figures on a German cathedral when the hour strikes—doors swing open, trumpeters appear, the archangels leave, and St. Christopher changes places with St. Boniface. Ritual is Wasp Catholicism transposed to the drawing room, the board room, and the bedroom.

The Wasp's reputation for fair play has created the erroneous impression that we do not lay guilt traps. True, we are not very good at long-term manipulation, but watch out: we have a lethal touch with hit-and-run guilt. The same fair play for which we are famed comes in handy when we do our Mr. Clean number.

Mary McCarthy analyzes the double-edged scruples of her Wasp heroine in *Birds of America*:

> He disapproved of her habit of leaving their posses-
> sions behind whenever she got a divorce. . . . It would
> have been a *kindness* to Hans, in Peter's opinion, to take the
> espresso pots and half the sheets and towels, to speak only
> of the baser items, instead of borrowing the sheets they
> were now sleeping on from Mrs. Curtis and drinking awful
> coffee from a dripolator. . . . Instead she had been "per-
> fect," taking only her mother's silver and Peter's baby cup
> and fork and spoon and every Christmas present Hans had
> ever given them, naturally—so as not to hurt his
> feelings—no matter how useless or hard to pack. The result
> was that it was Hans who was open to criticism, sitting out
> there with two cars in his garage and cupboards full of
> china and linen and glasses and kitchen stuff, while she,
> innocent and good, was "roughing it" with chipped plates
> and corny glasses with mottos and taking the bus to the
> nearest town twice a week to buy groceries in the super-
> market. His mother, he decided, was being so good she
> was bad, and this worried him. She must want Hans to feel
> that an *angel* had left him. . . .

12

THE WASP WOMAN'S LOOK
or
Calamity Jane Eyre Chic

Whether feminists are willing to admit it or not, women tend to look the way their men want them to, and the Wasp woman is no exception.

The typical Englishman, famed for traveling the world over and complaining every step of the way, is convinced of the superiority of everything English. He is certain that no cuisine can match his water-logged Brussels sprouts and no female beauty can stand up against the rosy, unspoiled perfection of the Englishwoman. In movies, the gruff, retired colonels and hearty squires portrayed by Nigel Bruce can always be counted on to voice some version of "Give me one of our fresh, simple English girls every time."

God and the Englishman have formed the Wasp woman, and the result of the partnership runs the gamut from *crème de la crème* to *folie à deux*.

A few women in every ethnic group are truly beautiful, but the Wasp woman's divine gift is prettiness. Her best feature is usually her face. As the seventeenth-century traveler James Howell wrote in *The Monarchy of Spain:* "To make a compleat woman, let her be English to the neck, French to the wast, and Dutch below. I have seen women in England look as youthfull at fifty as here at twenty-five."

The Wasp woman's youthfulness, what our men call "holding up well," is often amazing. The reasons are obvious: a long history of enthusiastic birth control, the absence of a rich native cuisine, the high-status habit of perpetual dieting, and her reluctance to cook anything at all if she can possibly avoid it, which results in a lot of eating out. Paradoxically this helps keep her slim thanks to the peculiar Wasp definition of embarrassment. She will not be caught eating pastries in a French restaurant or spaghetti in an Italian one because "people might think" that she was *not* dieting.

The two most prevalent physical types in Waspland both tend to look young. One is the spare tomboyish Yankee with legs-by-the-yard that Spencer Tracy called "not much meat, but choice" when describing Katharine Hepburn. She is the perpetually sun-tanned woman with the raspy laugh who is always yelling, "Tell them to open the pro shop!" as she unloads the trunk of her car in front of the country club. The only area of her glorious golden self that shows her age is her throat, which is full of ropy tendons. They are souvenirs of half a century of looking for lost balls, stretching out the car window to instruct policemen in etiquette, and, of course, all the yelling she does. Besides her eternal "Tell them," she yells, "Trim the jib sheets!" "Oh, God, I'm in the sand trap!" and if she fox hunts, she may spend a lifetime yelling, "There he goes!"

The Yankee tomboy's youthfulness is in her figure. The other Wasp type is the anachronistically pretty woman with a rarefied look about her that leads people to describe her with words like porcelain and alabaster. Her problem, ironically, is her pretti-ness. Prettiness is out now and has been for some time. The in thing to be is sexy, chic, glamorous, attractively scruffy, or smash-ing. The pretty woman went out with the pretty dress, so when she makes an appearance, onlookers experience pleasant surprise followed by that off-base sensation that anachronisms provoke, rousing in them an inchoate resentment of her differentness. Had she been around at the turn of the century she would have been a great beauty, but now her looks are threatening because they do not conform with current ideals.

She has that untouchable Deborah Kerr look that makes watch-ing *From Here to Eternity* such a heart-breaking experience. Even the most cynical viewer feels embarrassed for Miss Kerr as she mucks around on the beach, but worse are her futile attempts to look like an army-post tramp by holding a cigarette in her mouth. Nothing could make Deborah Kerr look like a tramp; the male viewer longs to yank the cigarette from her lips, and the female viewer merely cringes. Both end up vaguely angry at *her*.

In today's unrarefied atmosphere, the pretty Wasp makes a lot of people angry. When she enters a party, the more hang-loose men and women become suddenly uptight as what appears to be the last of the great ladies walks in. Sensing their reaction to her, she becomes uptight, growing more guarded, aloof, and defensive until she is quivering with what everyone interprets as haughtiness.

She is the special victim of what men are so fond of calling "the natural look," with the ironic result that she often looks far less fetching than she might. Constantly told by men that she does not need "all that junk" on her face, or that she needs nothing but that eternal male favorite, a little light-pink lipstick, she comes to believe it. As pretty as Joan Fontaine, she can look as dowdy and drab as Joan Fontaine used to look in the first seventy minutes of those moth-into-butterfly movies of the thirties and forties.

She tries to "red up" sometimes, but whenever she does she experiences vague little tendrils of uncertainty. She may use eye shadow, mascara, and lid liner, but she does not feel entirely comfortable with them, and thanks to the men in her life, she is convinced that they do not suit her. ("You're already pretty, darling; that war paint is for the women Nature forgot.")

Most of the time she sticks with powder, lipstick, and cheek glow, which she calls rouge. Her muteness earns her the resentment or the outright loathing of women who regularly do what Helen Gurley Brown so aptly calls a complete ring-and-valve job for every public appearance. They feel that she is criticizing them by silent example; that she is saying "*You* have to try but *I* don't." Thus she acquires a reputation for being a bitch and enemies that she really does not deserve.

She also acquires unwanted female counseling services. No visit to the powder room is complete without a run-in with the painted hussy who proffers her eye shadow and babbles about "highlights." The jealous and/or insecure woman who ostensibly wants to "help" the pretty Wasp drives her further into her shell, so that the prophecy is fulfilled: The pretty Wasp grows to despise such women; to get even with them she *becomes* the supercilious bitch with a superiority complex that she has so often been accused of being. Just as blacks grow Afros to emphasize their blackness, she emphasizes every Wasp characteristic she possesses. In both cases, it is a matter of aggressive self-defense.

Wasp or Waspy women have dominated advertisements for so long that everyone got the idea that the pretty Wasp is the girl who looks pretty while wind-blown, pretty while "sleep-tousled," and pretty while wringing wet. Thanks to all the blonde, vestigially nosed girls shown riding in convertibles, *her* hair was supposed to blow back from her face, with the wind, streaming out behind her head like Isadora Duncan's scarf; never forward, over her face and into her mouth. So whenever she looks like the wrath of God she becomes twice as self-conscious as the unidealized woman, who can more readily accept such mishaps philosophically. It would help if she could go to Madrid and spend a year doing nothing but watching TV and leafing through magazines, but since she is not likely to do so, her self-defeating attitude has no place to go but on. There are women of all races and ethnic groups in ads now, but the official wind-blown Wasp convertible rider still reigns—the blonde in the white coat in the white car with the white dog.

Men who cherish the dichotomy of the ice maiden with hot pants take one look at the pretty Wasp, think: "The ones who look like they wouldn't . . . " and then make a beeline for her. Being what is called a challenge means that she attracts a lot of insecure boors whose egos need constant nourishment. She also attracts classic Don Juans, power-mad impotent tycoons, psychotic Svengalis looking for a Trilby, and the kind of Jewish men who are constantly running down Jewish women. She really has a great social life.

Then there is the ethnic man who hates himself for being an ethnic man. Usually he is devastatingly handsome, but he will never believe in himself. Instead he spoils the entire evening by referring to himself jokingly as a "greasy Greek." Sometimes he takes a different tack and calls himself "your golden Greek" but the effect is the same, and just as depressing. He is compelled to call attention to his non-Waspness when he is with a Wasp woman. "You've got class" is another identifying sentence of the wistful non-Wasp male.

He knows his date is a Wasp and he wants to talk about it to feed his masochism, but somehow he can't bring himself to say the name Wasp. Instead he says, "Are you Swedish? . . . You look German. . . . Any Danish blood?" After his date breaks the horrible/wonderful news to him, he will say something like, "You probably can't tan, as blonde as you are," even though his date is not blonde at all. He means, of course, fair, but he sees what he wishes to see. It takes a Wasp man—Stephen Foster, for instance—to describe accurately the hair color most prevalent among non-brunette Wasps.

If he remains in this masochistic groove long enough, his date, being human, will feel flattered. The gulf widens and she becomes smugly proud of her Waspness, but for all the wrong reasons. The Wasp woman's fondest wish is that such men would shut up. As blacks who were lionized during the civil rights movement can verify, there is nothing more burdensome than someone who really doesn't like you but who nevertheless wants to eat you with a spoon.

It is ironic that such a stereotype of blondeness exists, for in the super-Wasp South a surprisingly different ideal prevails. In *Old Mortality*, Katherine Anne Porter tells us, "First, a beauty must be tall; whatever color the eyes, the hair must be dark, the darker the better; the skin must be pale and smooth."

Southerners love the so-called Irish coloring because black hair sets off white skin so well. It also suggests the temptress, which all Southern women are supposed to be, and also the streak of bitchiness that the true Southern belle requires to do her number —vase throwing, door slamming, face slapping, and, of course, "flouncing" out of rooms in a towering rage. The rule of historical-novel writing long ago decreed that the blonde is the sweet one, but in *Gone With the Wind* even Melanie Wilkes had black hair. It was described only once in a very minor scene, but black it was, the same as Scarlett's. It is interesting to note that nobody in *Gone With the Wind* was blonde except the luckless Ashley. The beautiful Ellen O'Hara, Scarlett's mother, had black hair, and so did Bonnie Blue Butler, who would have become a sexpot had she lived.

Having been raised on *Gone With the Wind*, I would sell my soul for black hair—which is precisely what I would have to do to get it. As you have already perceived, when Granny set out to bend a twig she gave the project her all. She was never explicit when she promulgated moral absolutes, but then neither was Jesus. Both preferred parables and subtle allusions to get their point across.

One day when I was about seven, I came home from school and happened to mention to Granny that I had seen Mrs. So-and-So on the street.

"She dyes her hair, but she's very nice."

Even in this day of dizzying social change, many Wasp women cling to such prejudices. We do not mind dyed hair as long as nobody can tell that it is dyed; that being impossible to manage, we cannot bring ourselves to take the plunge even though we may hate our natural color. As for going light, the very words *bleached blonde* set many a Wasp woman's teeth on edge; and many Wasp men firmly believe that bleached blondes are bad women. (Red dresses trigger the same opinion.) To women like me, raised by the United Grandmothers of Dixie, the only course is floods of lemon juice to *stay* blonde (brunettes use vinegar). It is perfectly all right to use *natural* products to preserve one's *natural* hair color, but if you were not born with your favorite hair shade, you are supposed to put it out of your mind and turn your attention to making calves-foot jelly for sick people.

Sitting in the beauty shop warding off age is anathema to a certain type of Southern woman, for legend has it that she is an ageless charmer. Rather than embark on the quest for sleek sophistication that makes the middle-aged Jewish woman so stunning, the Southern woman prefers to "grow old gracefully" and let her legend linger in the mouths of a garrulous cheering section: "She was ravishing in her day." Southerners love to hark back to the past, and they still use words like ravishing, so the ageless coquette gets what she wants. Her preferred image is that of the soft, pert, girlish fading belle, but if she cannot manage that she strives for the Agnes Moorehead image of the dignity-dripping doyenne. Either way, she is perfectly capable of keeping a straight face when she refers to gray temples as "swan's wings."

In matters of looks and charm, the Southern girl is subject to a gnawing fear of a former generation of kinswomen who just might have been prettier and sexier than she. She grows up hearing about legendary women who danced all night . . . never sat down once the whole time . . . drew men like moths to the flame, and on and on. To exacerbate her fears, there are three albums of yellowing photographs sitting on the coffee table, so that the growing Southern girl always has a trauma at her fingertips. Or in the more elegant words of Katherine Anne Porter, "She is drawn and held by the mysterious love of the living, who remembered and cherished these dead."

Edwardian in her preference for male company, the Wasp

woman sees herself as the mistress of a house in Berkeley Square, presiding over a table filled with political luminaries, a stag dinner with herself as the sole *petite différence*. Thanks to such an outsized Jennie Jerome complex, going to the beauty parlor, or any other place that features large collections of women, gets on her nerves. There are numerous outbursts of "Oh, God!" before her hair appointment or shopping trip, and mutterings about "those damn chattering women" afterwards.

Viewing shopping on a par with a trip to the dentist, she is not always the *dernier cri* of the fashion world. She may own a leather coat soft enough to pull through a ring (pulling things through rings is a favorite fantasy of the quality-conscious Wasp woman), but she gets so attached to it that she will wear it for years, with no thought for changing hemlines. A 1947 New Look coat that originally cost five hundred dollars will remain a beautiful coat, but it loses something in translation when worn with a 1965 miniskirt. But the Wasp woman simply does not care. With a shrug, she quotes Mrs. Winston Guest ("A good suit simply doesn't wear out") and goes on about her business.

Her everyday dressing habits recall that English-country practice that Daphne du Maurier calls "throwing on a mackintosh" and going out for—you guessed it—a good stretch of the legs. With the dogs. The wee beasties that follow her around produce some of the most glorious runs in the history of nylons, but that does not bother her, either. She loves dogs better than stockings. (She also loves dogs better than furniture.)

Such toilettes do not result in sleek soignée perfection but they can be quite dashing. There is always a scarf in the pocket of the mackintosh, and because it is a Balenciaga and because it is on her, it never looks like a babushka. A definite Wasp look emerges from her impromptu, couldn't-care-less ensembles, the most successful one being the Katharine Hepburn uniform of beige woolen slacks, car coat, and white silk turban.

The most incredible fashion coup I ever saw was pulled off by a Southern fox-hunt matron. A stickler for traditional rules who was seldom out of the saddle for very long, she held fast to that rule most despised by women who ride: Hair must be confined in a net so it won't get caught in overhanging branches and yank the rider out of the saddle (it happened to Absalom in the Bible).

The hunt matron reasoned that since she rode so often, she

might as well leave her hair in a net at all times, so she did. It was an ordinary hair net, the kind sold in envelopes in drugstores, but somehow it looked right on her—but then so did her nicotine-stained fingers.

Further down the social scale we have the Wasp earth mother. Maizie is often nobody's mother because she is too busy being everybody's mother. She is Margaret Mitchell's Belle Watling and Dorothy Parker's "Big Blonde." In old movies she was perfectly portrayed by Joan Blondell and Ann Sothern. Today she is best represented by several of the showier country music singers providing they tone down some of their glamor.

A lovable slob, Maizie is what used to be called blowsy. She is definitely one of the kindest and warmest Wasps of all and perhaps our best ambassadress to the non-Wasp world. Though she is often sexually loose, her sexiness is actually buried under an avalanche of maternity.

She irons a lot, but what happens to the clothes is a mystery because she never seems to get dressed. She spends her days clacking around in backless bedroom slippers, her hair in rollers and her big white thighs peeking through her buttonless wrapper.

Although Maizie has the warmth and concern of the Jewish mother, the similarity ends there, for Maizie does not know the meaning of guilt. No matter what outlandish confession you spill on her, her reply is "Chrissake, hon, don't give it another thought." This is just as well, for she gets a lot of phone calls from the kind of people who skip hello and get right down to cases: "I've just got to come over and talk to you, something terrible happened!"

Maizie does not push food but she is constantly wrapping it up. The amount of Baggies, Glad wrap, and Reynolds wrap she uses boggles the mind, until you realize that most of her missions of mercy involve people who are leaving town post haste. Legalized abortions have cut into her chief good deed. In days gone by, she was always matching hysterical beauty shop operators with alcoholic doctors, or—in the South—the perennial "old colored woman" she always knew, who used a green twig as a curette. But Maizie still hands out money. Never a lot of it and always in cash; she is famous for the grimy, much-folded dollar bill, proffered with her eternal "I *want* you to have this."

She deflowers a lot of virgins, the kind of overdue young man who never forgets her even though he always leaves her after she has saved him from homosexuality or whatever it was he needed to be saved from. She is much too kind hearted to be really good in bed, but there is a lot of her; she is the kind of woman a man can truly wallow in and the kind of woman men secretly crave in this era of skinny, suntanned string beans. She is big, white, and soft, and she smells like sugar from repeated applications of Quelques Fleurs.

My own version of the Wasp look makes my life a barrel of fun. My chief problem is the frustrated beauty operator who is offended by the fact that my hairdo is six thousand years old. Convinced that chignons belong on Greek statues, she gushes, "Oh, I'd just love to get my hands on your hair!" Somehow, it always sounds violent to me.

The chignon is part of a larger problem. Raised by a grandmother who believed that eternal discomfort is the mark of a lady, I have a stiff look. Even when I am comfortable I look as if I'm suffering. I sit up straight, fold my hands, and button all my buttons regardless of the weather. Taught that a button is meant to be buttoned, I believe it. Consequently, I am an irresistible target for those fashionably scroungy women, usually named Yvonne or Tania, who advise me to remove my bra, unbutton to the waist, and "take down your hair and mess it up a little." When Yvonne and Tania do these things they look sexy and voluptuous. I simply look deranged, like those harassed women in gothic novels who are always swooning in remote castles. *What terrible thing happened to Arabella in Favisham Manor?*

You would think that people would consider me unapproachable and leave me alone. Not so. I also have what is known as an American-looking face, which leads to enormous tribulations. Whenever the people who talk to themselves decide to talk to somebody else, they always buttonhole me.

The far-right nut is nearly always a woman of indeterminate age who wears twenty-five scarves, a Greta Garbo beret, and a one-eyed fox fur piece. Some of the ones who have taken a liking to me have also worn Washington Senators baseball caps, white rubber galoshes in August, and those crocheted babushkas with a Mary Stuart widow's peak that my grandmother called "fascinators."

The best time to meet those ladies is on a day when everything has gone right. The best place to meet them is in chain cafeterias, which they enter in full sail demanding, "Does the fish have bones?" Refusing to be parted from their shopping bags, they loop them over their wrists and, trays shaking perilously, they slosh forward eschewing all assistance and cawing, "I'm going to sit with this nice girl right here."

Advancing age has not saved me from them; at forty I am still "that nice girl." They take one look at my Waspy mug and think, *"This* one is going to agree with me."

Usually they open with "Now *you* know and *I* know . . . " but often they are so positive that they have found a friend that they skip all the introductory little nothings and barrel right into it: "I say bring back the public whipping post! They ought to take that Mary Hartman off the air and arrest everybody! Put 'em in jail and throw the key away!"

The far-left nut is usually an old man. If you would like to meet him, follow me until somebody shouts, "What do people like you know about starving? I was in the Bonus March!"

Waiting rooms are another problem for the Wasp who has an "honest looking," i.e., Wasp, face. People are constantly asking me to watch their luggage for them. Scanning the faces of the other travelers, they pick me and then disappear. Old ladies in bus stations who never believe what the information clerk tells them because "he's been drinking, I can smell it" verify schedules and departure gates with me. Women who put young children on public conveyances to travel alone want them to sit next to me. "I can tell you're all right," they whisper. Yes, I'm all right, but I hate children.

You simply cannot win if you are saddled with the face that launched a thousand assumptions. Merely by walking in and sitting down, I once emptied what I took to be a nice Schrafft's-like cocktail lounge that catered to women. As the bartender explained afterward, it was a Lesbian bar, and everybody thought I was a cop.

My best effect, though, is the one I managed in London. My seat partner on a bus decided to strike up a conversation: "I hate these bloody American tourists, don't you?"

13

GROUP vs. GROPE
or
Wasps in Novels

There are two kinds of Wasp novels: those written by Wasps and those written by non-Wasps. The former category is dominated by Taylor Caldwell, who can turn anybody into a Wasp. St. Paul, Pericles, Cicero, and Joseph Francis Armagh all have emerged naturalized after a trip through her typewriter, which must have *Property of U.S. Department of Immigration* stamped in blood on its poor quivering platen.

The non-Wasp writer Wasps like best is Mary McCarthy, who knows us like the back of her Irish hand. She has spent a great deal of time with us. A native of Seattle, she went east to Vassar at a time when such a move *ipso facto* bestowed Wasphood on young ladies. She has married three Wasps, divorced two, and produced a Wasp son, Reuel Kimball Wilson. While her personal life with us undoubtedly has helped her know her subject well, her real weapon is her own self-esteem. She does not care in the least that she herself is not a Wasp; in her novels, she never kowtows to us, never interrupts her own narrative to whine about her ethnic origins, and although she is acerbic to a pitiless degree, she never makes fun of Wasps as Wasps—she simply out-Wasps them.

Unburdened by the reverence for us that haunts so many non-Wasp writers, she extracts our essence without resorting to the trowel. Her short story "The Weeds," about an unhappy wife who is a gardening buff, opens with a sentence that sums up the hell-on-earth Wasp problem of emotional repression: "She would leave him, she thought, as soon as the petunias had bloomed."

In *The Group*, she took a tiresome, overworked Wasp cliché

the Vassar girl, and turned out the quintessential Wasp novel without once waving the Union Jack. The reader forgets that the eight heroines are Wasps, but he remembers Polly Andrews and her home-made Christmas gifts; Kay Petersen's intense brand-name loyalty; Pokey Prothero's career as a vet; Libby MacAusland's great-girl enthusiasm; Lakey's intriguing chill; Dottie Renfrew's orgasmic one-night stand; Priss Crockett's center-stage husband; and Helena Davison's congenital spinster-hood.

Other non-Wasp writers never stop tugging their forelock. Desperate to be accepted as bona fide Wasps, they keep writing the same book over and over, hoping somehow to inundate with Waspness until they have washed down the clubhouse doors.

The non-Wasp writer who irritates Wasps the most is Stanislaus McGillicuddy, author of that renowned door-stopper, *Tempest on the Terrace.* . . .

Situated on the banks of the Monomania River in Wildebeeste County, Pennsylvania, is the town. It is said that the Derby family shaped the town, but that is false; it was the town that shaped the Derbys. In order to understand the Derbys it is first necessary to understand the town, for without the town there would be no book—or at any rate, it would be much shorter.

All towns in Wildebeeste County are named for some important act that its founder committed on its original site. Thus the county can boast of Maitland's Landing, Richardson's Transfer, and even Thompson's Stream.

The name of our town is Derby's Hump.

After Captain Hiram Derby paid damages to Princess Lackawanna's father, he turned his attention to laying streets. He named the best street in town Esterhazy and the second best, Vercingetorix. No sooner was this done than a nouveau riche Dutchman named Schumacher moved to Esterhazy. So many *Landesmänner* followed his example that Esterhazy was soon full of rich Dutchmen, so Captain Derby decided to move his house brick by brick, stone by stone, to Vercingetorix where it still stands.

All the best people did the same. Now the second-best street in Derby's Hump was the best street, though of course no one ever called it that. On the contrary, the aristocracy of Derby's Hump are proud of living on the second-best street because it is *the* place to live. Of course they don't say this in so many words; instead they boast that no arrest has ever been made on Vercingetorix because Irish policemen cannot spell it. Their favorite boast concerns a policeman who found a dead horse on Vercingetorix and dragged it around the corner so he could file his report: *Dead horse on 4th Street.*

It is things like that that form a person's character.

Our story concerns the descendants of Captain Hiram. His grandson, Cedric Derby, married Abigail Prescott, daughter of Eben Prescott, owner of Prescott's Iron Works and master of The Hermitage. When their engagement was announced, Old Eben insisted that the newlyweds live in The Hermitage even though he and Cedric hated each other. Naturally Cedric wished to take his bride to his own family homestead, The Place, so the two men entered Eben's den for a gentlemanly battle of wills.

The decision was arrived at with no difficulty. Old Eben poured Madeira and said quietly, "This house is big enough for both of us."

Cedric had to admit that was true. The Hermitage contained twenty rooms, on three stories, and boasted the thinnest Irish maids in town. They were always rushing past Cedric on the stairs, gasping, "By your leave, sor."

Abigail Prescott Derby was a cultivated woman, whose interest in the arts gave Derby's Hump its sobriquet, "the Athens of Wildebeeste County." All the town's prominent women attended Abigail's Thursday Afternoons, where the chief topic of conversation was Fritzi Schumacher's Saturday Nights.

Nine months after Cedric and Abigail were married, their first child, Geoffrey, was born. After that, a year apart, came Ethelred, Isabel (called Sissy), Matilda, Quentin, and the twins, Lionel and Lucy.

One week after the birth of the twins, Abigail summoned Cedric to her side and said, "I want to talk to you." The following day the locksmith arrived, and Cedric's possessions were moved down the hall to what became known in the kitchen as "Himself's room."

The turn of the century saw servant problems at The Hermitage. Delia Flannigan had twins, Sean and Francis; Peggy O'Malley had a stillbirth named Baby Girl; and Theresa Armagh had a miscarriage right in the middle of Thursday Afternoon.

Once again Abigail summoned Cedric.

"Bastard!" she whispered.

"I know, my dear."

"I want your word of honor that you'll never touch any of the servants again."

"You have it."

The following year, Fritzi Schumacher paid an extended visit to her Hochsteiner relatives in St. Louis, and Abigail embarked on a habit euphemistically known in the kitchen as "Herself has took to her room to nurse her headache."

Cedric, constitutionally incapable of liking more than one child at a time, devoted himself to his eldest son Geoffrey. Ethelred, finding himself shunted aside, tried to turn to his mother, but unfortunately she was a mean drunk. When he asked her, "Mother, are we rich?" she snarled, "Go to your room!" Nobody liked Ethelred except the family coachman, Emil. They spent many happy hours together in the carriage house, and Emil explained the facts of life to his young charge.

Pointing to a mare's vagina, he said, "Ist hier der stallion his putz beschtickt."

Ethelred was not ready for this. The shock brought on an attack of rheumatic fever that would have killed him had not his nurse-maid, Mary Reilly, stripped off her uniform and gotten into bed with him. She lay with him all night, holding his delicate shivering little patrician body against her big warm Irish peasant one until the fever broke.

Bald as an egg, Ethelred began a long reflective convalescence filled with books. The sight of his wizened second son filled Cedric with loathing, but soon he was forced to reconsider his feelings and love Ethelred, for Geoffrey caught rheumatic fever and died. Cedric cloistered himself in his den with his sorrow and the telephone, calling schools to cancel Geoffrey's enrollments. (Geoffrey had been enrolled in Groton and Princeton even before his mother had expelled his placenta.) "Never mind," Cedric told Groton. "I have no son."

That done, he stopped by Ethelred's room and knocked on the door.

"Come in," piped the unmanly little egg.

The door opened and Cedric's head appeared.

"You killed your brother."

"Yes, sir."

The door closed softly.

"Don't take it too hard, Master Ethelred," said Mary Reilly. "That's how Himself shows his love."

Cedric mourned Geoffrey for the required decent interval, then he got on the telephone again and called all the schools back. Thus it was that Ethelred was enrolled in his father's mind at the age of ten. Cedric had reconsidered.

Ethelred Derby was Groton ('12) and Princeton ('16). He m. Harriet Landringham (Vassar '16) and they had a s. Geoffrey II ('20). But the most important event in Ethelred's life was the Percheron's erection ('06).

He was lying in his sickbed when he happened to look out the window at the carriage house just as the horse "dropped" it. The moment he saw it, Ethelred had his very own first erection. His character was formed.

Just then Mary Reilly entered his room and saw that he had become a man. She put her hand on him, then unbuttoned her uniform.

"You're ready, Master Ethelred."

"Yes, but am I rich?"

When he was recovered completely from both the rheumatic fever and Mary Reilly, Ethelred acquired his first friend, Rex Tinkham, nephew of that exalted personage universally known as Rex Tinkham's uncle, the town fixer. Anyone who wanted a strike broken, a wife trailed, or a daughter aborted always called in Rex Tinkham's uncle. Even children knew about him; whenever they needed a fourth for cowboys and Indians, they would stand outside his house and shout, "Rex Tinkham's uncle! Can Rex come out and play?"

No matter what dire contretemps Rex Tinkham's uncle was presented with, his invariable reply was "Let's have lunch." Lunching with this great man was a soothing experience, except for those inevitable interruptions when the steward walked through the club calling "Rex Tinkham's uncle! Please come to the telephone."

When lunch was over, he would say, "I'll take care of it," and a week or so later Sissy's musician lover had left town and Sissy was accepted by a school for bad girls of good family.

Cedric had been indebted to him for years because he even had pull at Catholic orphanages. To Rex Tinkham's uncle, finding a "place" was finding a "place," whether he found it at the Racquet Club, the Union Club, Groton, Miss Porter's, or the Little Sisters of the Poor. He was that democratic.

Now Cedric needed him for far more important matters. Abigail was having an affair with Herman Schumacher. Not only that, the previous Thursday they had gotten drunk together in Philadelphia, where they boarded a deserted railway car and screwed from one end of the Main Line to the other in front of an unshaded window. They had been recognized at every stop: Overbrook, Merion, Wynnewood, Ardmore, Haverford, Bryn Mawr, Rosemont, and Radnor.

"I'll take care of it," said Rex Tinkham's uncle.

A few days later, the society pages of the major Pennsylvania newspapers all recorded a notable event: Mrs. Cedric Derby had granted reporters a guided tour of her rose gardens on Thursday Afternoon last, followed by a tea.

Ethelred and Cedric were very close now. Madeira flowed in the den, paving the way for intimate father-son exchanges, such as the one that began, "My boy, it's time we had a talk about the kind of women who have sons in military school."

Cedric need not have worried, for Ethelred was in love with Harriet Landringham, d. of Mr. and Mrs. Horace LaFont Landringham of New York, Palm Beach, and "The Windbreakers." He had met her through his boyhood friend, Rex Tinkham, with whom he shared bachelor digs in the city. The first time he saw her he rocked on his heels with awed delight.

"That's the girl I'm going to marry, Rex!"

"Horseshit," said Rex Tinkham, as usual.

On their first date, Ethelred found himself escorting not only Harriet, but her best girlfriends, too. "Sage, Faith, and dear old Pru" clung to Harriet like burrs, an old habit that had begun in Nursery Arms and continued through Elementary Arms, Junior High Arms, Senior High Arms, and Vassar. They accompanied her up the aisle at Wedding Arms and very nearly enrolled in Honeymoon Arms as well.

Dear old Pru caught the bride's bouquet, as the charitable Harriet had intended, but it brought no luck. Dear old Pru had problems: The size of her fortune was matched by the size of her feet, the size of her teeth, and her outsized passion for Rex Tinkham. Harriet pleaded with him, and dear old Pru tried her best to seduce him, but to all their blandishments he replied, "Horseshit."

One day when Harriet and Ethelred had been married for about a year, she rushed into their Sutton Place apartment in tears.

"I just saw dear old Pru!"

"Fuck dear old Pru!" Ethelred shouted.

"That's exactly what somebody did. She's pregnant. What shall we do?"

Ethelred made no reply as he went to the phone and dialed a number.

"Hello, sir. Do you think we could have lunch at the club?"

Two weeks later, instead of the usual "It's all taken care of," Ethelred and Harriet received a cable from Paris:

DEAR OLD PRU AND I WERE MARRIED YESTERDAY. IF BOY WILL NAME HIM CEDRIC AFTER HIS FATHER. GOOD TO BE TAKING CARE OF MY OLD FRIEND'S BASTARDS AGAIN. FEEL POSITIVELY NOSTALGIC. KISS FRITZI SCHUMACHER FOR ME AND TELL HER NOT TO WORRY. EVERYTHING TAKEN CARE OF BEFORE SAILING. LOVE TO ALL.

SIGNED
REX TINKHAM'S UNCLE

14

WHAT MAKES SAM HICKHAM RUN?
or
The Watergate Wasp

Our strange conceptions of honesty begin early in life, the first time we are told, "Look people straight in the eye when you talk to them!" Our mothers worry so much about the clear-eyed gaze that they forget to instruct us on what to *say* and *do* in these eyeball-to-eyeball confrontations. It is never long before we get the point: shifty eyes are worse than shifty acts and words.

We produce the finest-looking criminals in the country. They draw a bead on you from the post office wall; like the eyes of old oil paintings, theirs follow you from General Delivery to the stamp machine.

The cult of the firm chin is another organization that Wasp mothers join. Whenever I brought home a new boyfriend who was not positively in the final stages of lockjaw, my mother took me into the kitchen and hissed, "I don't like that boy's chin." Going to the movies with Mama was a distracting trial if the star happened to be Dana Andrews. "Look at that chin! Now that's what I call a *chin*. You can tell he's all right." She dissolved in ecstasy over Charlton Heston, Kirk Douglas, and Charles Korvin, all of whom left her nearly incoherent. "Look. . . . See that?" Finally, thinking I would fix her once and for all, I showed her a picture of Charles V in all the glory of the Hapsburg underbite, but instead of laughing as the members of my history class had, she said, "He must have done a lot of good things."

The major stumbling block in Wasp honesty is our insistence upon a sentimental note—it must be touching. The story of Abe Lincoln walking ten miles to return a borrowed book on time wipes us out. The Wasp mother's fondest dream is being undercharged eleven cents in the middle of a snowstorm, for it gives her a golden opportunity to teach a moral lesson. That very minute, she can send Johnny back to the store with a dime and a penny clutched in his little mittened hand. This sort of thing is the Wasp trek; its purpose is not to make us honest but to make us *look* honest.

It also makes us feel honest. When Johnny, blinded by snow and knocking icicles off his eyebrows, enters the store, everybody exclaims: "Awww . . . look at the cute little thing." Enough of this and Johnny's self-image is formed: Quick, somebody go find Lot and Diogenes and tell them not to worry—I'm here!

The Wasp shoplifter has to be seen to be believed. After stealing everything she wants, she decides she needs a shopping bag to carry it all home in. Positioning herself at the self-service rack, which truly honest people regularly raid, she glances around to make sure people are looking; then she slowly deposits fifteen pennies in the slot. Never a dime and a nickel—that wouldn't take as long as the pennies, and she wants people to notice and watch her in admiration. If she can catch the eye of a few old ladies and exchange a sweet smile with them, her day is made.

Even amounts of money bring out all sorts of Wasp honor twitches. In *Jaws*, there is a minor character who, "whenever she wrote a check for an even-dollar amount, refused to write 'and 00/100.' She felt it would be an insult, as if she were suggesting that the person who cashed the check might try to steal a few cents."

If a Wasp needs to borrow forty-eight dollars and his creditor-friend rounds it off, as any sensible person would, to fifty, the Wasp worries about the two dollars. Often, instead of waiting and paying back the entire fifty dollars at once, he might force the two dollars on his friend.

We drive the French crazy with our casual manner of checking the bill. A few cents here or there is not worth a scene; moreover, quibbling about minute amounts is the most repulsive habit anyone can have as far as we are concerned. We do check the bill, but we are satisfied if it is "about right." If the total corresponds more or less to our mental addition, we pay it.

Southern Wasp women have a notorious Lady Bountiful complex. Often arch-conservatives politically, we disapprove of government welfare in all its myriad forms. But the reasons are not as you might think. Government mercy, you see, cuts into our own mercies. We gladly give away our money to deserving unfortunates, but we hate to give it to the government and let Uncle Sam give it away for us. As Scarlett O'Hara said, "What good is a sacrifice if no one knows about it?" We want to be *seen* being honorable in the manner of great ladies.

A writer with a Lady Bountiful complex is in deep trouble, because writers never pay. Publishing-world etiquette decrees that editors treat agents, and that both treat writers. My check-grabbing tendencies are constantly frustrated, and I return from my annual business trip to New York suffused in a vague free-floating guilt that takes weeks to get over. To my way of thinking, I am a freeloader.

Obligation haunts the Wasp. Like all women, I was told by my mother that a man's payment is "the pleasure of your company," but I never believed it. None of my friends did, either. To the money-obsessed Wasp, if a man spends a lot on you, you really ought to go to bed with him. After all, it's the only way to keep from getting *involved* with him.

The only way to keep things from getting sticky is to let them get sticky. As the Wasp woman thinks as she rises from the bed of a man she hardly knows, "Now we're even-Stephen." It is her version of liberation; the only way to preserve her freedom and integrity. It is an icy attitude, but it has its good points.: If she really cannot stand a man, she will never string him along simply to get dinner dates out of him. No matter how much money he has, she will refuse to go out with him or encourage him in any way. Furthermore, she will tell him point-blank to give up and stop calling her; she might even say, as kindly as possible, "Look, I'm sorry but I really want nothing to do with you." Juggling, manipulating, and games in general repel her and she will not play.

One of the worst mistakes a non-Wasp man can make is to give his Wasp date money for the powder room. She would not be averse to letting him set her up as his mistress in a thousand-dollar-a-month apartment, but she is mortified when he hands her a dollar as she rises from the table. I once knew a non-Wasp woman who confided that she spent the evening peeing as often as possible so that she could get what she called "little-girls'-room money." She deposited it the next day in a savings account she had opened for that express purpose. She had over two hundred dollars in it, *and* she actually showed me the balance. I nearly died. Whenever a man has offered me powder-room money, I've drawn myself up into a stiff little huff and said, "I have my own, thank you." It's a matter of honor.

We strive for the *little* honesty that shines like the morning star through a cesspool of malfeasance. The hero of *The Lost Weekend*, Don Birnam, would have done anything for a drink. He hocked his girl's fur coat. He ruined his brother's reputation in the neighborhood by borrowing money in his name. But at the family farm he was scrupulously honorable about the key to the applejack closet because he did not want the servants to think ill of him:

> This kind of honor had baffled the foolish psychiatrist as it baffled many another before from his mother on, but could it by any stretch of ethics be called honor at all? Or was it honor so honest that it transcended the human, so human that it had not been characterized by the convenient words in the catalog?

My own version of the Wasp little honesty caused a friend of mine to fall into hysterics and disturb the peace at the public library. I took back some overdue books. The librarian misread the due dates and thought they said July 1 instead of June 1. "Fifty cents, please," she said, whereupon I did my Trueheart number, saying, "Oh, no, they're more than a month overdue," which raised my fine to three dollars.

As we walked away from the desk, my friend said, "Why? *Why! Why didn't you keep your mouth shut?*"

I was about to say something public-spirited, when suddenly, as often happens in such moments, the truth simply popped out—out of my mouth and out of my unconscious mind.

"If ever I get involved in extortion or embezzlement or something really serious, I'll have a terrific backlog of character witnesses to call on. There's the lady at the drugstore, the lady at the cleaner's, the man in the hardware store, and now the librarian."

The most outstanding example of our Little Honest Abe hang-up in recent times was President Eisenhower's special assistant, former New Hampshire governor Sherman Adams. All the while he was involved with Bernard Goldfine and vicuña coats, Adams did his Wasp thing in the White House. "He scrupulously paid for office stamps he put on personal letters and insisted that he be billed for personal phone calls . . . . In New Hampshire . . . he had been known to wade through blizzards to get to work on time."[1] As assistant to the President, he demanded that underlings make the Wasp trek, too; when anyone was even a minute or two late, Adams bellowed at him.

How could such a Simon Pure become entangled with a known shady operator like Goldfine in the first place? One would think that a man like Adams could not even bear to look upon him, much less strike up the cozy friendship that led to the schemes. To say that Adams was simply a hypocrite is too pat; it goes deeper than that. He had had too much Wasp training; love of honor and its outward trappings was more highly developed in him than honor itself.

Writes William Manchester:

"The presidential assistant's failure to grasp the interpretation which others might place on his relationship with Goldfine stemmed in part from an inability to see himself as others might see him. Adams knew Adams to be honest—that was that."[2]

Wasps not only love honesty in themselves and other people, we even demand it of the weather. Early Yankee missionaries in Hawaii grumbled about something they named the "Polynesian curse." Claiming that idyllic climates "destroy character," they took grim pleasure in relating stories of formerly industrious and trustworthy merchants and sailing men who became "no good" after a tilt with the tradewinds. Seasons ought to be recognizable, like an honest face and a firm chin; if they are not, they are no damn good.

Distrust of Hawaii has never quite died. In William Bradford Huie's novel, *Hotel Mamie Stover*, a descendant of early Yankee missionaries quits the islands for the mainland because "There is something dishonest about places like this." (A few years ago I made a similar observation about Phoenix and in a huff moved to Seattle, telling a friend, "It's *not right* for it to be this hot!")

Naturally, it is always perpetually warm weather we distrust.

---

[1] William Manchester, *The Glory and the Dream.*
[2] *Ibid.*

The North or South Pole will do nicely for character building —snow, after all, is our most vital prop.

There is a certain kind of Wasp who insists upon sleeping with the windows open no matter how cold it is. The fresh-air hang-up runs through Queen Victoria's letters to her children and grandchildren, most of whom made dynastic marriages with foreigners who did not have healthy English habits. Victoria was a bear on the subject, especially in her letters to the Princess Royal, her oldest child and the first to marry. The princess married the Prussian emperor, and Victoria was convinced that German absolutism had been caused in part by stuffy rooms. A breath of fresh air was needed, she felt, both politically and atmospherically. True-blue people open the windows; keeping them closed is decadent, a sure way to wreck character.

Lolling in bed in the morning is dishonest, too. On the morning after their wedding, Prince Albert and Queen Victoria rose at dawn to take a brisk walk, causing her prime minister to remark, "We'll never get a Prince of Wales at this rate." The Wasp who is a night person suffers regular bouts of guilt and self-disgust. My great ambition is to get up "as soon as the sky is light," a favorite puritanical phrase that Wasps like to use. My problem is that I write until the sky is light, have a martini while I watch the Today Show, then go to bed. I hate myself.

My most severe problem with our cold-is-honest hang-up is the sauna. To me, it's a steaming jungle of laziness and sin.

The Wasp trying to weasel out of accusations lapses into embarassing hyperbole: "All that I hold sacred" and "I could not live with myself" are standard. He also becomes rococo, like Charles Van Doren in the 1958 quiz-show scandals. When asked why he did not respond to a subpoena, instead of saying simply that he and his wife had gone out of town for a brief New England vacation, he said that he had wanted "to gather my thoughts . . . in the October beauty of the region."[3] When he finally confessed his guilt, he said that while he had always known that what he had been doing was wrong, he had done it anyway, "because it was having such a good effect on the national attitude toward teachers, education, and the intellectual life."

[3] Direct quotes of Van Doren are from *The Glory and the Dream*.

The situation shifted into high Wasp gear during the congressional hearings that followed. Van Doren's emotional testimony included mention of a letter from a strange woman who advised that he tell the truth so that he could "live with himself"; a lawyer who said "God bless you" when he heard that Van Doren had decided to confess; bird-in-a-gilded-cage stories about begging the producers of the show to let him lose (he could have freed himself by missing a question); an analysis of good versus evil; references to "horror"; and that all-time favorite: "I was running away from myself."

When Van Doren had finished testifying, Committee Chairman Oren Harris complimented him on his "candor," of all things. Congressman William L. Springer said he hoped Columbia University would not fire him "prematurely" (everything was all over now). Congressman Peter F. Mack, Jr., hoped that NBC would "forgive" him; and others praised him for his "fortitude," his "forthrightness," and his "soul searching."

It was hard to tell if Van Doren had done anything wrong at all until Congressman Steven B. Derounian spoke up: "I don't think an adult of your intelligence should be commended for telling the truth."

Derounian obviously did not understand that congratulating witnesses for how they performed rather than for what they actually said and did is a Wasp must. It all began back in the days of the medieval tournament. Unfortunately, *"Quelle Chevalerie!"* has lost a lot in translation over the years, having degenerated to "The witness is to be commended for the manner in which he responded to the interrogatories." The principle, however, remains the same. Our code of honesty, like the code of chivalry, is more icing on the cake. The point of it all is to emerge a "parfit gentil" knight and the finest flower of Christendom regardless of what you did on the Crusades.

The Wasp confronted by dishonesty, his own or someone else's, takes refuge in what he hopes is flowery, chivalric language. More often than not, it is simply tangled language, like the syntax jungles that came out of Watergate.

Edwin Newman believes that any liar is bound to distort language by his efforts at concealment. Since most of the lumpen-linguists of Watergate were Wasps, it may be more correct to analyze the problem endemically, as Somerset Maugham does:

> [There is] something in the English temper, perhaps a
> native lack of precision in thought, perhaps a naive delight
> in fine words for their own sake, an innate eccentricity and
> love of embroidery. . . . English prose has had to struggle
> against the tendency to luxuriance.

Bible-oriented Protestants may not make the best witnesses,
either, according to Maugham:

> King James' Bible has been a very harmful influence on
> English prose. . . . The Bible is an oriental book. Its alien
> imagery has nothing to do with us. Those hyperboles,
> those luscious metaphors, are foreign to our genius. Those
> rhymes, that powerful vocabulary, that grandiloquence,
> became part and parcel of the national sensibility. The
> plain, honest English speech was overwhelmed with or-
> nament. Blunt Englishmen twisted their tongues to speak
> like Hebrew prophets.[4]

There is something to this theory. "The congregation shall
stone him with stones" sounds exactly like John Mitchell under
oath.

If the Wasp would only relax and be his blunt self in tight
moments, he would be much more likable, and he would not give
the rest of us a reputation for pomposity. The income of
stenotypist would, of course, be greatly reduced, since it takes a
heap of heaping to make a heap, but America would be spared two
years of "Yea, though I walk through this point in time."

There might not have been a Watergate at all had it not been for
a chivalric Wasp who could not stop talking. If Alger Hiss had shut
up, Richard Nixon might never have become President.

In 1948, Hiss was called before the House Committee on Un-
American Activities to respond to charges by Whittaker Chambers that he was a member of the Communist party. Hiss made a
statement to the committee denying it all. At the conclusion of his
statement he was a free man; it had been simply Chambers' word
against his own.

---

[4] Maugham quotations are from *The Summing Up*.

But then Hiss made his fatal error. Shown a photo of Chambers, instead of flatly saying he had never seen him before, "he looked at it with an elaborate air of concentration and said, 'If this is a picture of Mr. Chambers, he is not particularly unusual looking.' He paused and then, looking up at Congressman Karl Mundt . . . added, 'He looks like a lot of people. I might even mistake him for the Chairman of this Committee.'"

Nearly everyone in the room was on Hiss's side, and they laughed heartily at his dig. "Hiss acknowledged this reaction to his sally by turning his back on the Committee, tilting his head in a *courtly* bow, and smiling graciously at his supporters" [my italics].

It got even worse. Hiss then wanted to know if Chambers were present in the room. "He then looked from side to side, giving the impression that he did not have the slightest idea who this mysterious character might be and that he was anxious to see him in the flesh."

By being what Chambers later called "too mouthy," Hiss drew the suspicion of Richard Nixon. He went on being verbosely chivalric throughout the investigation. The car he had given Chambers "had a sassy little trunk in back." When asked if he had ever seen a prothonotary warbler, instead of saying yes, he said: "I have, right here on the Potomac. Do you know that place? They come back and nest in those swamps. Beautiful yellow head. A gorgeous bird."[5]

From prothonotary warblers to Checkers. Can Watergate be far behind?

[5] Hiss material from Richard M. Nixon, *Six Crises*.

15

ONE WASP'S FAMILY
or
The Ties That Bind

Died in her home at 92 Second Street, Fall River, Mass., on August 4, 1892, Abby D. Borden, second wife of Andrew Borden, age sixty-five; also died at eleven o'clock at the same time and place, Andrew Borden, age seventy.

Obituaries must be properly worded and tastefully tucked away where they belong regardless of blazing headlines containing the same information. That vital phrase, "she died in her home," is not likely to occur to headline writers describing a double hatchet murder, so it must appear elsewhere.

The Lizzie Borden case is pure Waspology, a cornucopia of all our tics and twitches, as well as our most admirable traits. With the exception of Bridget Sullivan, the Borden's maid, everyone involved in the entire hideous, zany mess was a Wasp.

It all began on July 19, 1860, when Lizzie was born—and christened with a nickname. Thirty-two years later at her inquest she stated her full name, Lizzie Andrew Borden, adding, "I was so christened."

Her father was a rich and miserly undertaker who was said to cut the feet off corpses to make them fit into smaller, cheaper coffins, for which he charged full-sized prices. When his first wife died two years after Lizzie's birth, Andrew was left with two daughters to raise. (A third daughter, Alice, had died in childhood.) Faced with the choice of hiring a housekeeper or remarrying, he chose the latter because it was cheaper. The lucky girl was a thirty-eight-year-old spinster named Abby Durfee Gray.

Three-year-old Lizzie obediently called the new wife Mother, but twelve-year-old Emma called her Abby. No one seemed to mind or tried to change it, so she persisted in her casual form of address.

Andrew Borden's sole interest in life was money. His operations expanded to include banking, cotton mills, and real estate but no matter how rich he got, he continued his practice of peddling eggs from his farms to his downtown business associates. Wicker basket on his arm, he set forth to board meetings, savoring joyous thoughts of earning yet a few more pennies.

It has been suggested that Borden was a Protestant celibate in his later years and never bothered to consummate his marriage of convenience, but let us look at what we *know* about Abby Borden's emotional outlets. She was five feet tall and weighed over two hundred pounds. Her favorite activity was staying home and eating. She hardly ever left the house except for rare occasions when she accepted a luncheon invitation from her sister, Mrs. Whitehead.

Emma Borden, the elder sister, was forty-two at the time of the murders. About all that can be said of her is that she was one of those spinsters who scurries. Mouselike in all respects, she did not speak above a whisper (she had to be asked many times to raise her voice at the trial), and wherever she went, there was a rustling sound. About the only place she went besides her room was the grocery store, or around the corner to Borden Street to visit her friend, another spinster, named Alice Russell. Unlike her sister, Emma was not a churchgoer.

Compared with the rest of her family, Lizzie comes through as a prom queen. Never known to go out with men, at least she went out. Most of her sorties were missions of mercy. A member of Central Congregational Church, she taught Sunday school to a class of Chinese laundry workers' children; she was secretary-treasurer of the Christian Endeavor Society; a member of the Ladies Fruit and Flower Mission, which visited shut-ins; and a member of the Fall River hospital board. She belonged to the Women's Christian Temperance Union, whose Carry Nation was later to adopt her MO; and she lent her services to the group that cooked and served an annual Christmas dinner for newsboys. In short, Lizzie was what is known as a pillar of the church.

What did she look like? Like everyone else in that inbred Wasp town. New York *Sun* reporter Julian Ralph, the Dan Rather of his day, wrote during the trial, "By the way, the strangers who are here begin to notice that Lizzie Borden's face is of a type quite common here in New Bedford. They meet Lizzie Borden every day and everywhere about town. Some here even come in the courtroom. Some are fairer, some are younger, some are coarser, but all have the same general cast of features—heavy in the lower face, high in the cheekbones, wide at the eyes, and with heavy lips and a deep line on each side of the mouth."

In 1892 Ralph could not write "sensual" lips, but Lizzie's were that. She was not bad at all. Plump by our standards, she had what her era called a good figure; her hair was red and her eyes very blue. The photo we see most often showing a heavy woman in pince nez was taken years after the crimes. At the time of the murders she was only thirty-two and looked even younger. The deep lines on either side of her nose had not yet produced those Richard Nixon jowls that come to aging Wasps. In her youth the lines resulted in what are known as clean-cut or "chiseled" features.

Like all blue-eyed women, she was well-supplied with blue dresses—an unparalleled convenience in her case since her life was to depend on the ability of an all-male jury to tell one blue dress from another. They also came in handy for changing clothes without appearing to have done so; the case is a vortex of bloody blue dresses—clean blue dresses, light-blue dresses with blood, dark-blue dresses without blood. Today, eighty-five years later, crime writers are still arguing about which blue dress she wore on that famous morning in 1892, but there is one thing we can be sure of: her best feature was her wardrobe. Newspaper stories of the trial all comment on her excellent taste; she was one of those unusual Wasp women who instinctively knows and loves clothes.

Five years before the murders, the Bordens had what would have been a family fight, if only they had let loose and fought like normal people. If they had, there would not have been any murders.

Andrew deeded a piece of real estate over to Abby in her own name. Lizzie and Emma went to him and said, "What you do for her, you must do for us." Unable to refuse anything so nicely put, he bought his daughters a house valued at exactly the same price as the one he had given his wife. Everybody was even—except that they were not. They all started smoldering, brooding, and seething over what they *wished* they had said. Instead of going to the mat with it and clearing the air, they played that fine Wasp game known as Silent Gestures. Emma and Lizzie stopped eating with the elder Bordens, requiring the maid to set two tables, serve two meals, and wash two sets of dishes. In addition, they eliminated "Abby" and "Mother" from their respective vocabularies and started calling her "Mrs. Borden." What a cathartic release that must have been.

They never got as far as Not Speaking. "We always *spoke*," as Emma was to put it at the trial, meaning that they said only what they absolutely had to say and no more. Lizzie, who was the most paranoid member of the clan, ticked away for four years until 1891, when she committed a daylight robbery. Entering the master bedroom through a door in her room (the house was a shotgun arrangement with no hallways), she stole her stepmother's jewelry, her father's loose cash, and— for whatever reasons—a book of horsecar tickets.

Andrew and Abby both knew that Lizzie was the culprit, and Lizzie knew that they knew, but the proprieties had to be preserved. Rather than "have words," Andrew chose to call in the police and let them go through a mock investigation to catch the person the whole family referred to as "the unknown thief."

The robbery launched a field day of Silent Gestures. Everybody quietly bought lots of locks. There were locks everywhere, three on the front door alone and at least one on every bedroom door. To supplement the key locks there were bolts, hooks, chains, and padlocks. The jails Lizzie visited on her Fruit and Flower missions could not have been more secured than her own home.

The best Silent Gesture was Andrew's. He put the strongest available lock on the master bedroom and then left the key on the mantelpiece in the sitting room downstairs in full view of everyone, where Lizzie could get it if she decided to rob the master bedroom again. Lizzie knew that she was on her honor not to touch it; she also knew that if the key disappeared, she would be suspected. In one Wasp swoop, Andrew made it clear that he was simultaneously trusting her and distrusting her and warning her without saying a word. Wasps call that sort of thing the "honor system."

Abby Borden's Silent Gesture to Lizzie was to lock and bolt her side of the door that led into Lizzie's room. Lizzie responded with her Silent Gesture—putting a hook on her side and shoving a huge claw-footed secretary in front of the door.

Since Emma Borden *was* a Silent Gesture, there was no need for her to do anything except keep scurrying.

The only normal person in the house was Bridget Sullivan, the maid. Twenty-six and pretty in a big-boned healthy way, at the time of the murders she had been in the Bordens' service for almost three years. Her brogue was so thick that she referred to the Silent Gesture on the mantelpiece as the "kay."

The most interesting thing about Bridget is her utter devotion to Lizzie. "*De haut en bas*, Lizzie was always kind," wrote novelist Victoria Lincoln, her one-time neighbor. Stories abound about the affection Lizzie always inspired in servants; whatever else she did, she never forgot her *noblesse oblige*. Her habit of calling Bridget "Maggie" has been attributed to laziness (Maggie was the name of a former servant) or to absent-mindedness and disinterest, but such attitudes toward servants would have been out of character for her. I believe it was an extremity of tact, one of those small but meticulously observed kindnesses that the aloof or hard Wasp exhibits. In that time and place, the name Bridget was synonymous with "Irish maid." Like Rastus in black jokes, it designated a figure of fun. Knowing this, Lizzie substituted another.

Anyone who studies the Borden case grows to like Lizzie, or at least admire her, for her rigid sense of honor and responsibility toward her social inferiors. It would have been so easy for her to have cast suspicion on Bridget or to have accused her outright of the murders. The two of them were alone in the house with Abby and Andrew when the crimes occurred. The Irish were disliked in Victorian Massachusetts; a Yankee jury would have bought the idea of Bridget's guilt very easily. Yet Lizzie never once tried to shift the blame, and she refused to name Bridget as a suspect. "A cramped, false world made Lizzie Borden, but she had her code," says Lincoln.

Lizzie did name a suspect, however—her uncle. There is no

code in Waspland that covers relatives. Hiram Harrington was the husband of Andrew Borden's sister and the center of controversy in a game of Not Speaking. Hiram and Andrew had never gotten along; a few years before the murders, they had had their final "falling out." Andrew announced that he was Not Speaking to Hiram and demanded that the rest of the family follow suit. Abby and Lizzie, in agreement for once, obeyed, but Emma, who liked her aunt and uncle, showed rare spirit and went on speaking to them.

Andrew was on the verge of not speaking to Emma when something happened to divert him. The city tax assessor, who was also a deacon in the Central Congregational Church, raised the levy on some of Andrew's downtown property holdings. Andrew stopped speaking to the assessor instead, and as a silent gesture, withdrew from Central Congregational and bought a pew in First Congregational—an excellent Silent Gesture as it happened, because there was a feud between the churches. Central Congregational was Not Speaking to First Congregational.

Lizzie, who had obediently stopped speaking to the Harringtons, refused to change churches, but Emma got back in her father's good graces by agreeing to attend the new church with him. It was, however, an *extremely* silent gesture on Emma's part since she hardly ever went to church.

The Borden house must have been a peaceful place. There is nothing on record to show that they ever had the slightest argument of the raised-voice sort. "Never a word," Bridget later testified, with obvious sincerity and not a little awe.

About a week before the murders, Emma did something incredible. She went to Fairhaven. Ten miles is a long way to scurry, but scurry she did to visit friends and escape the heat wave that had descended on Fall River. Lizzie had also been invited to share a beach house for a week with her Fruit and Flower friends in Marion, a vacation town on Buzzards Bay. "The girls," as they called themselves, were individually named Mary Holmes, Anna Holmes, Elizabeth Johnson, Isabel Frazer, and Louise Remington. A Waspier lineup could not be found. The girls are important in the case for the collective interview they gave to a reporter after the murders. Solidly on Lizzie's side, they showered her with what, to them, were ultimate compliments: "She always was self-contained, self-reliant, and very composed. Her conduct since her arrest is exactly what I should have expected. Lizzie and her father were, without being demonstrative, very fond of each other."

The climax of the interview came when the reporter asked the girls if they thought Lizzie was guilty. No, they said firmly, because she had pleaded *not* guilty: "It is more likely that Lizzie would commit a murder than that she would lie about it afterward." She had always been, they said, "a monument of straightforwardness."

Indeed she was. Shortly before she was due at the beach house, she marched into her friendly neighborhood drugstore in the middle of the day and tried to buy poison.

One of the most puzzling aspects of the case has always been Lizzie's choice of weapons. Upper-class ladies simply do not grab a hatchet and do an Apache number at nine o'clock in the morning. The unlikelihood of it all was a major point in her defense and one that her jury of respectable middle-aged-to-old Yankee men bought without reservation. Women just *don't*. Women *do* poison, however, and always have. Obviously, Lizzie had originally planned to use the ladylike means, turning to the hatchet as a last resort after being unable to buy the poison she wanted.

The jury did not hear about Lizzie's drugstore caper because the druggist's testimony was excluded on a legal technicality, but here is what happened. It is a classic example of Wasp forthrightness.

In the middle of a heat wave, Lizzie put a fur cape over her arm and walked three blocks through the bustling downtown business district, most of which her father owned, to Smith's drugstore. When she entered the store, pharmacist Eli Bence was talking to two friends. Big as life and toting the fur, Lizzie interrupted them, and in her monumentally straightforward way, announced that there were moths in her fur and asked for ten cents' worth of prussic acid to kill them with. (It is not on record, but I can just see her holding up the fur and saying, "See?" just in case no one had noticed it in that hundred-degree heat.)

Bence was stunned. Prussic acid is used by furriers, but even in the pharmaceutically casual nineties, when you could easily buy arsenic over the counter, prussic acid was a no-no. One of the most dangerous of all poisons, it is also the quickest acting; twenty seconds to two minutes after imbibing, it's all over.

Bence refused to sell it to her, but instead of folding her cape and stealing quietly away, Lizzie started an argument.

"But I've bought it many times before!"

Bence's incredulity increased in the face of this stouthearted Wasp lie. Undoubtedly, she looked him straight in the eye when she said it.

"Well, my good lady, it is something we don't sell except by prescription, as it is a very dangerous thing to handle."

Lizzie left. It never crossed her mind that she might have called attention to herself, for she pressed on in her search for prussic acid in the neighboring city of New Bedford, which was a transfer point in her trip to the beach; a tall, fashionably dressed redhead with eyes so blue that they would be mistaken today for tinted contacts, she went from drugstore to drugstore talking about moths.

At the beach the girls noticed that she seemed despondent and preoccupied the day she arrived and were further perplexed when she suddenly cut short her vacation and returned to Fall River, giving as her excuse some church work. The gospel truth, as things turned out. She *did* keep her minister busy preaching funerals.

Back home, in the stifling heat that still stands as Fall River's record, she sat in her airless room and brooded. What was she brooding about this time? The same thing she had brooded about the other time. Her stepmother was about to acquire some more real estate, a farm this time, one of several that Andrew Borden owned, but a very special one because Lizzie and Emma had spent their childhood there and considered it theirs. Andrew was planning to put the farm in Abby's name, and install his brother-in-law, John Morse, as caretaker.

This last was especially unpalatable, for Lizzie and Emma were Not Speaking to Uncle John. He had been involved, so they thought, in the other real estate transaction five years before, when Abby had acquired title to the gift house.

Now Lizzie was seething and pulsing with hatred for Abby, Uncle John, her father, and their "plot" to do her and Emma out of their rightful inheritance. At some point in her sweltering stay in her room, she must have decided to do murder-by-hatchet. That settled, she proceeded to cover her tracks with a Silent Gesture —on the day before the crimes, she ate lunch with her parents. To

Lizzie's way of thinking, no one who was planning to murder two people would dream of eating with them the day before; to an honor-bright Wasp, the dining-room ruse she pulled would add up to an airtight alibi.

Bridget must have been surprised, or at least happy not to have to serve twice in that heat. The incident stuck in her mind and she mentioned it at the inquest, the preliminary hearing, and at the trial, as Lizzie had undoubtedly wanted her to.

After lunch, Lizzie returned to her room for some more brooding. While she was there, Uncle John arrived with plans to spend the night. Since she was Not Speaking to him, she did not go down to greet him but she did position herself at the window and eavesdrop on his conversation with the elder Bordens in the sitting room, which was situated directly below her room. What they said is not on record, but we can be reasonably sure that they discussed real estate. As Victoria Lincoln put it so well, none of them was the type for small talk. At the inquest, Lizzie blurted out that their voices had "disturbed" her as she tried to take a nap, thus indicating that their words had been audible to her. Why they sat there with all the windows open, talking about things they wished to keep secret from Lizzie when they knew that she was directly over their heads, is almost as big a mystery as the murders themselves. But then, it was destined to be a klutzy week all around.

That evening, Lizzie went around the corner to Borden Street to see Alice Russell and cover her tracks some more. The moment she set foot in the door she announced, "I have a feeling that something is going to happen! A feeling that somebody is going to do something. There's a feeling hanging over me that I can't shake off."

Naturally Miss Russell was interested; women dearly love to swap feminine-intuition stories. Lizzie related a tangled saga about Andrew's "enemies," prowlers in the yard, attempts to break into the barn, and her belief that "someone" had poisoned the milk delivery as it sat on the steps. Her father was such a ruthless businessman, she said, that "they" all hated him, and she would not put it past "them" to burn down the house.

Having successfully deflected suspicion away from herself and given Miss Russell something to testify about, Lizzie said goodnight and returned home.

On August 4, 1892, the temperature was already in the eighties at dawn, but that did not change the Bordens' breakfast menu. It was destined to become the most famous breakfast in American history, printed in newspapers all over the country and discussed by aficionados of the case for years to come. Alexander Woollcott declared it to be the one and only motive for the murders.

The last breakfast of Abby and Andrew Borden's life consisted of mutton soup, sliced mutton, pancakes, bananas, pears, cookies, and coffee. Furthermore, the mutton had been around for four days, having begun as the Sunday roast. The family had been eating it steadily since, suggesting that it might have been an entire sheep when it made its first appearance on the table. Andrew did not believe in waste; given the heat and the primitive wooden icebox in the Borden kitchen, it sounds as if the family were engaged in a race against spoilage. We do not know if the mutton was already rotten, but we do know that the bananas were; further, it is also on record that Abby and Andrew had been very sick the previous day and that they had spent the last night of their lives vomiting into their slop pail.

It is quite possible that Andrew and Abby would have died in their home on August 4 *anyway:* Bridget later testified that the murder-day lunch, which was never eaten, was to have been mutton soup, sliced mutton, and potatoes. Even a Wasp stomach can take only so much.

The day of days began in blunt, no-nonsense Wasp fashion, i.e., it was marked by a certain lack of fastidiousness. Andrew came downstairs carrying the connubial slop pail,[1] which he emptied in the back yard. Then he got a basket from the barn and gathered pears that had fallen to the ground from the pear tree, not too far away from where he had emptied the slops. These were the breakfast pears; whether anyone washed them before putting them on the table is not known, but nowhere in Bridget's highly detailed account of her activities that morning is there any mention of pear washing.

After breakfast, Andrew brushed his teeth at the kitchen sink where Bridget was washing dishes. A few mintues later, Bridget went out in the back yard and vomited. Whether it was the mutton

---

[1] Not to be confused with a chamber pot. A slop pail was a tall metal can with a lid, into which the contents of the chamber pot were poured and kept overnight. Slop pails were usually emptied once a day.

or the tooth-brushing or something she had seen clinging to a pear, we shall never know; but when she returned to the house, Abby was waiting with a most uncharacteristic order for a Wasp housewife. She wanted the windows washed; all the ones on the ground floor, inside and out, that very day. In fact, she wanted it done *that very minute.*

Here is one of the strangest aspects of the case. Victoria Lincoln calls Abby "an indifferent housekeeper." She was well known as a very easy woman to work for, and her servants always felt lucky to have such an undemanding lady of the house. Why then would Abby order a sick Bridget to such a task on the hottest day of the year? Because, says Lincoln, she was going to the bank that day to sign the deed for the farm and she anticipated a scene with Lizzie who, knowing Abby's hermitlike ways, would immediately wonder why she was going out and be able to put two and two together. The mere thought of "having words" in front of a servant struck horror in Abby's Wasp heart, so she invented a task that would take Bridget outside. Had it not been for this Wasp tic, Abby might not have died; Lizzie would have lacked the opportunity to commit murder if Bridget had been in the house attending to her regular chores.

Around nine that morning, after Andrew and John had left, a bogus note came for Abby. Ostensibly a summons from her sister, Mrs. Whitehead, its purpose was to give her a reason for leaving the house. Lizzie opened the door to the messenger, and a few moments later Abby lay face-down in a pool of blood, the back of her head destroyed by nineteen (not forty) blows from a hatchet. She was killed in the upstairs guest room while making the bed that Uncle John had occupied, a job that Bridget might have helped her with had she not been busy washing the ground-floor windows on the other side of the house.

How did Lizzie cleanse herself of blood? What did she do with the bloody hatchet between murders? She used that beloved Wasp trait, horse sense. She put the hatchet in her slop pail, confident that if the police searched it—an unlikely thing for Victorian police to do—she could easily explain how there happened to be blood in it. She was menstruating that week.

Menstruation also gave her a perfect means of washing Abby's blood from her hands and face. She used the sanitary napkins of the time, which were something like diapers. When she finished, she put the napkins and the bloody water from her bureau pitcher into the slop pail, too. All women stored their soiled napkins in their slop pails, to await the next laundry day.

Abby was killed sometime between nine and nine-thirty; Andrew at eleven. Lizzie's behavior during those two hours between murders was unflappable. She maintained a battle-of-Britain calm that makes it impossible not to admire her. Straightforward to the point of suicidal clumsiness, she was also damned clever. Opinions differ as to her *modus operandi*, especially with regard to the dress question. While I disagree with Victoria Lincoln about which dress or dresses she wore, I think she is right about where Lizzie hid the one she was wearing when she murdered Abby.

Where would any honest Wasp hide a dress? In the dress closet, of course, just as Poe's hero hid the purloined letter in a box marked *Letters*. It's so forthrightly sneaky, honesty-within-dishonesty. In Lizzie's case it was also a dress-within-a-dress. Like any woman with more clothes than hangers, she was accustomed to making hangers do double-duty. A bloody summer dress hung underneath and inside a heavy winter dress is not likely to attract the attention of investigating policemen. Men do not run out of hangers the way women do, and they have either-or minds. It was summer; Lizzie knew that any man searching her closet for a summer dress would pay little or no attention to heavy woolens, cashmeres, and silks.

Lizzie's original plan may not have included the murder of her father; we will never know, but we do know that at ten-thirty when Andrew unexpectedly came home, she was dressed for the street and had a hat in her hand. No respectable woman in 1892 would have left the house without a hat, so she was going *somewhere*. Andrew was not expected back until lunchtime, so we can safely presume that she had been planning to go out and establish an alibi for Abby's murder when her father suddenly returned.

Here is the turning point in the case. Andrew had obviously come home to look for Abby, who had never showed up at the bank. Any moment he might go upstairs and find his wife's body. Bridget had finished the outside windows and was now back in the house washing the inside ones. Uncle John was due back at noon. Andrew was napping on the downstairs sitting room sofa. Lizzie had to do something, and she had to do it fast. What did she do? Anyone else would have broken down but Lizzie started ironing handkerchiefs.

As she ironed, she conversed calmly and pleasantly with Bridget. It was Thursday, the maid's afternoon off, so Lizzie asked casually, "Are you going out this afternoon, Maggie?"

"I don't know. I might and I might not. I don't feel so good."

"There's a sale of dress goods at Sargent's Only eight cents a yard."

Bridget expressed some interest, so Lizzie added, "If you do go out, be sure and lock the door, for Mrs. Borden has gone out, and I may go out, too."

She could not have intended for a *living* Andrew to be locked up in the house by himself with his wife's corpse. Apparently, at some point in the handkerchief ironing and the girlish conversation about dresses, she had calmly decided to chop her father up, too, and let Uncle John bang hopelessly on the locked doors of the charnel house, unable to get in.

At eleven, Bridget went up to her attic room to wash and rest. At eleven-ten, she heard Lizzie's voice call up to her.

"Maggie! Come down quick! Father's dead. Somebody came in and killed him."

Somebody certainly had. Murdered while dozing on the sitting room sofa, the entire left side of his face and head was a bloody pulp. The eye had been severed and hung down his cheek, and one of the blows had bisected a jaw tooth.

Lizzie sent Bridget for Miss Russell and Dr. Bowen, then sat on the back steps. The Bordens' next door neighbor, Adelaide Churchill, called over to her and got a priceless reply.

"Oh, Mrs. Churchill, do come over. Someone has killed father."

Mrs. Churchill came over and the two stepped inside the kitchen. Verifying the news, she then asked, "Where is your mother, Lizzie?"

The sensible thing to say was "I don't know," but as we shall see, everybody in this case was a stickler for the truth.

"I don't know but what she's been killed, too, for I thought I heard her come in."

Bridget returned with Alice Russell and Dr. Bowen, who examined Andrew and asked for a sheet to cover the body. Lizzie

directed Bridget to get it. Whether she said anything else is in
dispute; no one present testified to it, but the legend persists that
she added, "Better get two."

A few minutes later, Alice Russell suggested that somebody
look for Abby Borden, so Bridget and Mrs. Churchill went upstairs. They were not gone long. When they returned, a white-
faced but brave Mrs. Churchill looked at Alice Russell and nod-
ded.

"There is another?" asked Miss Russell.

"Yes, she is upstairs."

The only excited person in the house was Bridget.

Mrs. Churchill sent her yardman for the police. At noon, when
Uncle John returned, they were swarming over the house and
yard, and a large crowd of onlookers had gathered in front of the
homestead.

An exciting scene awaited Uncle John as he ambled back for
lunch. There is no way he could have missed it, but he chose to
exhibit so much Wasp nonchalance that he became the first suspect. Seeing the crowd and the police and knowing only too well
the hatred Lizzie felt for Abby, he must have guessed the truth.
But instead of rushing into the house, he continued ambling
straight into the back yard, where he picked up two of the ques-
tionable pears and ate them as he stood in the shade of the tree.
(Some writers on the case have suggested he merely wanted to dull
his appetite before another mutton confrontation.)

Meanwhile, the police were questioning Lizzie, who claimed
that she had gone to the barn, and that when she returned, she had
found her father dead.

What had she gone to the barn for, the officer wanter to know,
eliciting the first of a series of clumsy lies unparalleled in the
annals of crime.

"To get a piece of lead for a fishing sinker," she replied.

It was the first thing that popped into her head, obviously
inspired by the vacation she had been planning to take with the
beach house girls. Even today it would be difficult for a woman to
pass herself off as the compleat angler; in 1892 it was even more
incredible. No matter how emancipated women get, they seldom
take up fishing. It is something a woman does to keep a man
company. She does not go fishing by herself; and as for an entire

giggly group of Fruit and Flower Missionaries going on a fishing trip, worms and all, it is positively mind-boggling.

At this point, Lizzie was playing everything by ear. It never occurred to her that she could have solved her immediate problems by pretending to faint, like Richardon's Pamela, and thus postpone the interrogation until she got her thoughts straight. It would have worked; women fainted a lot in those days. But she even refused to take advantage of the detective's gallant offer to come back and question her later when she felt better.

"No," she blurted, with a fine Wasp thump. "I can tell you all I know now as well as at any other time."

Next, and worse, when the detective referred to Abby Borden as her mother, she snapped back, "She is *not* my mother, sir, she is my stepmother! My mother died when I was a child."

At that point, Alice Russell apparently decided to get this real winner upstairs before she harmed herself further. Summoning Dr. Bowen, they took Lizzie to her room. There, Lizzie asked the doctor to send a telegram to Emma in Fairhaven, adding, "Be sure to put it gently, as there is an old person there who might be disturbed." Thoughtful on the surface, the request shows a certain Wasp hardness as well as our priorities regarding our kin. It's all right to disturb your sister with shocking news just as long as you don't disturb people who mean nothing to you. Putting it gently for *Emma's* sake was the last thing in her mind.

Dr. Bowen must have sent the Waspiest wire on record, for Emma did not catch the next train, nor the one after that, nor the one after *that*. She took her own good time and finally showed up late that evening, presumably clutching the tactful telegram in her cool little hand.

Returning from the telegraph office, Dr. Bowen remained alone with Lizzie in her room, giving her a mild sedative. It has been suggested that there was "something between" Lizzie and the married doctor. I believe there was, for his actions after leaving her room prove that she had confided a very dangerous fact to him that she chose not to mention to her women friends on the scene.

She had torn up a note or a letter and put the pieces in a downstairs wastebasket. Dr. Bowen went directly to the wastebasket, fished out the pieces, and was in the process of putting them together in the kitchen when a detective walked in on him.

Seeing the name, "Emma" on one of the pieces, the detective asked Bowen what it was.

Here we have a really magnificent lie, clumsier even than any of Lizzie's.

"Oh, it is nothing," said Bowen with a nonchalant shrug. "It is something, I think, about my daughter going through somewhere."

Before the detective could figure that one out, Bowen tossed the pieces into the kitchen fire. Men do not destroy evidence in the presence of police for women who mean nothing to them.

When Bowen lifted the lid of the fire, the detective saw therein a foot-long stick lying on top of the flames. Later, in the cellar, police found a hatchet *head* that had been washed and rolled while wet in furnace ash to simulate dust. The hatchet head had been placed in a box of other, very dusty household tools. It was a clumsy attempt, but one that showed admirable common sense.

Obviously, Lizzie *had* been in the barn, but not to look for sinkers. There was a vise in the barn, and heavy blacksmithing tools, and a water pump. She had used her head and, more important, kept her head; metal can be washed, but blood soaks into wood very quickly. She had had to break the hatchet head from the handle and burn the latter. She did all these things in a very brief time, and without giving in to panic.

Because she had been in the barn, Lizzie's obsession with honesty compelled her to say so. As Victoria Lincoln points out, she had a powerful psychological need to *mention* everything, no matter how damaging it might be. Because she had in fact put the hatchet handle into the fire, she told police that she had "laid a stick on the fire" to heat the flatirons while she was doing her handkerchiefs. She lied about *why* and *when* she had done things, but she never denied having done them.

Alice Russel exhibited the same idiosyncrasy. "Alice's conscience forced her to *mention* things at the trial, but not to *stress* them," says Lincoln. Wasp talent for making vital matters sound trivial enabled Alice to testify that after the murders, when she and Lizzie went upstairs, she had seen Lizzie coming out of Emma's room, where she had no legitimate business; and that there had been a bundled-up blanket on the floor of Emma's closet. But she made it all sound so matter-of-fact that she was not even cross-examined on it. No one ever thought to ask what might have been rolled up in that blanket, nor what connection it had with Lizzie's never-explained presence in her sister's room. (Lincoln believes the blanket contained bloody stockings.)

At the inquest, Lizzie was asked by the district attorney if her parents had been happily married. She paused so long that it was noted in the transcript by the court reporter. "Why hesitate?" prompted the district attorney.

"Why, I don't know but what they were," she said at last.

"Did they seem to be affectionate?"

"I think so."

"Were they affectionate as a man and woman who are married ought to be?" he persisted.

He got a very forthright answer.

"So far as I have ever had a chance of judging." said Lizzie.

Did Lizzie suspect that her father and stepmother had been married in name only? Did she feel, therefore, that Abby, being less than a real wife, did not qualify as a wife in matters of inheritance? If so, Lizzie's greed is much more understandable.

Lizzie quickly became America's Wasp Princess. From the moment of her arrest, people could not say enough about her icy calm. Even the Fall River police chief praised her: "She is a remarkable woman and possessed of a wonderful power of fortitude." A Providence reporter and Civil War veteran: "Most women would faint at seeing her father dead, for I never saw a more horrible sight and I have walked over battlefields where thousands were dead and mangled. She is a woman of remarkable nerve and self-control. . . ."

Julian Ralph, who also sang praises to her ladylike demeanor in every dispatch, wrote, " . . . It was plain to see that she had complete mastery of herself, and could make her sensations and emotions invisible to an impertinent public."

Wasp cool was also uppermost in Lizzie's mind. In an interview in the New York *Recorder* while she was awaiting trial: "They say I don't show any grief. Certainly I don't in public. I never did reveal my feelings and I cannot change my nature now."

It never occurred to anybody that repressed feelings were the cause of the whole mess.

Certainly it was Wasp repression that gave us that marvelous "quarrel" between Lizzie and Emma that took place in the Taunton jail before her trial. Described by Mrs. Reagan, the police matron, it went like this:

"Emma, you have given me away, haven't you?" Lizzie whispered.

"No, Lizzie, I have not."

"You have, and I will let you see I won't give in one inch."

Finis. Lizzie turned over on her cot and lay with her back to Emma and Emma remained in her chair, neither of them saying another word, for the entire two hours and twenty minutes remaining until visiting hours were up.

When Mrs. Reagan spilled this sensational dialogue to the press, Lizzie's lawyers claimed she was lying and tried to get her to sign a retraction. Matters became so confused that we are not sure who heard and said what, but Victoria Lincoln believes Mrs. Reagan: "That terse exchange followed by a two-hour-and-twenty-minute sulking silence sounds more like a typical Borden family fight than the sort of quarrel an Irish police matron would dream up from her own experience."

The trial, which ran from June 5 to June 20, 1893, was a maze of blue dresses. The prosecution tried to prove that on the day of the murders Lizzie had worn a light-blue cotton dress with a dark-blue diamond figure in it. Lizzie claimed that she had worn a dark-blue silk dress with a light-blue figure in it. Both dresses, like all her others, had been made by the same dressmaker; to confuse matters even more, both the light-blue cotton and the dark-blue silk had been cut from the same pattern and were identical in style. Assistant prosecutor William Moody, who was to become a beau of Alice Roosevelt and a U.S. Supreme Court justice, had the impossible job of describing the finer points of female fashion to the all-male jury. At one point, as he struggled with the train of the dark-blue number, Lizzie burst out laughing.

The light-blue cotton was not available for display for the simple reason that Lizzie had burned it in the kitchen stove on the Sunday after the murders. For once, she had not gone to church. Instead, she had stayed home to do some very interesting chores. She claimed that she had burned the light blue because its hem was stained with brown paint, an accident that had occurred a few months before the murders when the house was painted. She was stuffing the last of the skirt into the fire when Alice Russell walked in and caught her in the act.

It was just like Lizzie to burn a dress in broad daylight when the yard was full of policemen still searching for clues. It was just like Alice Russell to be so tormented by her honor-bright conscience that she decided to go to the DA with the dress-burning information. It was a very Waspy Sunday morning indeed.

At the trial, the prosecution labored mightily to prove that Lizzie had worn the light-blue cotton on the murder day, but the person who had had the best chance to see her dress was Bridget Sullivan, and Bridget steadfastly refused to break on the witness stand. Try as he might, the DA could not get her to remember what Lizzie had worn. Bridget herself was suspiciously well-dressed at the trial, leading people to assume that Lizzie and Emma had bribed her to keep mum about the dress.

Lizzie was acquitted. She quickly bought a big new house in the best neighborhood for herself and Emma, but Fall River's upper crust shunned her. She lived in solitary glory with no visitors except the local librarian, Miss Leighton, who like Lizzie was a passionate supporter of the Animal Rescue League. Lizzie, who had never been permitted to keep pets by the tight-fisted Andrew Borden, acquired a series of bull terriers and an elaborate bird station for her huge lawn.

When she returned to Central Congregational after the trial, everyone was very polite to her, so she took the hint and stopped going. Now it was Emma who became a pillar of the church, scurrying back and forth every Sunday.

Things remained quiet for several years after the trial, then Lizzie caused another sensation. She was charged with shoplifting in Providence, an incident that shocked Fall River far more than had the murders. In Waspland, murder is one thing but stealing is something else. The town might eventually have come around and accepted her, but the theft sealed her social doom once and for all.

Taking up with "theater people," she threw a whing-dinger of a house party that went on for an entire week. No one knows exactly what happened, but something most assuredly did, for Emma moved out in the middle of the night and never spoke to Lizzie again. Maybe she found out that Lizzie had really committed the murders, but I doubt it. The Protestant conscience is not programmed for meaningless confessions. It sounds more as if Emma discovered that her sister had a sex life.

Lizzie had acquired what appears to have been a girlfriend. Her name was Nance O'Neil, which could not have gone down very well with Lizzie's neighbors on the Hill. An actress of some note on the Boston stage, Nance was present at the party the night Emma stalked out of the house. It was probably Nance who was the recipient of that extant letter Lizzie wrote beginning, "Dear Friend," and going on to juicier sentiments: "I dreamed of you the other night but I do not dare to put my dreams on paper."

Lizzie had enough money to live wherever she wanted, but she chose to stay in Fall River and brave it out as the town's leading pariah. As she had once sworn to Emma, she refused to give one inch. It is impossible not to admire her for her guts. She lived alone in her mansion until her death in 1927.

Emma, who had been living alone in New Hampshire for years, read of her sister's death in the paper. She did not attend the funeral or even send flowers—good Silent Gestures, to be sure, but not nearly so good as the ultimate Silent Gesture she made ten days later. She died.

Her body was brought back to Fall River and placed in the family plot, next to Lizzie's fresh grave. All the Bordens lie together now, closer in death than they ever were in life. Andrew and Abby with their identical death dates; Andrew's first wife, Sarah Morse; Lizzie; Emma; and the daughter, Alice, who died in childhood. It is the only kind of family reunion they were emotionally capable of having.

As a final Wasp touch, Lizzie and Emma both left most of their money to the Animal Rescue League. Nothing could be Waspier, except perhaps the explanation little Victoria Lincoln got when she asked her elders why nobody ever spoke to their neighbor, Miss Lizzie Borden.

"Well, dear, she was very unkind to her mother and father."

16

THE NON-WASP WASP
or
How to Win Your Spurs

America is full of non-Wasp Wasps. The Protestant group known as Scotch-Irish is considered Wasp in America even though they are Celts. They have names like Buchanan, Conway, Murray; or Irish names that do not sound Irish, like Quigley, Harrington, Hart, Walsh, or Walker. Orange Irish are looked upon as Wasps; to Americans, an Irishman is not really Irish unless he is Catholic. Scots also become Wasps when they cross the ocean. To the ethnic ear, the two Waspiest names in America are probably Cunningham and Hamilton, but both are quintessentially Scottish.

People named Morgan, Pritchard, Jenkins, Williams, and Davies are Wasps, too. When the Welshman emigrates to America he becomes a Wasp because he is a Protestant and he has a familiar, pronouncable name.

Then there are German Protestants whose families have been in the Midwest for a century or more. Carl Hauser is a Wasp, and so is Winifred Ackerman. They are Wasps because they look the part, and because they are no longer noticably German in customs and habits. Scandinavians in the Far West also "pass."

All the foregoing examples are obvious and self-explanatory. The real fun begins when the Wasp alchemist decides to transform himself into the real article. Thus we have the black Wasp— James Bayard Patterson, anchorman of your local news station. It's easy for a black to become a Wasp because they have the most Anglo-Saxon names in the entire country. A black anchorman especially has it made because *all* anchormen are assumed to be Wasps.

James Bayard Patterson exudes a cool prep-school air, which is why the studio executives hand-picked him in the first place. ("The government says we've got to have one.") When James Bayard Patterson beams his diffident smile into the camera and intones, "This is James Bayard Patterson wishing you a most pleasant good evening," he sounds just like the rector of St. Paul's greeting visiting alumni. Soon, by some mysterious American psychological process, he becomes a Wasp look-alike, which means he is ready for his final coup: he is chosen for the ad.

> Name: James Bayard Patterson
> Profession: News analyst
> Favorite sports: Tennis, skiing, squash, lacrosse
> Hobby: Collecting rare books
> Drink: Dewar's Scotch

The Hebrew Anglo-Saxon Protestant (HASP) is perhaps our greatest burden. Believe it or not, most Wasps aren't nearly so dull as David Susskind, but he regularly ruins our reputation. No matter what media sin Il Ponderoso commits, it never detracts from the Jewish reputation for lively wit; instead, it adds to *our* reputation for genteel, stultifying death-in-life. His interviews positively crackle with Waspiness: "Ummm, really? . . . Er, tell me . . . Is that so? . . . How interesting." Worse, he wears the Wasp uniform— beautiful, expensive dark suits—and no matter how he crosses his legs he never shows any calf flesh. His socks extend all the way up to his rarefied atmosphere. If he took off his shirt on camera, we would see a sock top around his neck. Susskind would make Charles Bovary look like a hyperkinetic wit, but the Jews never suffer for it. *We* suffer for it.

Every Wasp of my vintage has had to explain Herman Wouk. No, he *isn't* a Wasp even though he loves the navy, conventional sexual behavior, and conformity and hates mouthy intellectuals. Noel Airman in *Marjorie Morningstar* and Tom Keefer in *The Caine Mutiny* got the same kind of contemptuous treatment from Wouk that Wasps give to all intellectuals so that a lot of people, including some Wasps, have long assumed that Wouk is ours. Mistaking *The Caine Mutiny* for a Wasp novel is easy to do, but would you believe *Marjorie Morningstar?* Cocktail party sages in the fifties regularly called Marjorie's sexual agony and Wouk's solution for it "our Anglo-Saxon Puritan morality."

There is also a Jewish Good Ole Boy. He is the cab driver who talks all the way from La Guardia to the Plaza about "defending our shores against the Commies." A man among men, Stretch Ginsburg belongs to Jewish War Veterans, at whose meetings he drinks Seven & Seven and slaps other men on the behind, football-coach fashion, when they tell farmer's-daughter jokes. Any Jewish man who worries occasionally about his lack of *goyish* machismo runs the risk of lapsing into Good Ole Boyhood. Alex Portnoy's ecstatic references to Jewish men "with black hair on their balls" playing baseball with their sons brushed perilously close to male-club misogyny. After all, Wasp women depend upon Jewish men to reject stag night. Seeing them turn into rough-and-ready male-bonding artists upsets us; we have enough of that with our own men.

The Papal Wasp makes life difficult for us, too. Grace Kelly and Bill Buckley are both Irish Catholics whose appearance and crypto-Wasp ways give us a bad name. Whenever she lets loose with one of her serene sneers, or whenever he drops a ten-dollar word, real Wasps are accused of mandarin snobbery.

Should you wish to pass for a Wasp, there are a number of ways to do it. One is to become a Republican. The poor old GOP has been foundering on Waspy shoals for years, unable to work around its white, male, monied, non-ethnic image. They also fail at the precinct level because they are not good ward heelers; ringing doorbells, chatting easily with working people, and *asking* for votes are hard for Republicans to manage unless they have ethnics to help them out, which they seldom do. The Republican way is the Wasp way: have lunch with the big-wigs. Whenever you have a problem, political or otherwise, the Wasp way to solve it is to have lunch.

You can also drop classic Waspisms into your conversation. At the stroke of five, say, "The sun is over the yard arm. God, do I need a drink!" In the middle of the afternoon, tell your office mates that you are going to call your mother. Dial the weather or the time check, then say, "For God's sake, Julia, aren't you up *yet?*"

Or tell your friends you are going shopping with your father's mistress: "I'm so grateful to her because she helps Daddy unwind." Send an Ivy League college a check for ten dollars and mark it "Alumni Fund." The bookkeeper won't know the difference and the check will be processed automatically before they find out that they never heard of you. Take the cancelled check to work and leave it lying around where someone will see it.

Or go to the dog show. Take the program to a party and say, "Matilda's Pride of Claphamstall is really a marvelous bitch." And when your friends announce their impending trip to Europe and wax ecstatic about all the great art they're planning to see, say, "I hope you're taking some American toilet paper."

Nothing is more Wasp than broken bones. When you arrive at work in your sling, don't admit that you fell down the stairs. Instead say, "Skittish mare." Our equestrian image simply will not go away, so you may as well take advantage of it. The only thing more Wasp then riding horses is falling off horses. If you want to be Haut Wasp, break your collarbone. It is *the* riding mishap, bar none. Be like the debutante I knew who had broken her collarbone in four places and always wore strapless evening dresses to show off the clots of shattered bone that ran from shoulder to shoulder. *That* is Wasp status.